PORTABLE C
AND UNIX® SYSTEM
PROGRAMMING

D1713178

PORTABLE C
AND UNIX® SYSTEM
PROGRAMMING

J. E. Lapin

Rabbit
SOFTWARE

PRENTICE-HALL, INC., Englewood Cliffs, New Jersey 07632

Library of Congress Cataloging-in-Publication Data

Lapin, J. E.   (date)
   Portable C and UNIX system programming.

   Bibliography: p.
   Includes index.
   1. C (Computer program language)   2. UNIX
(Computer operating system)   3. Software
compatibility.   I. Title.
QA76.73.C15L36 1987   005.13′3   86-25231
ISBN 0-13-686494-5

Prentice-Hall Software Series
Brian W. Kernighan, Advisor

Editorial/production supervision: *Lisa Schulz Garboski*
Cover design: *Lundgren Graphics Ltd.*
Manufacturing buyer: *Gordon Osbourne*

© 1987 by Prentice-Hall, Inc.
A division of Simon & Schuster
Englewood Cliffs, New Jersey 07632

UNIX is a trademark of Bell Laboratories.
PDP, DEC, and VT100 are trademarks of the Digital Equipment Corporation.
IBM and PC/AT are trademarks of International Business Machines.
XENIX and MS-DOS are trademarks of Microsoft.
CP/M is a trademark of Digital Research.
MULTICS is a trademark of the Honeywell Corporation.
FOR:PRO is a trademark of Fortune Systems.
IS/3 is a trademark of Interactive Systems Corporation.
SCO is a trademark of the Santa Cruz Operation.
IDRIS is a trademark of Whitesmiths, Ltd.

The author and publisher of this book have used their best efforts in preparing this
book. These efforts include the development, research, and testing of
the theories and programs to determine their effectiveness. The author and publisher
make no warranty of any kind, expressed or implied, with regard to these programs
or the documentation contained in this book. The author and publisher shall not
be liable in any event for incidental or consequential damages in connection with,
or arising out of, the furnishing, performance, or use of these programs.

Printed in the United States of America

10   9   8   7   6   5   4   3   2

ISBN 0-13-686494-5   025

Prentice-Hall International (UK) Limited, *London*
Prentice-Hall of Australia Pty. Limited, *Sydney*
Prentice-Hall Canada Inc., *Toronto*
Prentice-Hall Hispanoamericana, S.A., *Mexico*
Prentice-Hall of India Private Limited, *New Delhi*
Prentice-Hall of Japan, Inc., *Tokyo*
Prentice-Hall of Southeast Asia Pte. Ltd., *Singapore*
Editora Prentice-Hall do Brasil, Ltda., *Rio de Janeiro*

CONTENTS

FOREWORD

This book is the outgrowth of over three years of work at Rabbit Software Corporation. Rabbit was incorporated in 1982, with the business mission of creating software for the (then) new generation of 16- and 32-bit microcomputers—in particular, data communications and distributed processing software allowing integration of such micros into large scale computer networks. It was clear at that time that increased address space, CPU performance, and availability of Winchester disks would allow minicomputer power on a desktop. It was also clear that multitasking operating systems would be a necessity.

At that time, there were two clear directions for Rabbit. First, a company named Convergent Technologies had introduced the first such desktop microcomputer, which was based on a proprietary multitasking network-based operating system called CTOS. Second, based on prior experience of the founders, it was clear that the UNIX system would be a leading candidate for incorporation on these new computers.

The latter direction was not as obvious then as it is today in retrospect. Many industry people believed the UNIX system was too old, not user-friendly enough, and inadequately supported to allow commercial introduction. We at Rabbit, however, felt that despite these problems there was a vacuum that had to be filled with some multitasking, minicomputer-type operating system. The UNIX system was such an operating system. It was easily ported to machines, and clearly could (and would) become a major presence there.

It is important to note that Rabbit has never been solely wedded to any operating system. Our software, which allows microcomputers and mainframe computers (especially IBM computers) to work in conjunction, was intended to run on any reasonable operating system. And that's where this book comes in.

Rabbit is a service-oriented development company, which means that we don't just develop a product or package, but we also port (i.e., move) our software to multiple microcomputers on behalf of hardware manufacturers, qualify the software, and work onsite with Fortune 1000 companies and other large organizations. This creates a critical challenge: Our software must be flexible, rich in functions, easily tested and maintained, and supportable across a range of products, users, computers, and operating systems. This is a potentially large matrix.

To solve this problem, Rabbit created a development and architectural approach called "Middleware." Middleware is a methodology allowing construction of big systems from small, separable, generic software subsystems, which can be used as components to build products or used directly by end-users. These are the building blocks that allow our systems to grow continually in a modular rather than monolithic fashion.

As part of this approach, Rabbit needed to create portable software. Portability was desired to cross between sufficiently rich operating systems and hardware. Even interprocess communications and data transfer were involved, since Rabbit's software must also run in distributed environments (i.e., multiple boards or computers that may have dissimilar internal data formats). Also studied were language-level compatibility, environmental compatibility (e.g., terminal I/O, disk I/O, operating systems routines), and generic subsystems (e.g., our "Help" system, profile parsers, queue managers, "Virtual Terminal System").

The result of these studies was a set of internal standards for software construction intended to result in generic, flexible, expandable software which could be used stand-alone or integrated into bigger applications (either our own or a user's), and would be testable and portable to many environments without creating a huge albatross of dissimilar versions.

In creating this standard, Rabbit discovered that no good reference material existed on how to write software to be transportable, especially between UNIX system variants. In particular, we found it necessary to create our own documents defining portable usage for our programmers.

In this book, we discuss issues of construction and performance for the UNIX system and C, but the broad issue of construction of large-scale software for distributed processing applications is not covered. It is our intent that this book be of direct service to those who need to build or choose software once to run on different machines and UNIX system variants.

Charles Robins
Vice President of Development
Rabbit Software Corporation

PREFACE

The remarkable success of the C language and the UNIX operating system during the last decade has demonstrated that true software portability between machines ranging from desktop micros up to the largest supercomputers is practical. No other operating system runs on the variety of hardware architectures the UNIX system does, nor with the degree of compatibility it provides.

With C and the UNIX system, software portability is practical—but it is not automatic. The UNIX system's evolutionary path has zigzagged from commercial software shops to the universities and back again, leaving several major dialects and a fair amount of confusion in its wake. Only now are true industry-wide standards being established.

This book may be used to understand both the underlying causes of portability problems and the philosophy and techniques that create portability. It also serves as a reference manual describing a detailed set of C standards and UNIX system comparisons that define portable usage for a broad range of C compilers, UNIX system variants, and micro- or minicomputers. The reader can apply the principles described herein to create similar standards for other languages, operating systems, or hardware environments.

The techniques described in this book (founded on an underlying belief that quality is the highest priority in developing software systems) can significantly decrease the development/test cycle and reduce the cost of long-term support by improving the overall reliability, readability, and maintainability of the product.

This is not an introductory text on C or the UNIX system. While the reader need have no familiarity with portability issues, some knowledge of the

C language and at least one version of the UNIX system is necessary to take advantage of the material presented herein. A bibliography listing our formal sources and a number of excellent tutorials has been included.

Chapter 1 summarizes obstacles to portability, a conceptual framework for thinking about portability, and general approaches for solutions. It also gives historical information on both C and the UNIX system.

Chapter 2 discusses some specific causes of portability problems in C programs then describes the Portable C Standard (beginning in Section 2.7). This is a set of C conventions and usage rules that has enabled Rabbit to achieve a very high degree of applications portability across both UNIX system variants and other systems. These guidelines are the distillation of many staff-years of research and development experience.

Chapter 3 begins with an introduction to the dialect groups and genealogy of the UNIX system. It then compares many major versions: Version 7, BSD 4.1, 4.2, and 4.3 (from pre-release documents), System III, XENIX 2.3, 3.0 and 5.0, System V, and AT&T's System V Interface Definition. Information that clarifies the relationship of the X3J11 ANSI C standard (now in preparation) to the UNIX system is also given.

Chapter 4 gives a more detailed treatment of three specific portability problems: the UNIX system's *ioctl*(2) call, the handling of signals, and the portable exchange of data.

Chapter 5 deals with the higher level of maintaining and porting the software once developed, including discussions of: isolating nonportable code; using *make*(1) and SCCS to advantage; the use of shell scripts; and some useful scripts for maintaining interface files and object archives.

Appendix A gives a full listing of a basic version of *portable.h*, the portability definitions file (introduced in Chapter 2).

Appendix B is a quick reference list of the names of all UNIX system features deemed portable according to the comparison charts presented in Chapter 3.

Appendix C describes several UNIX system dialects for which there was not enough room in the charts of Chapter 3.

Appendix D illustrates a method of compatibly handling differences in directory structure between 4.2BSD and other UNIX system versions.

UNIX system comparison information was gathered mostly from system manuals. The 4.3BSD information was based on a formal pre-release report from the developers on differences from 4.2; the system is not yet released at this writing. Some information on undocumented features of various dialects came from various sources in the general UNIX system user community and sometimes directly from the source code itself. We have used and developed programs on each of the major dialects described here. Information derived from folklore, the USENET, and other "soft" sources is so marked in each case.

Every functional difference discovered in UNIX system manual sections 2 through 5 is indicated in the notes; no such thing as an "unimportant" change was assumed. We are necessarily somewhat less strict about reporting differences between commands and applications programs (manual section 1). Relationships between these in different versions are much more complex and (in some cases) obscure.

Comparison tables for the traditional sections 6 (games) and 1M/8 (maintenance) have been included for completeness. Notice that much of Section 1M/8 is machine dependent; only relatively machine-independent utilities have been listed here.

Readers are encouraged to use the code examples contained herein as a basis for developing their own portable include files and libraries.

Suggestions, corrections, and commentaries may be mailed to the authors. As with any book of this type, there are likely to be many potential improvements or suggestions noted by readers. Please feel free to forward any such to our offices via UUCP mail at {burdvax,cbmvax}!hutch!book or via regular mail to:

> Rabbit Software Corporation
> 7 Great Valley Parkway East
> Malvern, PA 19355

The authors wish to thank Sheldon Newman and Charles Robins, the founders of Rabbit Software Corporation, for creating the environment in which we were able to follow through with this project.

> Jon Tulk
> Eric Raymond

ACKNOWLEDGMENTS

This book is the outgrowth of a set of studies done at Rabbit Software Corporation by our internal standards committee. One of the things that we are proudest of at Rabbit is that results (such as this book, or a quality software product) at our company stem from group interaction and constructive criticism. Given that, there are several people worth mentioning relative to this book:

Jon Tulk,   co-author and manager of the development of our study, brings a wealth of experience and insight on software design and architecture. Jon is both a member of the Rabbit Standards Committee and a delegate to the ANSI X3J11 Committee.

Eric Raymond,   co-author and principal researcher of this study, knows UNIX system internals, systems tools, and variants like the back of his hand. His knowledge of and affection for the UNIX system are reflected in this document. (Eric, a former full-time employee of Rabbit Software, has gone independent as a UNIX system consultant.)

Steve Barber,   who spent long hours studying UNIX system manuals to ensure that the final book had a thorough technical edit. Steve gained UNIX system experience from MIT's Project Athena, while earning his degree in Computer Science.

Charles Robins,   a cofounder of Rabbit, filled the margins of early
                       drafts with comments that helped turn our notes
                       into a book.

Dennis Warman,   an English major in his long-gone college days,
                       reworked some of the more obscure sections of the
                       manuscript and made certain that our commas
                       were at least proximate to their optimal locations.

The other members of Rabbit's internal C Standards Committee, which
drafted both the philosophy and original version of these standards, are:

David Langdon,   one of the original employees of Rabbit and a
                       delegate to the ANSI X3J11 Committee.

Gil Jacobsen,   whose intense belief in good standards pressed these
                       efforts forward.

Dave Tollefson,   our second employee, and a very strong advocate of
                       quality.

Additionally, every member of our technical development staff deserves
mention, since they contributed based on their experiences at Rabbit with
dozens of machines and operating systems. They use these standards and
ensure that they are kept accurate and up-to-date. Specifically, Tom Donohue
contributed to mklib and cx, and John Gooding helped with error handling
and reporting. And a special thanks to Bill Scholz who compiled the index.

Many other members of the UNIX system community have been of
help to us. We particularly wish to thank: Ken Thompson and Dennis Ritchie,
the inventors of the UNIX system, who contributed to the histories of C and
the UNIX system; Gordon Waidhofer, who supplied invaluable suggestions;
David Oster, who contributed historical and philosophical perspective; Fred
Pickard and Carl Waldspurger, who wrote test C code to verify some of our
facts; and, finally, Dave Schroeder and Paul Gumerman, who proofread the
final draft.

PORTABLE C
AND UNIX® SYSTEM
PROGRAMMING

1

INTRODUCTION

This chapter introduces the subject of C and operating system portability. However, the applicability of the concepts presented is by no means limited to C and UNIX software. The types of problems encountered and the techniques for their solution are, in principle, the same for any language or operating system. We also present, for background, brief histories of the development of the UNIX operating system and the C language.

Section 1.1 discusses the need for standards—not only in terms of portability, but in relation to overall quality.

Section 1.2 introduces the "Portability Range" concept which is fundamental to defining appropriate portability standards. It also describes the range of portability addressed by Rabbit's Portable C Standard and the Portable UNIX Software Standard.

Section 1.3 examines levels of compatibility and discusses the forms of incompatibility that typically arise from each.

Section 1.4 gives an overview of techniques. We present six general rules that we use as a guide to achieve portability and discuss four specific areas that are typically incompatible.

Section 1.5 presents a history of the development of the UNIX operating system to give the user a background against which to understand the differences in the versions discussed in this book.

Section 1.6 presents a history of the development of the C language, providing a background for the Portable C Standard.

1.1 An Overview of Portability Issues

It is well documented that the cost of long-term support of a major software system is much more than the cost of its development. This cost is multiplied when several essentially identical versions of the same package are supported on various hardware or operating systems. There is also the probable cost of redesigning and rewriting involved when a package is ported to a distributed or multiprocessor environment not originally planned for.

Obviously, planning for portability should begin in the earliest design phases and continue through implementation. Portability is inseparable from general quality and maintainability. Systems that are unstructured, badly organized, or difficult for a maintainer to comprehend will also be difficult to port cleanly and quickly; conversely, practices that lead to portability enhance the maintainability and quality of code. The extra effort required by good portability practices is justified by the increased maintainability—even for systems for which no port is ever expected.

1.2 Portability Ranges

Before creating standards for portability, it is essential to define the set of target machines, operating systems, and language versions to which it will apply. We call this the "range of portability." If the range of portability is restricted to, say, 16- and 32-bit processors running AT&T UNIX System V, the standard may not need to be very tight. If the range is broadened to include 8-bit processors running CP/M and C compilers that do not support, for example, bit fields and floating-point, the standards will obviously be much more restrictive. Effective planning for portability requires that one choose a range of target systems and be aware of the different levels in hardware and software systems at which portability problems can arise.

This book is primarily intended to support portability of C programs and shell command usage (hence, scripts) among processors running any of the major varieties of UNIX systems.

The C standards chapter specifies practices that should, in addition, facilitate ports of operating-system-independent modules of C code between systems supporting a full C compiler (i.e., a compiler that faithfully reflects the specification found in *The C Programming Language*; see Appendix A: C Reference Manual). We have used these standards to port successfully to both UNIX systems and other C environments on a variety of 32-, 16-, and even 8-bit microcomputers. The reader may wish to consider making these standards more or less restrictive to suit portability for a broader or narrower range of portability. Our only warning is that it is much more difficult to tighten a loose standard than to loosen a tight one.

We have organized the UNIX system material so that it can be used to evaluate the portability of code within various UNIX system dialect groups, most particularly within the AT&T dialects (System III; System V, Release 1; and System V, Release 2), the Version 7/Berkeley dialects (Version 7, Berkeley 4.1, Berkeley 4.2, and Berkeley 4.3), and the XENIX versions 2.3, 3.0, and 5.0.

1.3 Portability Levels

There are several levels of portability of programs and data between systems. Between systems based on similar hardware and the same operating system, one may have *runfile compatibility*; binary executables may be moved between systems and will run correctly. Since almost all porting situations allow one to recompile, and since applications programmers can do nothing to force runfile compatibility in any case, this level will not be discussed further.

Two key aspects of compatibility depend primarily on the machine's hardware architecture (i.e., register length, internal representations of data types, and the like). These are:

- *Data file compatibility*—Exists when binary data images corresponding to any C structure or data type can be exchanged between systems. This requires that data type sizes, structure padding conventions, byte orders within word data, and floating-point representations all be compatible among the systems involved. This is sometimes achievable between similar processors using standard transport media formats.

- *Compiler compatibility*—Exists when any operating-system-independent portions of C code have identical execution semantics on different systems. C compilers fulfilling the **[K&R]** specification are, in practice, sufficiently compatible; C porting difficulties almost always spring from underlying hardware differences.

The Portable C Standard primarily addresses compiler compatibility in the above sense; it may be used independently of the UNIX system material.

A third key aspect of compatibility depends on the system software, and is:

- *Operating-system compatibility* — Exists when two operating systems support or can emulate a sufficiently complete mutual subset of kernel and support library functions. "Sufficiently complete" includes features necessary for the development of target applications, but need not include facilities that are hardware-dependent in principle or used only for system maintenance.

Strong operating-system compatibility theoretically exists among all Version 7-descended UNIX system dialects. The feature tables given later in this book will help identify a subset of portable UNIX system features.

Strong compatibility also exists among all C environments supporting the ANSI X3J11 C standard and IEEE P1003 Operating System Environment.

1.4 An Overview of Portability Techniques

The essence of portability is restraint. The objective of portability is maximum independence from the host environment. This implies not using host features that, though attractive, would tie the application too strongly to a specific host environment. Portability further implies a design style and coding practices that isolate system dependencies into small, well-defined areas.

Here are the essential elements of application portability:

1. **Write in the subset of C defined by the intersection of the capabilities of all C compilers in the target range of systems.** This may involve foregoing the use of long identifier names, advanced features like the `enum` or X3J11 `const` and `volatile`, and nonunique structure member names.

2. **Avoid machine dependencies in the manipulation of internal data structures.** For instance, do not use multicharacter `char` constants or code that makes assumptions about padding or byte order internal to structure elements.

3. **Define the formats of interprogram data transfers in a hardware-independent way** whether the transfers take place indirectly via disk files or directly via an interprocess communication mechanism. The programs may well need to be distributed to differing hardware and/or operating systems on local area networks or tightly coupled multiprocessors. Distributed systems are becoming more common; it is wise to plan for them now.

4. **Where possible, use only the common subset of library and system calls.** Most C implementations support a large subset of the UNIX I/O library. In X3J11 and P1003 conforming environments or under any UNIX system, a much larger set is available (see Appendix B for a list of functions in the Portable UNIX Software Standard).

5. **Where nonportable features are essential, use the "Portability Library" approach.** Define a generic version of the required feature and implement a version of it in terms of the nonportable functions available under each of the operating systems in the range of portability. Develop a library of such dependent features to effectively create an operating system environment that is a superset of the target operating systems.

6. **Isolate any version-dependent features needed.** Despite all of the foregoing techniques, there will still be code that differs slightly from one implementation to the next—typically, in initialization—because the software is in a different environment. Confine version-dependent

nonportable code to a small version-dependent module that has a common interface in all implementations. This module (and any in 5, above) will be documented as needing attention during ports, whereas the rest of the software should require no changes.

These points outline the theory of portability on which this book bases detailed advice. As a practical matter, there are several specific areas in which C portability problems concentrate:

- **Control of I/O to terminals and other serial-port devices.** UNIX systems have two different control protocols for terminals, neither of which has set a standard for other C environments. Furthermore, the RS-232C control signals are defined for computer- or terminal-to-modem connections and are ignored or misused in a variety of ways when directly connecting terminals to computers. Finally, despite the existence of an ANSI 3.64 terminal-control standard (largely based on the DEC VT100), there is no standard for escape sequences for control of CRT display functions. These combine to create a dismal swamp of portability problems.

- **Text file format incompatibilities.** UNIX systems use a single ASCII line feed as a line separator and do not distinguish between text and binary file types (all are modelled as arrays of characters). Other operating systems often use the sequence of a carriage return followed by line feed as a line separator, and/or implement access to text and binary files differently.

- **Filesystem name space semantics.** Again, this is not usually a problem among UNIX systems (except that 4.2BSD supports longer filename segments than other versions), but ports from an operating system with a hierarchical directory structure to one with a flat directory structure can be difficult.

- **Program size and segmentation constraints.** Eight-bit machines or segmented 16-bit architectures such as the PDP-11, Z8000, or Intel 8088/8086 family often impose 64K addressing constraints on program and data space sizes. This difficulty is sometimes addressed by making different memory models available in compiler-generated code; unfortunately, access to larger models usually hurts performance. In either case, ports of large applications to machines with limited program size are likely to be fraught with difficulties and may even require redesign.

Methods of bridging the differences between the two UNIX protocols for terminal and serial-port control are addressed later in this book. Detailed discussion of the filesystem problems will not be addressed. Limitations and tradeoffs due to segmented memory architectures must be taken into account during system design; fortunately, microcomputer chips are universally moving toward intrinsic support of larger program sizes.

1.5 A Brief History of the UNIX System

No discussion of UNIX system dialect differences would be complete without touching on the historical causes of the incompatibilities among the various dialects. In this section, we examine the genealogy of modern UNIX systems and the history of the divergence between the Bell Labs and Berkeley traditions. For more detail, the reader is referred to [DMR] for a view of early UNIX system history by one of its principals.

1.5.1 The Beginnings of the UNIX System

The UNIX system originated in 1969 as the personal project of a Bell Labs computer scientist named Ken Thompson. He had been one of the researchers from Bell Labs working with others from M.I.T. and General Electric on an experimental operating system called MULTICS. When Bell withdrew from the project, Thompson found himself at loose ends and with an itch to write an operating system based on some MULTICS-inspired ideas about filesystem design that he had been speculating about with Dennis Ritchie and several other colleagues.

During this time, Thompson acquired an available PDP-7 minicomputer for use as a host for the interactive game he had written while on MULTICS. He and Dennis Ritchie rewrote "Space Travel" for the machine. The contrast between the interactive flexibility of MULTICS and the clumsy technology being used to develop programs for the PDP-7 (cross-assembling programs on the GE 635 development machine and using paper tape to transfer the results) convinced Thompson to implement his filesystem design on the PDP-7. After the addition of various simple utility programs and an assembler, this became the first UNIX system, although it was not so named until the following year (1970).

In 1970, Thompson, Ritchie, and friends were able to justify the purchase of an early PDP-11 minicomputer in exchange for a commitment to develop a word-processing system for Bell's Patent organization. The system was up and running by mid-1971, and was a success. This gave the nascent UNIX system group enough leverage to get a bigger machine (a PDP-11/45) and was responsible for the inclusion of text manipulation tools in the UNIX system.

In 1973, the Version 4 UNIX system was rewritten in C. This greatly facilitated maintenance, porting, and extension of the system. Many early users contributed useful tools, and interest began to spread rapidly. The UNIX system began to replace other operating systems on the PDP-11 systems at Bell Labs. Computer science departments at a number of universities began to use the UNIX environment as a teaching aid and laboratory for systems design.

The expanded user community worked marvels with a poorly documented, often buggy system that nevertheless displayed enough unique strengths to make loyal friends. The growing set of development and communication tools encouraged the growth of a subculture of UNIX system aficionados. Since AT&T did not yet offer support, it was necessary for early users to become expert at the internals of the UNIX system. They added tools in profusion to versions 5 and 6 and established the UNIX system's early reputation as a hacker's system (and administrator's headache!).

All present-day UNIX system implementations are descendants of the Version 7 UNIX system for the PDP-11 first informally released by Bell Labs in the spring of 1978. Version 7 addressed most of the reliability problems and gaps in the Version 6 design, and earlier versions quickly became history. The Version 7 facilities effectively provided the portability standard of the UNIX system world.

1.5.2 The AT&T/Berkeley Connection

Ken Thompson spent a sabbatical at the University of California at Berkeley in 1979. There was considerable interest there in porting the UNIX system to the newly released Digital Equipment Corporation VAX minicomputer. Bell Labs gave the Berkeley Computer Science Department an early version of their experimental port to the VAX (UNIX/32V). A group of enthusiasts was soon hard at work.

In October 1980, after development of a number of preliminary versions, the Computer Science Department at Berkeley publicly released Berkeley System Distribution 4.1 (4.1BSD) for the Digital Equipment Corporation VAX. Many new facilities and tools (including the C shell with job control, *termcap*, and *vi*) had been added, making it a considerably more powerful and mature environment than V7. Many universities, software houses, and government installations subsequently bought VAX machines specifically to run UNIX systems, and 4.1BSD was widely identified as the state-of-the-art in UNIX systems (indeed, even various research groups within Bell Labs converted to it).

AT&T's own development of UNIX versions had gone more slowly. Uncertainties about the legality of selling computer products under the 1956 consent decree (regarding the businesses AT&T could engage in and the licensing of its patents) resulted in no group at Bell having a charter to develop UNIX systems except for internal use.

The release of System III for the PDP-11 and VAX in 1982 finally provided formal AT&T support, but the system incorporated very few of the many enhancements the UNIX system user community had come to expect in the BSD releases. System III had instead been heavily influenced by an offshoot of Version 6 called "Programmer's Workbench" (PWB), used internally at Bell Labs for software development.

General reaction in the user community was one of disappointment. Nevertheless, the potential economic advantages of portability (and an active underground of UNIX system partisans) generated interest in a supported, stable UNIX system at many commercial shops that had previously considered the system an interesting but overly risky proposition.

System III triggered a split in the user community. It had evolved in different directions than the BSD versions; most notably, the terminal control software had been rewritten to provide an interface that was more elegant than, but completely incompatible with, Version 7 and even more alien to the elaborate enhancements that had been added to BSD to support job control and other functions.

In a larger sense, the split between the Version 7/Berkeley world and AT&T System III reflected widespread uncertainties about the UNIX system's role and its future. The quirky, hacker-spawned ingenuity of the BSD version clashed with the safe-and-sane corporate respectability of AT&T's "official" supported version. The debates that followed often reflected more than purely technical differences of opinion.

The growing importance of microcomputers did nothing to simplify matters. Early microcomputer ports of the UNIX system (such as Microsoft's original XENIX, first released in 1980) tended to be based on the Version 7 kernel, with enhancements modelled after the Berkeley systems. The appearance of System III created a quandary for UNIX system suppliers in the commercial micro market: Bell or Berkeley?

The first concerted attempt to address the problem came in February 1983 from */usr/group*, an influential UNIX system user's organization. Their UniForum 1983 Draft Standard (UDS 83) attempted to define a "core UNIX system" consisting of a subset of System III kernel and library calls plus a record-locking primitive. AT&T declared that it would support the UniForum effort.

The division was exacerbated by the release of 4.2BSD in July 1983. The second Berkeley release widened the gap between the AT&T version and the BSD version by introducing many more facilities and some subtle but significant incompatibilities with the Version 7 that had previously served as common ground. It began to look as though hopes for a standard UNIX system might dissolve due to ideological differences.

1.5.3 After the AT&T Divestiture

Meanwhile, AT&T announced UNIX System V, which included a major expansion of C library support, new development tools, and significantly, some major Berkeley utilities such as *termcap* and *vi*. In the late summer of 1983, AT&T announced an agreement with Intel, Motorola, Zilog, and National Semiconductor that committed the chipmakers to support compatible versions of the newly released System V for all of their (sufficiently powerful) microprocessors.

In January 1984, AT&T announced Release 2 of System V and declared its intent to cooperate with user groups to set formal standards for UNIX software. Release 2 converged with the 1984 revision of the UniForum Draft Standard (UDS 84) and with the IEEE standards proposals that grew out of it.

Release 2 added Berkeley-style enhancements like C flexnames, job control, and interprocess communication facilities. It became clear that AT&T was ready to co-opt useful developments from Berkeley and elsewhere.

That same month, DEC announced formal support for 4.2BSD-derived ULTRIX on the VAX, and IBM announced System III support for its personal computers. Industry pundits claimed that IBM's endorsement of System III established AT&T-derived industry standards, and most observers expected that System V-based products from IBM would soon follow.

Nevertheless, 4.2BSD was still favored over System V by many academic, software development, and scientific sites for its richer set of tools and features. Two major vendors released systems that offered the option to switch between System V and 4.2BSD interfaces at will, and it was notable that these systems were built as 4.2BSD systems that emulated System V rather than the other way around. Berkeley's TCP/IP networking features gave it another advantage over System V in a market increasingly concerned with data-sharing and telecommunications capabilities.

The standards momentum did not definitely swing to AT&T's System V until early 1985, when the release of the *System V Interface Definition* document provided a formalized and hardware-independent description of the System V, Release 2 facilities. The nearly simultaneous AT&T/Microsoft announcement of the marriage of System V and a projected XENIX 5.0 for the IBM PC/AT united AT&T's standard with the most successful of the microcomputer ports.

The controversy was kept alive by the adoption of the Networked File Standard (NFS) by a consortium of influential 4.2BSD vendors. AT&T responded by announcing plans for a similar transparent file-system-sharing feature for System V, Release 3.

1.5.4 The Standardization of UNIX Systems

Presentations at the 1985 USENIX Conference indicated a new spirit of cooperation between the Berkeley Computer Science Research Group and the Bell Labs team, with suggestions that the next major Berkeley version and the upcoming System V, Release 3, would converge significantly. The Berkeley 4.3 announced in September turned out to be a performance tuneup with little in the way of new features and no new challenges to AT&T's announced networking enhancements for Release 3.

That same month, AT&T and Sun Microsystems (home of Bill Joy, BSD's principal developer) announced an agreement to converge their system interfaces within the following year. It seemed clear that other 4.2BSD vendors would follow suit.

Standards-making bodies displayed a similar degree of consensus. The X3J11 ANSI Draft Proposed C Standard and IEEE P1003 Portable Operating System Environment committee (based on the work of the disbanded UniForum UNIX system standards group) both issued progress reports describing interfaces essentially identical to System V, Release 2. The AT&T System V Interface Definition included a summary of differences from the UniForum/P1003 standard, manifesting AT&T's intention to work with user-driven standards efforts. With formal cooperation between these groups being arranged, the way was cleared for an ANSI/ISO operating system and language environment standard mirroring the System V Interface Definition.

IBM's pre-announcement of System V support for its new high-end mainframes had provided the signal many in the commercial world had been waiting for. A public commitment to System V by the six largest European computer vendors stimulated hopes that the day of one international standard operating system might soon be arriving.

1.6 The Evolution of C

The evolution of the C language has been smoother, but not without divergences and a little controversy. A major advantage that C enjoyed from earliest public exposure was that the minimum C design plus standard libraries was sufficiently powerful so that there was little incentive for compiler implementors to proliferate incompatible extensions. This, together with the inertia generated by the need to support old code, has kept the language relatively compatible through its lifetime. We emphasize history and interaction with UNIX systems in the following pages; for a look at more detail of past and possible future languages, see [LR].

1.6.1 C Compiler Families

High-level language support had been an early goal of the UNIX system developers. Thompson had written an interpreter for the B language (an invention of his based on the BCPL language) for the PDP-7 version of the UNIX system; it was one of the first tools moved to the PDP-11. Some features of B made it a poor match for the PDP-11 hardware, and the interpretation overhead made it impractical for systems programming. In 1971, therefore, Ritchie and Thompson began design of a successor language, C. Ritchie subsequently designed and built the first compiler for C on the UNIX system on a PDP-11. As we have noted above, the recoding of the UNIX system in C in 1973 was a major watershed in the system's evolution.

C code was intended to replace PDP-11 machine language in UNIX systems programming. The language was designed as a sort of structured assembler for an idealized processor and memory architecture that could be efficiently modelled on most conventional machines. The effectiveness of this design may be judged by the remarkable success and stability of C on a wide range of hardware running many operating systems.

Descendants of the original C compiler (often called the "DMR compiler" after Dennis M. Ritchie's initials) provided the development language for the rapidly growing community around Versions 5, 6, and 7. In 1978, Brian Kernighan and Ritchie released *The C Programming Language* [K & R], a book that filled a much-needed role as a tutorial and description of the language. The book catalyzed interest in C outside of the UNIX system community and stimulated the growth of a number of independent implementations of the language.

Prominent among these was the Whitesmiths' compiler, an implementation developed by P. J. Plauger and others based on Version 6 C that became fairly widespread on real-time control systems and other specialized minicomputer environments, despite some significant incompatibilities with later C environments modelled on Version 7. It was later used to develop a Version 6 lookalike named IDRIS and ported to a number of microcomputers.

Meanwhile, S. C. Johnson had been developing a "Portable C Compiler" (PCC) compatible with the DMR compiler but designed to be easily retargetable to machines other than the PDP-11. Version 7 and System III supported it (as *pcc*(1)) in parallel with the DMR compiler (*cc*(1)), and the two were kept fairly closely in step as the language evolved. On the Berkeley and System V versions and in most microcomputer ports, it replaced the original DMR compiler entirely.

While C continued as the development language of choice on the exploding numbers of UNIX systems during the years following Version 7's release, it also grew in popularity in the CP/M and MS/DOS world of personal and business microcomputers. Pioneer partial implementations such as Ron Cain's Z80 public-domain "Small C" compiler prepared the way for complete, well-supported versions of the language such as Aztec, BDS, and Lattice C. The degree of source code portability between these versions remained quite high, due partly to a tradition of making C I/O and support libraries conform to the de facto UNIX system standard that had developed in the wake of Version 7.

Work began in 1983 on an ANSI standard for the C language and associated support libraries. As this book was in final preparation, the ANSI X3J11 committee was preparing the formal issue of a Draft Proposed Standard for public comment. AT&T's involvement in X3J11 was such that the final standard seemed certain to be reflected in future UNIX system releases.

The ANSI Draft Proposed Standard for C included significant enhancements to the language, but much more radical changes may be on the way from an AT&T development project called C++. The next section includes some technical discussion of both these indicators of C's future.

1.6.2 Evolution of Language Features

The C language settled into an approximation of its modern form in 1977 with the release of the phototypesetter enhancement to Version 6. That tape included the then-new version of the DMR compiler enhanced to support the *troff*(1) phototypesetting software, which was at that point the largest C application the developers had supported.

This C introduced the `typedef`, `union`, and `unsigned` (for `int`s only) constructs; the approved syntaxes for initialization and some compound operators were also changed. With one major exception, it was the language described by [K&R]. For more detail on the differences between it and earlier versions, see [K&R], Appendix A, Section 17 (Anachronisms).

That one major difference concerned the treatment of public storage. Ritchie's original intent had been to model C's public storage handling after the FORTRAN COMMON model, on the theory that any machine with a linker that could handle FORTRAN would then be able to support C.

Two early C ports (to the Honeywell and IBM 360) happened to be to machines that severely limited the use of common storage. Ritchie and others concluded that, for portability, the language design needed to be changed to incorporate the stricter definition-reference model described in [K&R], only to discover that enough existing source depended on the common model to make the change impractical.

Version 7 returned to the original common storage model. It introduced the `enum` type and support for structure assignment, structure arguments to functions, and structure returns from functions. Johnson's *pcc*(1) became important at this time in facilitating ports of the new version to a wider range of machines.

Significant new features appeared in System III. One concerned the handling of structure names. Older compilers kept structure member names in the same name space as other identifiers, so that two members of the same name in different structures caused a clash. System III relaxed this restriction; each structure template defined its own miniature name space for its member names. The `void` and `unsigned char` declarations were also introduced. The scope of `extern` declarations within a function was narrowed to the body of the function.

The first 4.1BSD C compiler was originally a port of an early System III C. Accordingly, its successors on the various Berkeley versions included all these features. Support for very long names (flexnames) was added.

AT&T's System V brought further changes. An attempt in Release 1 to reinstate the definition-reference model had to be abandoned due to heavy user pressure against it. Other changes completely removed the old Version 6 syntaxes for compound operators and initializations, and required complete qualification of structure and union name references. System V, Release 2, added Berkeley-style flexnames.

The ANSI Draft Proposed Standard for C included substantial enhancements, including: the new storage classes `const` (for read-only objects) and `volatile` (for locations such as memory-mapped control registers that may be modified at any time by the host hardware); the enhancement of `unsigned` to be a legal qualifier of any integral type; the introduction of a `signed` keyword analogous to `unsigned`; new syntax for specifying the expected argument type profiles for imported `extern` functions; initialization allowed for `auto` aggregates and `unions`; and a number of other minor changes. It also added another twist to one thread of C's history by specifying a definition-reference linkage model, with common-model linkage as a described permissible extension.

Further down the road, the future of C includes some exciting possibilities. Bjarne Stroustrup (an AT&T researcher) has produced and is developing a proposed successor language to C called C++. Publications ([**BS1**], [**BS2**], [**BS3**]) describe a superset of existing C that adds powerful facilities for object-oriented programming modelled on SIMULA-67 and Smalltalk. Since the C++ compiler can generate C code (including a C version of itself), it should prove just as portable, and potentially as widely distributed and popular as C itself.

2

PORTABLE C STANDARD

This chapter presents the rules and guidelines that constitute Rabbit's Portable C Standard. It is organized as follows:

Section 2.1 describes the philosophy that we used in developing and refining our C standards. This philosophy, which is summarized in three concise statements, has repeatedly proven itself in practice. Next we discuss four categories of rules: portability, maintenance, style, and performance. For each of these categories we indicate the degree of flexibility extended to the individual programmer.

Section 2.2 introduces the Portability Definitions File (*portable.h*), which represents one technique for realizing portable and standard C software. Examples from the Portability Definitions File are used liberally throughout the remainder of this chapter, and the entire file is presented in Appendix A.

Section 2.3 introduces the `public` and `private` keywords in the context of a discussion of the historical semantic problems of C scope declaration keywords.

Section 2.4 discusses three storage allocation models used by different compiler/linker combinations.

Section 2.5 discusses memory addressing models that arise from differences in hardware addressing architectures.

Section 2.6 describes the manner in which the number of significant characters of symbols varies in different compilers and linkers.

Sections 2.7 through 2.16 provide full details on Rabbit's Portable C Standard. Each section covers a single aspect of C programming and is subdivided into the categories discussed in section 2.1—i.e., portability, maintenance, style, and performance. The topics addressed are:

    The Preprocessor
    Names and Initialization
    Declaration and Use of Types
    Data Representation
    Character Sets
    Expression Evaluation
    Control Flow Constructs
    Managing Multiple Modules
    Modularization, Commenting, and Documentation
    Error Handling and Reporting

Section 2.17 presents a complete example function that illustrates some of the rules that have been discussed.

2.1 Overview

To be useful, any coding standard must win over programmers on its merits. No amount of cajoling or threatening will enforce a poor standard; pressures for compliance simply cause resentment and increase the ingenuity of developers' excuses. Too often, standards are an effort to create a boiler-plate intended to extract reasonable quality from mediocre programmers; such standards generally both fail their purpose and become straitjackets to competent, creative individuals.

At Rabbit, we've had consistent and even enthusiastic support for our development of coding standards, largely because of the controlling philosophy we developed at the outset and then stuck to throughout. The framework of this standard was created by a group experienced with a wide variety of hardware, applications, languages, and operating systems; details are added (even now) as new information is gained. We believe that good standards are coordinated, not imposed, and will be perceived as an aid rather than an irritation. A good standard persuades people to live up to its spirit as well as observing its letter. The guiding principles used to achieve this are:

1. **The benefits of a rule must significantly outweigh any extra effort required to follow it.** And it must be *seen* to do so by those it will constrain.
2. **The reasons for each rule must be clearly understandable.** Typically we've included these reasons with the statement of each rule or guideline, and have often added motivating examples.

3. A standard should not arbitrarily restrict programming style. Design and coding skills flourish where developers work well in teams, but take individual pride and care in their work. The standards writer should respect this by constraining developers no more than is consistent with agreed-upon goals. Stylistic freedom will also help convince developers to respect the standard.

These standards were created to increase the portability and maintainability of C programs. Related subgoals were to increase code quality and encourage consistency of style. The standard is divided into four levels of conformance as follows:

a. Portability Rules—These rules solve known portability problems by avoiding known areas of incompatibility or by establishing techniques that create portability. These rules are very explicit; they must be rigidly followed during development and code reviews. Any errors made in the application of Portability Rules will be detected by the hardware, compiler, or operating system during a future port to a new system. It is much more painful to retrofit changes once several versions have been released than to do it right the first time.

b. Maintenance Rules—These rules are designed to ensure high-quality code in order to speed initial development and/or future maintenance. Maintenance of existing systems is usually far more expensive than development, and especially so if the coding style is opaque, poorly commented, and badly structured. These rules deal with program modularity and layout, internal documentation and comments, and use of language constructs.

c. Stylistic Guidelines—As the name implies, these are advisories aimed at giving the code a somewhat consistent overall style. If, no matter who wrote a piece of code, it has a familiar look and is in a readable style, learning and maintaining it will be simpler. Careful visual layout can make the difference between a program that anyone can maintain and one that everyone wants to rewrite. Our approach is to teach good habits and encourage consistency without unnecessarily restricting personal stylistic choice.

d. Performance Techniques—Where applicable we comment on coding practices that improve performance. However, since C was well designed to generate optimized code, any C compiler with a good code generator or optimizer will generate sufficiently tight code that many supposedly "optimizing" source changes will have little effect.

Performance should be addressed first during the system design phase: the largest improvements usually come from a change to the algorithms, not the code. Initial development must concentrate on getting the structure and function correct; nobody needs a fast program that doesn't work. Once the code is functional, apply available measurement and profiling techniques to determine where to make optimizations. There will probably be several well-restricted areas that need to be optimized, in which case it may be worthwhile considering the use of one or two carefully selected assembler routines in order to leave the bulk of the C code uncompromised.

Since our coding standards all have a clear payoff in reduced suffering for both programmers and maintainers, we find that initial education followed by positive and natural reinforcement from peers are sufficient to establish, propagate, and enforce them.

The base-level C supported by all UNIX system dialects in this study is defined by Kernighan and Ritchie's *The C Programming Language* [K&R]. Where applicable, we discuss differences from the X3J11 ANSI Draft Proposed Standard for C (referred to as "ANSI C").

2.2 Portability Definitions File

Throughout the book, we refer to *portable.h*, the "Portability Definitions File". This file contains definitions of types, macros, and constants that support the conventions recommended in the portability and practices rules. It is recommended that the file be available in the "/usr/include" directory on UNIX systems.

Details of various parts of this file are discussed in the appropriate sections of this book. A complete listing of *portable.h* suitable as a starting point is reproduced in Appendix A. Modify or add to this as necessary to customize a version for any target UNIX system.

2.3 The `public` and `private` Conventions

For historical reasons, the terminology and keywords used for declarations in C tend to confuse a variable's *scope* (where it's visible from) with its *declaration level* (whether it's declared inside a function or outside at the file level) and its *storage class* (what kind of storage is allocated for it).

A variable's scope may be *function* (within one function), *file* (from its declaration to the end of a source file), or *program* (file-scoped and visible to all modules linked to the defining one). A variable's storage may be *static* (at a fixed location in data space), *auto* (on the stack in a function activation frame), or *register* (in a processor register).

Many expositions of C describe function-scoped declarations as "internal", and file- or program-scoped declarations as "external" in terms of their declaration level. This is confusing, because declarations using the keyword `extern` (to declare an item as defined in a different module or later in the same module) can also be described as "external".

The declaration syntax is just as confusing. In archaic (Version 6) C, the `static`, `auto`, and `register` keywords all described storage classes and were only legal in declarations within functions. All "external" definitions (outside functions) had program scope.

During development of the *troff*(1) phototypesetter, the need for variables with file scope was realized. Rather than add a new keyword, the developers decreed that `static` on a file-level declaration would give the declaration file scope. This new kind of declaration was called "external static," completing the confusion.

To clarify the terminology and scope of "external" declarations, we define two pseudo-keywords in *portable.h*:

```
/* Scope control pseudo-keywords */
#define public                 /* public is C default scope   */
#define private   static       /* static really means private */
```

With these extra declarators, we can redefine our terminology for scope and storage class. Function-scoped declarations may have `static`, `auto`, or `register` storage; file- or program-scoped declarations may not include storage class keywords (they are always static) but always include `public`, `private`, or `extern` to indicate their actual scope.

As another benefit of this approach, we are able to write a tool that scans a C source file for all `public` declarations and creates a small file of corresponding `extern` declarations. This interface file—often referred to as a ".x" file because of its filename extension—is included in other source files that will reference functions or variables in the original file. With this method, error-prone manual generation of `extern` declarations is eliminated. We shall see in Chapter 5 that makefiles can be set up to use this tool to ensure automatic updating of interface files whenever necessary.

2.4 Public Storage Models

One major source of problems in porting C programs made up of more than one source module is the different models used by compilers and linkers to interpret definitions of and references to storage that is visible to several modules.

The three distinct models commonly encountered are listed below from least to most restrictive.

1. *Common-storage model* — A given name may be defined multiple times, possibly with different sizes; all definitions will be combined by the linker, and a single area of the largest size will be allocated in the runfile. All references will be to this area.
2. *Definition-reference model* — A given named storage area may be defined only once; further definitions are illegal and raise an error. Thus, all but one declaration of any variable must be preceded by an `extern` keyword.
3. *Whitesmiths model* — There may be any number of `extern` and any number of unqualified (`public`) declarations of a variable. Exactly one must be initialized and is taken to be the definition, determining the size and initial contents of the data area in the runfile.

The greatest impact of the differing models is in the use of include files. UNIX software traditionally takes advantage of the looseness of the common-storage model by declaring all common storage for a multiple-module program in a single include file and then including it in every module. This fails rather messily on systems that use any stricter model (most notably, on System V, Release 1).

To ensure compatibility, assume restrictions of the definition-reference model and initialize at the single `public` **declaration.** That is, in any collection of modules, there should be exactly one definition (an initialized `public`); all other declarations should be preceded by the keyword `extern`. Use of the `public` and `private` pseudo-keywords and the ".x" file convention recommended in the C standards section tends to alleviate most of the confusions in this area.

Notice that although **[K & R]** describes and uses a definition-reference model, and the Draft ANSI C Standard prescribes the same, almost all UNIX system compilers use the looser common-storage model (System V, Release 1, the exception, uses definition-reference).

The Whitesmiths model is found exclusively on compilers from Whitesmiths, Ltd, which run on Z-80, 8088, and 68000 micros and the PDP-11 family.

2.5 Memory Addressing Models

An aspect of hardware architecture that can affect the portability of C programs is the manner in which memory addresses are specified. The PDP-11 on which C was designed had a memory organization that encouraged C programmers to treat its data segment as a linear sequence of addressible byte-sized cells including the procedure's stack. Many of the machines on which C and the UNIX system have been most successful (e.g., the DEC VAX, Motorola 680xx, National Semiconductor 320xx, and Western Electric

32000 series) have large, flat, byte-addressable data spaces and addressable stacks.

Although C's formal definition almost entirely sidesteps dependence on any underlying processor model, traditional C usage and much standard library code and conventions derived from UNIX systems assume these features. Processors with a very different memory model may cause or expose portability problems.

Some processors do not have a linear address space. As an example, the Intel 8088/86 processors have a 16-bit offset register that is used in conjunction with a 16-bit segment register to determine the actual address. The offset register is not sufficiently large to span the entire address space; therefore, no more than 64K bytes may be addressed contiguously. To access the full range of memory, it is also necessary to modify the contents of the segment register. This results in a choice of memory addressing modes that can be used: specifying only the offset and accepting the 64K limit, or specifying the offset and the segment address.

Compilers typically address this problem by offering a choice of memory models. On Intel machines, there are separate segment registers for the code and data segments. Compilers offer a choice of offset (small, fast code restricted to 64K) or segment/offset (larger, slower code with access to all memory) addressing, for each of the code and data spaces. There are thus four distinct memory models, as follows:

Code	Data	Model
64K	64K	Small
64K	all	Large Data
all	64K	Large Code
all	all	Large

In a small-model program, pointer handling is similar to that of a machine with 64K maximum memory (such as the 8080); although long integers may be 32-bits, pointers are 16-bit objects and thus these objects are not interchangeable.

In a large-model program, all of the machine's memory is available. Both long integers and pointers may be 32-bit objects, but pointers are internally composed of two 16-bit parts that combine arithmetically to form the final address value. The special arithmetic necessary to operate upon these pointers (e.g., incrementing, subtracting) can be hidden by the compiler. Casting a pointer value into a long integer and then performing arithmetic upon it is almost certain to give invalid results.

The two mixed-size models provide a special problem: it is possible that the pointers for code and data segments may be of different sizes (32-bit for data and 16-bit for code or vice versa). In this situation, the programmer must be especially careful to use the correct type of pointer for the object to which it points (i.e., pointer to variable versus pointer to function). Further, code generated using different models cannot necessarily be linked together, so support libraries may have to be available in each of the models.

Regardless of the memory model used, porting from such a machine is generally easier than porting to it.

2.6 Significance Lengths of C Identifiers

An important pair of compiler/linker parameters that differ among systems is the maximum number of initial characters in an identifier that are significant for either private (static global and local) or public (non-static global) identifiers. The following table gives these figures.

In the table, the entries for *private* give the number of significant characters used by the compiler to distinguish identifiers; the entries for *public* give the number of significant characters used by the linker. The ANSI column describes the proposals of the X3J11 Draft Proposed Standard for C.

Scope	V7	BSD	SIII	SV1	SV2	XENIX	ANSI
Private	8	256	8	8	256[2]	31[3]	31
Public	7[1]	256	8	8	256[2]	31[3]	6

[1] This is the figure for PDP-11s. Some machines, such as the Honeywell 6000, have a six-character limit.

[2] System V, Release 2, has options to enable strict (eight-character) checking.

[3] This figure describes XENIX 3.0; 2.3 has an eight-character limit. Early releases of PC/AT XENIX 3.0 allow multiple public declarations without complaint, but have a compiler bug in the declaration code that prevents storage from being allocated unless one of the declarations is initialized.

2.7 The Preprocessor

Although defined in [K&R], the preprocessor is often treated as separate from the C language proper; consequently, it varies somewhat more than the compiler does from one implementation to another. Its purpose is to perform literal string replacement of single tokens or of macros that resemble "call by name" functions. While the preprocessor is a very powerful tool, it can lead to a variety of unusual errors and has the potential for major abuse. This section gives rules for realizing the benefits of the preprocessor while avoiding the pitfalls.

2.7.1 Portability

Due to variation in support of preprocessor capabilities and due to the possible unexpected results when expansions occur, macros must be defined very carefully. The following rules assist the definition of safe, portable macros.

The definition must fit on a single line. The use of backslash as a continuation character is not accepted by some compilers.

The macro text should not include C keywords. This restriction is due to the nonobvious nature of macro expansions. By embedding a C keyword such as return, case, or break in a macro, the programmer hides part of the program's structure. This can create bugs that are very difficult to see at the source level, especially by a person other than the original programmer.

Each usage of a parameter must be parenthesized. This protects against unexpected interactions of the expanded parameter with the surrounding macro text. Given the code fragment

```
#define SCALE(x)  x * 5

    z = SCALE(y + 1);
```

the expansion will be y + 1 * 5. If the parameter is parenthesized, as in

```
#define SCALE(x)  (x) * 5

    z = SCALE(y + 1);
```

the expansion will be (y + 1) * 5, which is the intended result.

The overall replacement text must be enclosed in parentheses or braces. This protects against unexpected interactions of the expansion text with the surrounding original text by guaranteeing that the expansion is always itself a syntactically correct C expression or statement. Given the code fragment

```
#define ODD(x)  (x) & 1  /* Nonzero if value of x is odd */

    if (ODD(y) == ODD(z)) ...
```

the expansion will be

```
    if ((y) & 1 == (z) & 1)
```

where the == will take precedence, giving results very different from the expected. If the expansion text is parenthesized, as in

```
#define ODD(x)   ((x) & 1)    /* Nonzero if value of x is odd */

    if (ODD(y) == ODD(z))  ...
```

the expansion will be

```
    if (((y) & 1) == ((z) & 1))
```

which is the intended result.
Examples of well-formed macro definitions are:

```
#define BYTE(x)      ((x) & 0x0ff)
#define FATAL(s, c)  {puts((s), stderr); exit(c);}
```

**Beware of passing a side-effect-generating expression (e.g., i++ or an
I/O function call) into a macro;** it may well be evaluated more times than
expected. This is one reason for requiring that a macro's name be all uppercase: its nature is clearly indicated (see Maintainability, Section 2.7.2).
Notice that in UNIX systems some commonly used "functions," such as
getchar() and *putchar()*, are actually implemented as macros.

Use #define to give mnemonic names to constant expressions.
Magic numbers (compiled-in numeric constants for program parameters) lead
to cryptic and unmaintainable code. Using #define to name them not only
makes the code more intelligible, but also eases adaptation to different operating system or machine environments when porting; most code changes occur
in header files and the compiler takes care of propagating the change
throughout the source code. When the expansion is an expression, not a single
value, remember to parenthesize the replacement text:

```
#define ROWS      24                  /* number of rows       */
#define COLUMNS   80                  /* number of columns    */
#define BUFSIZE   ((ROWS)*(COLUMNS))  /* size of screen buffer */
```

System constants are defined in *stdio.h*. Some additional constants that should
be in *portable.h* are:

```
/* Standard constants */
#define TRUE      1                  /* for use with booleans   */
#define FALSE     0

#define SUCCEED   0                  /* for use in exit() & return */
#define FAIL      (-1)               /* for exit() & error returns */

#define EOL       '\n'               /* end of line (line feed) */
#define EOS       '\0'               /* end of string (ASCII NUL) */
#define EOP       '\14'              /* end of page (form feed) */
```

TRUE and **FALSE** are names for the values C generates from relational expressions; SUCCEED and FAIL are names for values traditionally used as program exit values in UNIX software and function return values in C; EOL, EOS, and EOP are names for several common delimiter/control characters. Other useful constants should be added to *portable.h* as needed.

Avoid #elif, the defined() pseudo-function, and the ## concatenation operator. These are new in ANSI C and a few recent System V-conforming implementations; they should be avoided for maximum portability to older C implementations.

2.7.2 Maintainability

Names used in #define (constants and macros) should be uppercase (possibly with underscores and digits embedded) and must be unique within seven characters. The length limit is imposed because some compilers treat these names in the same manner as private symbol names (i.e., names not visible to the linker); on UNIX systems the lower limit is at least 8, and in ANSI C-conforming environments it is 31.

A one- or two-character lowercase prefix may be used to show grouping of constants, to indicate a common usage, or to avoid a possible naming conflict. An uppercase name indicates to the programmer that this is not a C function or variable. For macros, this is especially important since they look syntactically the same as functions but behave very differently due to the string replacement done by the preprocessor. Consider the following code fragment using typical macros supplied with most C compilers:

```
#define islower(c)   (_ctype[(c)] & _L)
#define toupper(c)   (islower(c)? ((c)-040) : (c))

    if (toupper(*p++) == 'A')
        return 1;
```

Assume that the if statement is part of a loop searching for an occurrence of 'A' or 'a' in a string pointed to by p. The expectation is that p is incremented by 1 at each execution of the statement, but look at the expanded code:

```
    if (((_ctype[(*p++)] & _L)? ((*p++)-040) : (*p++)) == 'A')
        return 1;
```

Upon careful inspection, it is clear that *p++ will execute two times for every execution of the statement; furthermore, the value of p may or may not be the same for those two executions, depending on the order of side-effect evaluation.

This insidious type of bug is very difficult to find by inspection of the source code but could be more easily noticed if the macros were called isLOWER and toUPPER, drawing the developer's attention to their true nature.

Do not create ad hoc syntax extensions. It is possible via `#define` to make C look like ALGOL, PASCAL, or some other language. Indeed, it is possible to make a C program totally unreadable by anyone but the author. Language extensions can be very powerful tools when properly handled (witness `public` and `private` in *portable.h*).

As an example of undesirable syntax extensions, consider:

```
#define IF      if (
#define THEN    ) {
#define ELSE    } else {
#define ENDIF   }

    IF a == b THEN
        IF a == 0 THEN
            printf("both zero");
            ENDIF
        printf("equal");
    ELSE
        printf("zero");
        ENDIF
```

The generated code is correct, but the syntax rules of the language have been drastically changed. This significantly increases the difficulty of maintenance for anyone other than the original programmer.

We recommend that such extensions be created only where they:

- serve to extend the usefulness of the language or to allow further tools to supplement C's capabilities (see *cx* in Chapter 5)
- will become part of the local idiom to the extent that programmers know them as well as they know the base language
- have sufficiently wide applicability that they will be defined in *portable.h*, not just in the source files of a specific application
- meet all of the guidelines set down in Section 2.7.1.

2.8 Names and Initializations

Portability problems affecting the naming of identifiers in C arise mostly from three areas:

- the number of characters within which names must be unique
- whether structure and union member names are kept separate from other names by the compiler

• the rules for names to be considered unique by the linker

We give rules for naming that avoid all of these problems. This section also deals with the writing of initializers and the maintenance/stylistic considerations of names.

2.8.1 Portability

Externally visible names must be unique within six characters regardless of case and should be composed only of letters, digits, and underscores. This applies to the names of variables and functions declared at the module level which are not private (`static`). This is required because some older linkers, especially on smaller systems, truncate symbols to six characters and use a case-blind comparison technique (i.e., 'A' and 'a' are considered to be the same). ANSI C has retained this requirement.

Internal names must be unique within seven characters for maximum portability to old UNIX systems and other C environments. ANSI C requires uniqueness within 31 characters. This applies to names of `static` and `auto` variables, private (`static`) functions, type declarations, structure and union tags, and names used in `#define` statements. C is case-sensitive, so mixed-case names can be used to advantage, but names should not be distinguished solely by a difference in case.

Do not use names that begin or end with an underscore. UNIX support libraries and C compilers commonly use names distinguished by a leading or trailing underscore; this form should be avoided in application code.

Names of members of structures or unions must be unique within the program. Compilers differ in handling structure and union tags and member names; some maintain a separate name space for each structure or union, while some put them in the same name space as variables and functions. The portable method assumes that there is only one name space and that all symbols must be unique. To achieve uniqueness without sacrificing meaningfulness, consider adding a prefix to member names derived from the structure or union name:

```
struct EmplRec        /* Employee Record structure */
    {
    char erName[20];
    int   erAge;
    };
```

The ANSI C standard requires a separate name space for the member names of each structure.

An initializer must be given for the definition of any public variable. This requirement stems from the difference in storage models described fully in Section 2.4. If it is necessary to write an initializer that is not truly meaningful (e.g., where no value is valid until set during a runtime initialization), document this with a comment so that maintainers will not be misled.

Initializers should be written using the equals sign. Some compilers still support the Version 6 syntax, which does not require the equals sign but many do not. Obsolete syntax should never be considered portable.

2.8.2 Maintainability

Names should be chosen to reflect the purpose of the variable or function they identify. In addition, local names should not conflict with global names; the C compiler will correctly override the global but a maintainer may miss or forget the local redefinition and become confused.

2.8.3 Style

The following single-character names, sometimes followed by a digit, are conventional for scratch variables (typically **auto** variables). It is not appropriate to use these names as global or public variables (see the preceding rule); it is best to use mnemonically meaningful names wherever possible. It is also not appropriate to use these names for variables whose scope can be (loosely) defined as "farther than the eye can see."

c	character values
i, j, k	indices
m, n	maximum counts
p	pointers
s	string values

The use of one or more of the following letters as a prefix is recommended as a way to indicate the use of the rest of a name:

c	character
p	pointer to
l	length of
n	number of
b	byte
w	word
i	index of
f	flag
s	string

As an aid to readability, for names beginning with a lowercase letter, the use of an underscore is recommended to set off the prefix (e.g., l_name). Names beginning with uppercase do not need the underscore (e.g., lName), an advantage considering the six- and seven-character uniqueness requirements.

2.9 Declaration and Use of Types

Most problems relating to types arise from the use of nonportable declarations or misuse of the types. According to [K & R], C does not allow for the application of the keyword `unsigned` to any type other than `int` but many compilers do (ANSI C allows for all meaningful combinations of declarators). Whether or not `char` is a signed type is explicitly implementation-dependent, leading to irregular behavior of `char` values that have the high-order bit set.

The C language is relatively loose in type checking and, further, provides several mechanisms (casts, unions, pointers) for bypassing the type rules. When types are used in a straightforward way, no problems arise except variations in the sizes of variables, but use of any of these bypass mechanisms may cause portability problems by creating dependencies on the machine architecture.

In this section, we point out nonportable declarations, explain which data manipulations will lead to problems, and give some pointers on using C types to improve maintainability and performance.

2.9.1 Portability

Don't use `register` **declarations for** `short` **or** `char` **variables.** Some compilers will simply ignore such declarations but others occasionally generate bad code when the object in a register is less than an `int` in size. Although compiler bugs should not normally be taken as a reason for restricting usage, this is a practice that is frequently a source of trouble and is therefore best avoided.

Don't use the `enum` **data type.** ANSI C and many of the more recent and complete compilers do support this type, but many others do not. Because the enumerated type is not as completely implemented and strictly type-checked in C as in Pascal, not much is lost by ignoring it. The major advantage of `enum` is an improvement in code readability; similar benefit may be gained by careful use of `typedef` and `#define` constants.

Be wary of using ANSI C's new `signed`, `const`, **and** `volatile` **declarations** in code intended to be ported to older C versions. The `signed` keyword solves the signed versus unsigned implementation-dependency of the `char` type. `Const` is used to declare read-only variables. `Volatile` is used to declare variables that are changed by something external to the declaring program (e.g., memory-mapped I/O ports or variables shared with other programs). In most cases, the preprocessor can be used to translate them to null strings for compilers that do not support them without affecting the code or the design.

Pointers should be explicitly declared with the type of the objects to which they point. This applies to pointer-valued function returns as well as to pointer variables. In the rare case in which a multiple-type pointer is needed, declare it as a union of pointer types. Further, the (void *) type of ANSI C should be considered non-portable to all older C versions.

Cast NULL (which is arithmetically 0) to the appropriate pointer type any time it is used in expressions or as a function argument. On processors such as the 8086, the representation of a null pointer may differ from the arithmetic (integer-sized) constant 0. On the 68000, code generation that exploits the difference between data and address registers may break code that expects the null pointer to be identical to an integer zero.

Programs should contain no pointer assignments other than the following "safe" expressions:

1. NULL
2. another pointer variable
3. an address generated by &
4. an array name
5. a function name
6. a pointer-valued function call

Anything else will certainly not be portable and may be the source of very subtle errors.

Don't use the right shift (>>) operator on signed quantities. This operator may perform an arithmetic shift or a logical shift depending on the size of the variable, the compiler, and the hardware. When a right shift is performed, the high-order bit (sign bit) is vacated and must be filled with a one or a zero. In an arithmetic shift, it is filled with a copy of the sign bit, thus preserving the sign of the value and resulting in the equivalent of a signed divide by 2. In a logical shift, it is filled with a zero, thus modifying the sign of the value. For arithmetic right-shifts, divide by 2 to the nth power for an n-bit shift. For logical right-shifts, >> is safe for unsigned short or int variables, but not necessarily for long data.

To perform portable logical right shifts of long data, use the following macro (defined in *portable.h*):

```
/* long unsigned right shift */
#define LURSHIFT(n, b) \
        (((long)(n) >> (b)) & (0x7fffffff >> ((b)-1)))
```

This macro ensures that the inserted high-order bits are set to zero by performing a "bitwise AND" of the result with a similarly shifted bit-mask. Note that this example applies to machines with 32-bit-long integers. For other word sizes, the LURSHIFT macro must be adjusted accordingly.

Never extract data from a variable in a manner other than that in which it was stored. Using a union to store data and then to retrieve parts of it using different type interpretations will generally not be portable. Also, taking the address of a variable, casting it to some other type, then accessing the value via this pointer is not a portable technique for data conversion. For instance, storing a value in an `int` and then attempting to access the least-significant byte of that `int` using a trick involving unions or pointers will yield very different results on different machines because the byte-order may be reversed and because the length of an int can differ.

The only safe form of pointer casting is in using a character pointer to copy data from one scalar, array, or structure to another of identical type and size. This works because internal byte-ordering, padding, and so on, is maintained between different instances of variables of the same type. The important point is that no attempt be made to interpret or operate upon the data, only to copy it.

No bitfield may be larger than an `int` **or overlap an** `int` **boundary in memory.** Individual fields should be no larger than 16 bits, since an `int` may be only 16 bits on some machines (this assumption should be confirmed if a broader range of portability is planned). Notice that C does not guarantee the order of bits in the physical memory, only that bit fields may be accessed as stored.

Use type `char` **only for seven bit unsigned data.** (Notice that the seven-bit ASCII character set meets this requirement.) The C language does not define whether `char` variables contain signed or unsigned values: The choice is explicitly left as implementation-dependent. This means that `char` values that have the high-order bit set will be treated as negative numbers on some machines and positive numbers on others.

On a machine that treats `char` as unsigned data, there is no easy way to force sign-extension; thus, the use of `char` for signed data is completely unportable. The ANSI C standard deals with this problem by adding the keyword `signed`, which may be applied to `char`. The next rule deals with a way of handling 8-bit unsigned quantities.

For 8-bit unsigned data, use type `byte` **and the** `BYTE` **macro to avoid sign-extension problems.** (`byte` and `BYTE` are defined below.) This applies to constants as well as variables. For example, on machines that treat `char` as signed:

```
char c;

c = 0x80;
if (c == 0x80)
    puts("equal");
else
    puts("unequal");
```

will always print "unequal" since c will be converted to `int` (with sign-extension) before comparison to the `0x80` constant. This can be rewritten as

```
byte c;

c = 0x80;
if (BYTE(c) == 0x80)
    puts("equal");
else
    puts("unequal");
```

which will print "equal" because the combination of the `byte` type and the `BYTE` macro will ensure that data is treated as unsigned.

Octal character constants are subject to the same sign-extension. Thus, on some machines, `printf("%x", '\200')` will output "ff80".

Type conversion also takes place when arguments are passed to functions: `char` and `short` become `int`. Again, this coercion can lead to surprises. For example, if `c` is a `char` initialized to "128", the `printf("%d", c)` may print "−128", because `c` was sign-extended when it was moved to the stack.

The `byte` type and `BYTE` macro operate together to mask these differences. Variables intended to store 8-bit unsigned data are declared as `byte` and every access to the variable is via the `BYTE` macro. Character constants that have the high-order bit set should also be referenced using `BYTE`. In the following code fragment, the expression `BYTE('\200')` ensures that `i` is set to 128 regardless of sign-extension rules, `b1` is also set to 128, and the expression `BYTE(b1)+1` ensures that the output will be "129, 129" regardless of sign-extension rules.

```
int  i;
byte b1;

i = BYTE('\200');
b1 = i;
printf("%d, %d", i+1, BYTE(b1)+1);
```

Definitions for the `byte` type and `BYTE` macro appear in *portable.h*; their definitions are selected for the target environment. Where the C compiler supports `unsigned char`, they are:

```
typedef   unsigned char   byte
#define   BYTE(x)         (x)
```

In this situation, the `byte` type directly supports the needed function and the `BYTE` macro does nothing.

Where the C compiler does not support `unsigned char` and characters are unsigned by default, they are:

```
typedef   char      byte
#define   BYTE(x)   (x)
```

Here again, the `byte` type directly supports the needed function and the `BYTE` macro does nothing.

Where the C compiler does not support `unsigned char` and characters are signed by default, they are:

```
typedef   char        byte
#define   BYTE(x)      ((x) & 0xff)
```

Here, the `byte` type is signed since no other option is available, but the `BYTE` macro will strip all high-order bits, effectively undoing the sign extension.

2.9.2 Maintainability

Use `typedef` to create names for commonly used types. If the usage is common to more than an application, place the definitions in *portable.h*. Some types defined in *portable.h* in Appendix A are:

```
typedef int           bool;    /* >= 16 bits used as boolean  */
typedef char          flag;    /* >=8  bits used as boolean   */

typedef int           rchar;   /* I/O function return values  */
typedef char          *string; /* for readability             */

/* Use this length and type for filename variables; use
   256 on 4.2BSD since it is defined as such in dir.h          */
#ifndef MAXPATHLEN
#define MAXPATHLEN    64
#endif
typedef char          path[MAXPATHLEN];
```

Use `byte` for variables holding 8-bit unsigned data, `bool` and `flag` for logical values, and `rchar` for the `int` values returned by functions dealing with signed character data or character data plus "out-of-band" values (e.g., −1 for EOF in C library I/O functions). The `string` type is purely for mnemonic value; the `path` type is used for names of files and directories, providing a common definition with a constant defining its length. Using these types makes the purpose and real data type of the variable more obvious.

Use `typedef` to make `struct` declarations more readable and uniform with declarations of scalar types. A structure tag declaration compounded with a suitable `typedef`, as:

```
typedef struct
    {
    int     stype;
    char    *name;
    }
    sample;
```

permits use of the declaration `sample newone;` instead of the usual `struct sample newone;`. The former often is more readable, especially when it is in the middle of a list of scalar-type declarations. Notice also that the new type, `sample`, may be used in `sizeof( )` expressions.

The extended form of structure tag declaration in which instances of a structure are declared following the closing brace, as in:

```
struct sample
    {
    int     stype;
    char    *name;
    }
    newone;
```

should be avoided, especially if the tag will be used for other declarations. It is less clear and less versatile than the approach recommended here.

Every function and variable must be explicitly typed. Don't use C's default implicit type of `int`. This simple rule produces more reliable, easier-to-read code, and facilitates the building of automated source-analysis tools. Use of `typedef` to assign mnemonic type names to commonly used definitions is recommended.

Wherever reasonable, declare functions as returning `int, not short` **or** `char`. Function returns are typically passed in registers (which are `int` width almost by definition); the `int` declaration avoids the need for an extra `extern` declaration to get the type correct when the function is linked from a library. The more usual case in which it is brought in from an object module is handled by the interface (".x") file created by `cx` (see Chapter 5).

There is a very nasty form of bug that can occur from mistyped function returns. Assuming a machine with 32-bit `int` and 16-bit `short`, consider a function `short func( )` called from a module that does not have an extern for `func( )`. The `return` statement in `func( )` may generate code that moves a (short) value into the lower 16 bits of a 32-bit register without clearing the upper 16 bits. The reference to `func( )` will generate code that treats the whole 32-bit register as the result (it expects an `int`), thereby picking up garbage in the upper 16 bits.

Functions that do not return a value should be declared type `void`. This enables *lint* to do sharper correctness tests. Where the C compiler does not support `void`, `#define` it as `int` in *portable.h*.

Note that many C compiler code generators derived from the Portable C Compiler (including those on 4.1BSD and System V) become very confused if the program uses the value of a function declared `void`, to the point of emitting a cryptic error message and crashing, so be careful to be consistent between declarations and references.

Expressions in `while, for, if, and ? :` **should have boolean results.** Reliance on the C rule that nonzero values are equivalent to TRUE can lead to code that is not completely clear. For instance, the meaning of

```
while (i-- && !j)
```

is more quickly grasped when it is written

```
while (i-- > 0 && j != 0)
```

Not only is readability enhanced, but a potential bug is avoided (if `i` is initially negative). Typically, a compiler will generate almost exactly the same code for both versions so there is little or no cost in terms of code size or performance.

2.9.3 Performance

For integer variables, use `int` **whenever space doesn't matter.** The size of an `int` is normally selected to be the most efficient for any given hardware. `Short` and `char` variables are always converted to `int` size values when used in expressions, so using `int` may shrink code size and aid performance considerably.

For floating-point variables, use `double` **whenever space doesn't matter.** For the same reasons given above for `int`, `double` should be used for scalar variables.

In structures, arrays, and other aggregate objects, use an explicit type closely suited to the size of the data. The trade-off is storage space versus the automatic conversion which occurs when the data is accessed. Using an `int` where a `char` would suffice can create an array up to four times larger. Furthermore, the size of an `int` may vary between two or four bytes (typically). Plan ahead and use a size that will not become restrictive in the future; for instance, if the values to be stored may someday overflow a 16-bit signed integer, use of `long` (not just `int`) is advisable.

Declare frequently used automatic or argument variables as `register`. Getting pointers and loop counters into registers can significantly increase performance. On entry to a function, for each variable to be placed in a register, that register's previous contents must be saved, thereby incurring some overhead. If `register` is used indiscriminately, this overhead could outweigh the expected savings. The primary candidates for `register` declaration are variables that are referenced within a loop.

Since C compilers will ignore register declarations after available registers have been used, declare them in the order that puts the most intensively used variables first. The following technique makes the priority of register declaration explicit. Given a machine that typically has three available registers, put the following in *portable.h*:

```
#define REG1    register
#define REG2    register
#define REG3    register
#define REG4
#define REG5
#define REG6
#define REG7
#define REG8
```

Subsequently, instead of writing `register` for each register declaration, use one of the macros, declaring the most critical to be `REG1`, the next most critical to be `REG2`, and so on. Up to eight variables may be declared this way since each `REGx` macro should apply to a single variable.

Putting scalar variables before arrays in `auto` **declaration lists may generate better code** on machines that access stacked values using a limited indexed addressing mode. As an example, the Z80 IX or IY registers can be used as stack frame pointers, providing indexed addressing to 128 bytes of stack data. When accessing data beyond the 128-byte limit, several instructions must be used to compute the stack address.

2.10 Data Representation

The major considerations of this section are the number of bytes in a data object and the order of the bytes. Remember that the specific rules apply to the range of portability that we have selected—they are not universal. In particular, the assumptions about the size of various types may need to be changed if a broader range is assumed.

2.10.1 Portability

Assume that `char` **is at least 8 bits,** `short` **at least 16 bits, and** `long` **at least 32 bits.** Experience with a number of 16- and 32-bit machines has shown that these are reasonable, but some 8-bit machines use 16 bits for `long`. Also, notice that on a 36-bit word machine, `short` may be 18 bits and `char` 9 bits. This should present no problem if the code has been written to be independent of exact sizes.

Do not assume that a pointer and a long integer are interchangeable. Pointers are normally the size necessary for memory addressing on the target machine. This may well be different from the size supported for `long`. Segmented machines, such as the Intel 80186, use two 16-bit values for segment/offset addressing. On these machines, the size of a pointer may be 16 bits for the small memory model and 32 bits for the large memory model; in a mixed model, pointers to data and functions may be of different sizes.

An `int` is always at least as large as a `short` and never larger than a `long`. According to **[K&R]**, the only guaranteed relationship is that "`short` is no longer than `long`," but it is reasonable to assume that `int` will fall within that range.

Never depend on the order of bytes in a variable. In particular, don't cast an address into a pointer to a different type for the purpose of operating upon the data.

Addresses passed to functions must point to types that exactly match the declared formal parameters: Be careful not to pass an (`int *`) to a function that is expecting (`char *`) or vice versa. Making this mistake may cause the function to read or to store more or less bytes than the variable can accommodate.

Never use multiple-character `char` constants. Some compilers allow this, some don't, and it is not clear that the results will be consistent across those compilers that do. The only portable use of character constants on current compilers is for single character values.

The `sizeof` operator always yields the amount of space an instance of an aggregate object would occupy in an array. Thus, on machines with alignment requirements, it will count in whatever padding would be required for its argument in an array—whether or not the argument is an array element.

2.11 Character Sets

Although most computers supporting the UNIX system and/or C use the ASCII (American Standard Code for Information Interchange) character set representation, complete portability demands that code not depend on the collating sequence or bit encoding of any particular character set. In particular, code depending on the ASCII character set is not portable to IBM or IBM plug-compatible machines that use the EBCDIC (Extended Binary-Coded Decimal) character set. This section considers character set portability specifically with respect to ASCII and EBCDIC.

Even though it may seem unlikely that a software product will ever be ported to one of these systems, it is worthwhile planning for such portability. The modification of existing software to retrofit character set independence can be a significant problem; by comparison, the initial effort required to write code portably is small.

2.11.1 Portability

Where possible, use the standard character-type functions or macros of *ctype*(3) **rather than comparisons or bit checks.** Almost all C environments provide at least the Version 7 macros *isalpha*(3), *isupper*(3), *islower*(3), *isdigit*(3), *isalnum*(3), *isspace*(3), *ispunct*(3), *isprint*(3), *iscntrl*(3), and *isascii*(3), defined appropriately for the system's character set. Most also support System III's *toupper*(3) and *tolower*(3) macros, which offer portable conversion between alphabetic cases. Any of these that do not exist on a system can easily be defined.

Do not depend on the results of arithmetic expressions which use character values. Since the collating sequences of ASCII, EBCDIC, and other character sets differ, a given source character may have various binary internal representations. For example, the character "A" has the value 0x41 in ASCII and the value 0xC1 in EBCDIC.

Comparing characters using other than the = = and != operators is not portable. Again, this is a direct result of collating sequence differences. In ASCII, for example, 'A' is greater than '0'; while in EBCDIC, 'A' is less than '0' (the value of '0' is 0x30 in ASCII and 0xF0 in EBCDIC). On the other hand, all ASCII and EBCDIC variants have 'A' less than 'Z', 'a' less than 'z', and '0' less than '9'; hence, *for these two character sets*, two digits or two alphabetics of the same case may be portably compared.

Do not rely on the binary values of alphabetics to be a contiguous sequence. In ASCII, the ranges 'A'...'Z' and 'a'...'z' correspond to contiguous ascending sequences of values, but in EBCDIC there are large gaps between segments of the alphabet.

2.12 Expression Evaluation

This section deals more with understanding the evaluation order rules of C than with portability per se. C's rules of expression evaluation differ from those of most other procedural languages, partly because of the lack of a "left-to-right" default order and partly because of the presence of "side-effect-generating" operators. Although there may be differences in evaluation order from one compiler to another, these are due to the language definition, and if the language rules are understood, they should not be a cause of trouble.

2.12.1 Portability

Evaluation order is guaranteed only for the following operators:

expr1, expr2	comma operator
expr1 ? expr2 : expr3	conditional
expr1 && expr2	logical and
expr1 || expr2	logical or

all of which guarantee evaluation from left to right (notice that some of these do not always evaluate their right-hand arguments). These constructs, along with the semicolon, are sometimes called "sequence points" because they give C's only guarantees of evaluation order.

Notice that the comma in function headers, argument lists, and declaration lists is not the comma operator and evaluation order is not guaranteed.

The order of side-effect evaluation is undefined. Except for the four "sequence point" operators, C compilers do not guarantee left-to-right evaluation of equal precedence operators as some other languages do. Compilers may rearrange subexpressions at will in order to improve efficiency. Further, the specific timing of evaluation of side effect generating operators is not defined. To avoid unexpected behavior, never write expressions that involve more than one side-effect-generating operator or function call, and don't use a variable more than once in an expression if it is subject to a side effect.

This means that expressions such as e1 + e2 may be evaluated as e2 + e1. Problems arise when one or more of e1 or e2 calls a function with side effects or uses a side-effect operator such as ++. The expression

```
z = a[i] + b[i++];
```

where i is initially 0 could be evaluated as though it were

```
z = a[0] + b[0];
```

as is the intention, or as

```
z = b[0] + a[1];
```

due to rearranging performed by the compiler.

Use explicit temporaries when order of evaluation is important, not parentheses. In particular, notice the following from **[K&R]**, page 185: "Expressions involving a commutative and associative operator (*, +, &, |, ^) may be rearranged arbitrarily, even in the presence of parentheses; to force a particular order of evaluation an explicit temporary must be used." This is a reasonable result given the lack of a definition of evaluation order discussed above. It does not impose any further restrictions on the programmer but bears noting for those whose past experience leads them to expect parentheses to be sacred.

ANSI C specifies that a unary plus before a left parenthesis will cause the parentheses to be respected; however, this still does not guarantee evaluation order within the parentheses.

Do not pass structures as function arguments. Structure-passing (the passing of an entire structure, not a pointer to it) is supported by post-V7 UNIX C compilers and by ANSI C but is by no means universal. Even on implementations that support it, insidious bugs in stack handling may result from the nonatomic nature of the copy operation (this was a documented problem in early AT&T versions).

2.12.2 Maintainability

The comma separator in declarations does not guarantee an evaluation order; declarations such as

```
int   a = 0, b = a+1;
```

are unwise. Further, on a machine with only three available registers, the declaration

```
register int a, b, c, d;
```

could place any three of the variables in registers. (Refer to Section 2.9.3 for a method of handling register declarations.)

Don't use comma where a compound statement will do. The comma operator in C provides a method of constructing compound statements parallel to the use of brace brackets. In most cases, it leads to poor coding practices including the writing of more than one statement on a line. Statements such as

```
if (pass++, i == 0) i++, init(pass);
```

are much less obvious than the equivalent

```
pass++;
if (i == 0)
     {
     i++;
     init(pass);
     }
```

Also, this allows for better commenting and easier addition of statements if the code is later modified.

The only place where the comma operator is undoubtedly appropriate is within the control expressions of do, while, and for statements, as in:

```
/*  Compress blanks out of a string  */

len = strlen(s) + 1;
for (i = 0, j = 0; j < len; j++)
     if (s[j] != ' ')
          s[i++] = s[j];
```

Use parentheses to force evaluation order when using any operators beyond the common arithmetic (+ − ∗ /), relational (> < >= <= ==

!=), and logical (&& ¦¦) ones. C has 44 operators arranged in 15 priority levels, some grouping left to right and some right to left. It is easier to code an expression correctly when parentheses are used; code becomes more explicit and easier to maintain.

For example: the expression

```
( c & 0xf == 0 )
```

is not a comparison of the lower order four bits of c to zero as might be expected. The implicit order of evaluation is

```
( c & ( 0xf == 0 ) )
```

so parentheses must be used, as in

```
( ( c & 0xf ) == 0 )
```

to get the desired result.

Additionally, for very complex expressions, consider breaking them into simpler subexpressions using intermediate variables. Not only does this enhance the understandability and the maintainability of the code, but some compilers have been known to become confused by sufficiently complex expressions.

2.13 Control Flow Constructs

Whole texts have been written on the subject of structured programming and design, which the reader should consider in addition to this book. A full treatment of the subject is beyond our scope, but we make some recommendations designed to guide programmers toward the best use of available constructs. C provides a sufficient set of constructs to allow for the writing of well-structured code, but there are one or two nonstructured temptations to avoid.

2.13.1 Maintainability

Never use goto **to transfer control to a point inside a more deeply nested block.** If control is transferred into a loop that has not been initialized or has previously terminated, the criteria for loop termination will not necessarily succeed.

In general, the goto **statement (hence, labels) should be avoided as much as possible;** use break and continue instead. In particular, avoid transferring control to points earlier in the source file. Furthermore, functions that use more than one label probably do not fully use the available structured control statements and should be rewritten.

A guideline for multiple choice constructs: use "if ... else if" if the order of evaluation is significant, the conditions are not mutually exclusive, or if they test different variables. Use switch if the choice depends on a single variable or expression.

Document any "fall-through" cases of a switch. In C, the cases of a switch are not mutually independent compound statements as they are in some languages. Advantage often is taken of this by allowing control to "fall-through" from one case to the next. Whenever this is done, it should be clearly documented in the comments because a maintainer can be very confused as to whether this is deliberate or is an accidentally omitted break (a common bug).

2.13.2 Performance

Usually for(; ;) **generates faster code than** while(1). This is because the null expressions in the for(; ;) will generate no code, whereas the constant value in the while(1) will still generate a test on some (but not all) compilers.

Often "if ... else if ..." is faster than switch. This is because compilers differ in their ability to optimize a search of the case values of a switch. The switch often is implemented as a table search and the order of the search is not always identical to the order of the cases in the source file. The best performance usually is achieved by evaluating the switch expression into a temporary variable and testing it using a chain of if ... else if ... statements, looking for the most likely cases first.

2.14 Managing Multiple Modules

In this section, we recommend practices that affect the portability and, especially, maintainability of programs that are implemented using more than one source module. This is always the case for well-structured, nontrivial software.

2.14.1 Portability

Do not declare public variables in #include **files.** It is common practice to declare storage for variables in a header file that is then included by several source modules. Effectively, each source module declares a public instance of each variable, then depends on the linker to merge identically named blocks of storage in the generated object files. This technique fails if the compiler uses the stricter definition-reference model (see Section 2.4) as does the System V, Release 1, compiler.

The portable approach is to declare public variables once, using the
`public` keyword, in the source module that most properly "owns" them.
For a file *prog.c*, a separate file, *prog.x*, is created containing an `#include`
of the *prog.h* file, if any, and appropriate `extern` declarations for each of
the `public` variables and functions in *prog.c*. This interface file should be
included by all other source modules that use the variables or functions
defined in the originating source module.

Here is an example of how this works. If *prog.h* contains:

```
/*
     prog.h — definitions needed by prog.c and its users
*/

#define SAME       1
#define DIFFERENT  0
```

and the (trivial) function, `prog.c`, contains:

```
#include "prog.h"

public int n_matches = 0;   /* number of matches found */

public int match(a, b)  /* count and report matches */
int a, b;
     {
     if (a == b)
         {
         ++n_matches;
         return SAME;
         }
     return DIFFERENT;
     }
```

The corresponding interface file should contain:

```
/*
     prog.x — external definitions for prog.c
*/

#include "prog.h"

extern int n_matches;
extern int match();
```

If this file is included by programs that link to *prog.c*, all necessary information is acquired. In Chapter 5, we describe a shell script, *cx*, that automates
the creation of interface files.

Absolute path names should not appear in `#include` **directives.** Any
remote file (i.e., outside the current directory) referenced by an `#include`

should be referred to by the last segment of its pathname; its directory should be given in an include-path (−I) option to the compiler. Adherence to this rule means that no changes need be made to source code files if the files that they #include move to different directories.

2.14.2 Maintainability

If a constant is used in only one module, it should be defined at the head of that module. If it is used in several modules, it should be defined in a header (".h") file included by each.

Use one of extern, public, **or** private **(or its synonym** static) **for every module level declaration.** This practice controls the visibility of declarations in an obvious way and also provides keywords for use by source manipulation tools such as *cx* (see Chapter 5). Public and private are defined in *portable.h*.

Data and functions should be private unless cross-module reference is needed. Allowing names to be public unnecessarily increases the number of symbols in the linker tables, increases the chance that function names will conflict, and violates the modular programming rule of publicizing only the defined interface.

Library modules should, where practical, have a test driver built in. This usually will take the form of a conditionally compiled main program at the end of the module:

```
#ifdef TEST
main(argc, argv)
int    argc;
char *argv[];
    {
    /* The test driver goes here. */
    }
#endif
```

Compilation of the module with the −DTEST option on the command line will generate a standalone program that exercises the library function. Recompilation without −DTEST will generate the object for the library function with no space or performance penalty due to the test driver. Where the −DTEST command line option is not supported, it may be necessary to enable compilation of the test driver by editing the source file to (temporarily) define TEST or remove the #ifdef ... #endif pair.

It is all too common for test drivers to be written separately, as an afterthought, and then lost. This approach encourages writing a test driver as an integral part of development and updating the test code as a natural part of the maintenance process.

In general, avoid nesting #include **files.** Some C compilers handle a limited number of nesting levels and it may be confusing to a maintainer

trying to determine what is included in a source module. One explicit exception to this rule is that interface files may (and usually should) #include
their associated header files. We make this exception both because the relationship is well-defined and because, if necessary, *cx* (see Chapter 5) can be
redefined to copy the text of the header file into the interface file in place of
the #include.

**Non-int functions linked from a library must be explicitly declared with
an extern.** Particularly insidious bugs may result from using *malloc(3)*
and other (char *)-valued functions without explicit declarations.

For example, compilers for the Motorola 68000 often return pointer
values in the A0 register and nonpointer values in the D0 register. Omitting
the extern declaration for *malloc(3)* in this case will result in the calling
routine picking up garbage from D0 while ignoring the returned value in A0,
creating a subtle and nasty bug.

Strictly speaking, good practice would require declaring the type of all
externally defined functions (even int), but as a practical matter that
becomes too cumbersome. Also, creating and including a interface file that
defines all of the members of a library may cause linkage of all members (this
is implementation-dependent) and, therefore, is not useful.

A "module" should consist of three source components:

- A C source code file (".c" extension)
- A header file (".h" extension)
- An interface file (".x" extension)

The first component is required, the second and third may be optional.
No header file is required if the module doesn't export definitions; no interface
file is required if the module has no public variables or functions.

The ".c" file contains the C source code. The interface file contains an
#include of the header file, if any, and an extern declaration for each
public function and variable in the source code file. The header file contains
whatever constant, macro, type, structure, or union definitions are needed by
both the module and its users.

2.14.3 Style

**It is recommended that the first comment of every released module be in
the form of a manual page.** The format was designed for programmers by programmers to be easy to use and create. It is a well-established UNIX
software convention; examples of this style are found throughout the UNIX
reference manuals.

A well-written manual page comment works well as both internal and external documentation. The general format is:

```
/*************************************************************
NAME
    docexample —— illustrate manual page format
SYNOPSIS
    (List declarations of module entry points.)
DESCRIPTION
    Describe the module's function from the user perspective. Document the
    black—box function; don't describe implementation details unless the in-
    formation is necessary to use the module.
RETURNS
    Document shell status returns for a command or the return type and
    value for a function. Diagnostics may be listed and explained in depth
    here.
CAVEATS
    Describe known and rumored bugs in the code, and warn of any docu-
    mented but unimplemented features.
FILES
    If the module uses particular files or devices, list them with comments.
    Make it clear where the data comes from and goes to.
NOTES
    Discuss design limitations and environment dependencies (i.e., on
    operating system, compiler, or machine). Notes for future enhancements
    often go here also.
SEE ALSO
    Reference other modules used with or related to this module.
HISTORY
    This part should list names of authors and maintainers, the date(s) on
    which they wrote/modified the code, and notes on changes made.
COPYRIGHT
    This is where a copyright notice, if any, should be placed.
*************************************************************/
```

Use a common, consistent approach to source file organization. If source files are organized in a logical fashion, finding a particular definition, function, and so on, will be simplified. This will increase the productivity of maintainers and of the original author.

To gain the maximum benefit, it is best if a consistent approach to source file organization is adopted by all members of a programming staff. Absolute rigidity of structure is not required, simply an overall consistency. One possible such organization is:

```
/**************************************************************

NAME

     sample.c  —  a sample source file organization

     ... the manual page comment goes here (see above) ...

 **************************************************************/
/*
 * This is an optional module comment, which may contain a
 * maintainer's perspective of the module's control flow
 * and global data structures. It should be complementary
 * to the manual page.
 */

#include <portable.h>     /* Portability Definitions File */

#include "project1.x"    /* Header/extern file includes  */
#include "project2.x"
          :
#include "projectn.x"

extern  bool ext1;      /* Module externs. Few of these  */
extern  char ext2;      /*  are needed if the .x files    */
          :
extern  char ext3;      /*  have been used.               */

#include "sample.h"     /* This module's .h file, if any. */

#define DEF1  1         /* Local defines, if any.         */
#define DEF2  2
          :
#define DEF3  3

typedef char  type1;    /* Local typedefs, if any.        */
          :
typedef int   typen;

public  short pub1;     /* Public variable declarations.  */
public  char  pub2;
          :
public  int   pubn;
```

```
private char  priv1;   /* Private variable declarations. */
private long  priv2;
            :
private bool  privn;

/* Functions and procedures start here:    */
            :
            :
/* The module's main should be at the end. */

/* End of sample.c */
```

As indicated in the foregoing example, a natural ordering for functions in C is to define a function before it is referenced. This avoids the necessity of writing many `extern` declarations, which act as forward declarations and which can become out-of-date with respect to the actual function.

Where common sense dictates deviation from the normal organization, it should be done. For instance, if a public and a private variable are logically a pair, place them together in the file. The goal is to improve the maintainability, not simply to follow a rigid structure.

2.15 Modularization, Commenting, and Documentation

The visual layout of a program, the relevance of comments, and the accuracy and completeness of documentation are as important to the maintenance of software as the quality of its implementation. Even the original programmer may have trouble understanding (remembering) the intent and method of a piece of code after a year has passed. How, then, is another person to maintain that code unless attention was paid by the original author to making it transparently understandable? The recommendations of this section are a guide to clear layout and documentation.

2.15.1 Maintainability

Keep down the length and complexity of functions. Large, complex functions are difficult to understand completely—a prerequisite to successful maintenance. There is a limit to the amount of simultaneous detail with which humans can cope; functions are a tool for hiding complexity beneath a well-defined interface that may then be considered as a primitive.

Each function should address a clearly defined task; if a function grows large and complex or rambling, there are probably subtasks within it that can be made into separate functions. A good test for the conciseness of a function is whether its purpose can be described by a simple sentence of the form "verb" + "object(s)."

Another criterion to consider in deciding whether a function is overly complex or poorly defined is the complexity of the argument list. As a practical rule-of-thumb, try to keep to no more than four arguments so that the call semantics can be easily comprehended and remembered. Some arguments (e.g., x-y coordinate pairs) form natural groupings and may count as one argument for purposes of this rule.

Also note that a function of fifty lines or less can fit on a single printed page; one of twenty-four lines or less can fit on a standard size CRT screen. This is advantageous for maintenance simply because the programmer can see the entire function at one time and not have to visualize part of it while paging forward or backward to see the rest.

Each function should have a header comment, documenting its function. A good explanatory comment should be located with the header to describe basic functionality. The "verb" + "object(s)" description could appear as part of this comment. Nontrivial internal data structures and algorithms should also be explained.

Comment the purpose of the code, not the implementation. Always try to relate comments to the intent rather than the mechanics of the code. Comments such as

```
/*  If ch1 is EOF, assign FALSE to fDone  */

if (ch1 == EOF)
    fDone = FALSE;
```

are not very useful. At best, they say nothing; at worst, they clutter up the code. Instead, describe what is going on:

```
/*  When end-of-file is reached, set fDone
    flag so the main loop will terminate.  */

if (ch1 == EOF)
    fDone = FALSE;
```

This principle requires particular effort at the line-by-line level.

Comment special coding techniques. Using nonobvious techniques (clever coding "tricks" or "hacks") should be avoided unless absolutely necessary for space or performance. In the event that such code is necessary, comment liberally to describe the intended function, the mechanics of the trick, and any dangers foreseen in maintaining the code. Remember that code must be built to be maintained by those other than the original writers and designers; it must be internally constructed and documented so that any nonstandard techniques are easily understood by those who come later.

2.15.2 Style

Keep source lines under 80 characters long. This makes editing on a CRT easier and allows for printing on an 80-column printer.

Comment each logical group (paragraph) of statements. Within a function, brief comments of one or two lines can be very effective for explaining the purpose of the following section of code.

Comment declarations on the same line. Most declarations can be described with a brief phrase regarding their purpose. This form can also be used in the code text but has two drawbacks: Comments may run beyond column 80, and if code lines are added, deleted, or reordered, more effort is required to keep the comments valid.

Arrange arguments as input-only arguments first, input-output arguments next, and output-only arguments last. This is simply a convention to create consistency for the sake of maintenance.

2.16 Error Handling and Reporting

Most of the recommendations below are based on UNIX software conventions for error handling. The principles, however, are also sound for other C environments since the three standard I/O streams (stdin, stdout, stderr) are usually supported by the C library regardless of the underlying operating system.

2.16.1 Portability

Unless an application design specifically demands otherwise, write error and log messages to the stderr (standard error) stream rather than standard output. This is conventional usage and allows for the segregation of error messages to a log file, leaving the standard output stream unpolluted. This is especially important for programs designed to be "filters" (standard input and/or output streams come from and go to other programs, not files), because the program receiving the output will probably be confused by error messages and because only the error stream will be seen at the terminal.

2.16.2 Maintainability

Preface error messages with the name of the originating program. Most UNIX utilities preface their error messages with their names followed by a colon and space. This practice is recommended for C in general so that messages from different programs can be distinguished in an error log.

2.16.3 Style

By convention, UNIX utilities return an exit status of 0 to indicate successful completion. Nonzero values are commonly used as status or error indi-
cations, but may sometimes be item counts. This practice is recommended for
any C environment that supports an *exit()* function. Notice that the constant
SUCCEED (0) is defined in the *portable.h* for this purpose.

A program that can detect an invalid command line should display at
least a one line message prefixed "usage:" showing the SYNOPSIS entry
from its manual page—i.e., an indication of the correct calling sequence
and/or options. This message should be written to the standard error stream.

By convention, many C functions and UNIX system calls return values
outside their valid result ranges to indicate error conditions. It is also common
to return a fixed "impossible value", often −1 (defined as FAIL in
portable.h), and place a specific error indication in the system variable *errno*.
This is particularly useful if there are more error conditions than can con-
veniently be returned or if an error condition may have to be seen by functions further up in the call hierarchy.

We recommend that applications follow this practice. Each product or
major subsystem can be assigned a range of error numbers (but notice that
errors 1 to 99 should be left to the UNIX system; at present, various dialects
use approximately forty of them). In some implementations, errno may be
a signed 16-bit integer so error numbers should not be greater than 32767.

2.17 An Example

The following example illustrates many of the points made in the rules
defined above. In particular, it shows a manual page, a test driver, commenting practices, and use of the public and private keywords. This
function, *itoa()*, is part of the Rabbit Standard Library, a group of functions,
programs, and include files that support a portable environment across operating systems in our range of portability.

```
/*

NAME

    itoa  --  integer to ascii string conversion


SYNOPSIS

    int itoa(num, pBuf, lBuf)
    int   num;          - Number to be converted
    char *pBuf;         - Pointer to output buffer
    int   lBuf;         - Length of output buffer


DESCRIPTION

    itoa converts an integer value (num) to an ascii
    digit string in pBuf.  If the string length (lBuf)
    is not sufficient to hold all of the digits plus a
    string terminator and a minus sign (if needed), the
    result string is truncated on the left.

RETURNS

    itoa returns the length of the result string, not
    counting the string delimiter.  If the value of
    lBuf is zero or negative, nothing is stored at
    pBuf and FAIL (-1) is returned.

HISTORY

    21 Jul 83 - Les Shuda - Original coding

*/

#include <portable.h>


public int itoa(num, pBuf, lBuf)  /* Convert int to string */
int   num;              /* Number to be converted  */
char *pBuf;             /* Pointer to output buffer */
int   lBuf;             /* Length of output buffer  */
    {
    register int i;     /* Buffer index       */
    int sign;           /* Hold sign of num */

    /*  If the buffer length is invalid,
        return an error indication (FAIL).  */
    if (lBuf <= 0)
        return FAIL;

    /*  Store an end of string marker at
        the end of the output buffer.          */
```

```
    pBuf[lBuf — 1] = EOS;

    /*  Exit now if output buffer is too
        small to put any digits into.        */
    if (lBuf < 2)
        return 0;

    /*  Store the sign and make sure num is positive */
    if ((sign = num) < 0)
        num = —num;

    /*  Set i to index the last position in the buffer
        then loop to store converted digits until the
        number is done or the string is full. The digits
        are converted starting at the least significant
        and are right—justified in the buffer.          */
    i = lBuf — 1;
    do
        {
        pBuf[——i] = num % 10 + '0';
        }
        while ((num /= 10) > 0 && i > 0);

    /*  Store a '—' if num was negative and there
        is still room in the buffer.              */
    if (sign < 0 && i > 0)
        pBuf[——i] = '—';

    /*  Now, left—justify the result string
        in the output buffer.                */
    if (i > 0)
        strcpy(pBuf, &pBuf[i]);

    /*  Return the length of the result string,
        not counting the string delimiter.      */
    return (lBuf — i — 1);
    }


#ifdef TEST
#include <stdio.h>

private char s1[10];      /* test output area    */
private int i;            /* integer test value  */
private short h;          /* short int test value */
private int res;          /* return from itoa    */
```

```
main()
     {
     printf("Test run of itoa.\n");

     /*  Test conversion of values throughout the range
         -1,000,000 to 1,000,000, using different size
         variables and output buffers.                        */
     printf("\nLarge #s (int) with buffer len = 10...\n");
     for (i = -1000000; i < 1000000; i += 12345)
          {
          res = itoa(i, s1, 10);
          printf("i = %d, string = %s, return = %d\n",
                  i, s1, res);
          }

     printf("\nLarge #s (int) with buffer len = 7...\n");
     for (i = -1000000; i < 1000000; i += 12345)
          {
          res = itoa(i, s1, 7);
          printf("i = %d, string = %s, return = %d\n",
                  i, s1, res);
          }

     printf("\nSmall #s (short) with buffer len = 10...\n");
     for (i = -32767; i < 32767; i += 319)
          {
          h = (short) i;
          res = itoa(h, s1, 10);
          printf("h = %d, string = %s, return = %d\n",
                  h, s1, res);
          }

     printf("\nSmall #s (short) with buffer len = 5...\n");
     for (i = -32767; i < 32767; i += 319)
          {
          h = (short) i;
          res = itoa(h, s1, 5);
          printf("h = %d, string = %s, return = %d\n",
                  h, s1, res);
          }

     printf("\nSome special cases...\n");

     /* Test conversion of zero */

     printf("\nConvert zero with buffer len = 5...\n");
     i = 0;
     res = itoa(i, s1, 5);
     printf("i = %d, string = %s, return = %d\n",
             i, s1, res);

     /* Test convert -99 into a buffer with
        length increasing from -1 to 5.          */
```

```
    printf("\nConvert -99 with buffer len = -1, 0, ... ,5\n");
    s1[0] = EOS;
    for (h = -1; h < 6; h++)
        {
        i = -99;
        res = itoa(i, s1, h);
        printf("i = %d, (len = %d), buffer = %s, return = %d\n",
            i, h, s1, res);
        }
    }
#endif
/* End of itoa.c */
```

This function provides a capability missing from the standard UNIX library: the complement of *atoi()*, converting an integer to a string. Notice that the program verifies validity of the length of the output buffer before modifying that buffer. Its natural range of return value is from 0 to 1Buf−1; therefore, −1 is chosen as the error indicator. The test driver exercises a variety of common cases through a wide range of inputs, then specifically tests some boundary conditions.

3

UNIX SYSTEM DIALECTS AND PORTABILITY

In this chapter, we describe the UNIX system dialect divergences that are the consequences of the evolutionary history described in Chapter 1. Detailed feature-by-feature comparisons of major current dialects are then given.

The aim of the tables presented in this chapter is to provide a supplement to your UNIX system manuals, enabling you to determine precisely what system features are portable between different pairs of dialects.

The following are the dialect abbreviations used in both the tables and notes, and in the genealogy chart included in the next section.

Label	Version
V7	Bell Labs Version 7
4.1BSD	Berkeley System Distribution 4.1
4.2BSD	Berkeley System Distribution 4.2
4.3BSD	Berkeley System Distribution 4.3
BSD	Berkeley System Distribution 4.1, 4.2, and 4.3
SIII	AT&T System III
SV1	AT&T System V, Release 1
SV2	AT&T System V, Release 2
SVID	AT&T System V Interface Definition
SV	SV1, SV2, and SVID
AT&T	SV and SIII
XE2.3	Microsoft XENIX 2.3
XE3.0	Microsoft XENIX 3.0
XE5.0	Microsoft XENIX 5.0
XENIX	Microsoft XENIX 2.3, 3.0, and 5.0

3.1 Dialect Groups and UNIX System Genealogy

From an application developer's point of view, the most significant differences between UNIX system dialects are found between dialects descended from AT&T System III, on the one hand, and those that derive from Berkeley 4.1 and Version 7 on the other. All these divergences will be specified in detail later in this book.

Following is the ancestry chart for UNIX system dialects. Italicized names indicate versions that are now defunct and are included for historical interest only.

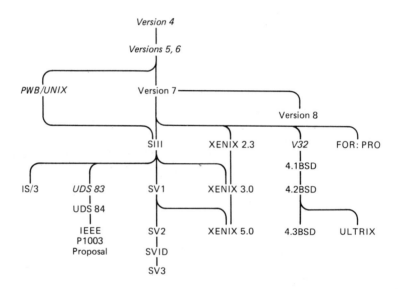

The chart indicates only relationships between kernels. Tools and libraries from more advanced versions have been ported to V7 implementations as a "value-added" tactic often enough to completely confuse the picture otherwise.

Version 8 was alive and in use at Bell Labs as of late 1985 as the operating system of about sixty machines, mostly at Murray Hill. Some concepts of the system (most notably the streams I/O organization) are expected to show up in descendants of System V, but V8 itself is no longer in the mainstream of commercial UNIX system evolution.

This chart lists a few versions not included in the tables. ULTRIX is Digital Equipment Corporation's 4.2BSD-based port for their PDP-11 and VAX minicomputers. IS/3 is a System III version offered by Interactive Systems Corporation; we describe it further in Appendix C. FOR:PRO is Fortune Systems's Version 7 port for the Fortune desktop micros, also described in Appendix C.

3.2 UNIX Feature Tables

The following tables give a very detailed feature-by-feature comparison of the major UNIX system dialects. In each section, names of features run down the left side (in ASCII collating order) and dialects run across the top. The dialects are arranged in approximate chronological order—the predecessor of a given dialect is to its left. The meanings of the table columns are as follows:

1. Name of the item (*Name*)

Gives the name of the tool, system call, library function, driver, or special file format being documented.

2. Where to look (*Under*)

If a name is given in this column, it is the name of the command, command group, or library section under which the item is actually listed—also see the note on the "n" notation below.

3. Degree of item's portability (*?*)

A "Y" entry in this column indicates that the item is in the Portable UNIX Software Standard. An "M" in this column indicates a machine-dependent feature. A "*" indicates that there is a note for this command. In the Section 3 table only, a "@" in this column indicates a call described in the ANSI X3J11 Draft Proposed Standard for C (Information Bulletin) [**X3J11**].

4. UNIX system family resemblances

The remaining columns describe the item's status in the dialects (labeled at the top of each column). The table entries describe the relationship between an item in a given dialect and the item of the same name in the predecessor dialect, i.e., the one from which the dialect under consideration derived. The notation is as follows:

F   This is the first UNIX system dialect in which this item exists under the given name. If two dialects both have "F", the command exists in two functionally different, unrelated versions.

>   The item is compatible with its previous version but has added features. See below for definitions of "compatible."

=   The item has the same features as the previous version, but the documentation has changed (usually this means detail has been added).

≡   The item has the same features, and the documentation is the same.

X   The call is incompatible with its previous version.

$ This call is not found in the first release of this dialect. Notice that 4.3BSD features are tagged in this way also and distinguished in the notes.

n   For this dialect, the item has a separate listing in manual section "n."

?   Documentation for this item is missing in the documentation for this dialect, even though it is present and referenced elsewhere.

.   The item is not supported in the given dialect.

O   The item is labeled "obsolete" and/or "not supported" and will probably never be seen again.

P   The feature is marked "PDP-11 only."

V   This indicates a BSD or System V feature marked "VAX only."

B   This indicates a System V feature marked "3B20 only."

C   This indicates a feature supported only on System V under processors that use the Common Object File Format (COFF).

D   This indicates a feature supported by DEC processors only (i.e., the PDP-11 and VAX).

Two or more processor codes indicate separate versions for each processor. A note will indicate differences between these versions.

Following are the criteria used to determine if a feature is "compatible with its previous version":

- For a function, the calling sequence and semantics are compatible with the function of the same name in the predecessor of this UNIX system dialect.

- For an I/O driver, it recognizes a superset of the requests valid in the previous dialect.

- For a file format, it is defined by the same C structures and/or constants with the same symbolic names as its previous dialect (though not necessarily the same values). Programs that include the header file corresponding to the format will run correctly. Notice that this does not imply portability of the binary data layout between machines.

- For a utility program, it accepts a superset of the commands and options valid in the previous dialect.

For purposes of this study, two versions of a call were considered to have the same documentation if their name, synopsis, and description sections contained equivalent text, or if the sole change was to split some portion of the description or notes into a section with its own heading.

3.3 Option Switch Tables

The notes sections contain tables of option switches that use the same conventions as the main tables, including the uses of the $\equiv$, $>$, X, F, and $ indicators.

3.4 General Notes and Caveats

3.4.1 Version 7

Version 7 is the ancestor and least common denominator of all current UNIX system dialects; we often describe features in the table notes in terms of their enhancements over Version 7, so if your system is of a more recent vintage it may be helpful to have a Version 7 manual such as [V7] (our source) handy.

3.4.2 4.1BSD and 4.2BSD

These are the much-elaborated descendants of V7 developed at UC Berkeley. Our sources were primarily [4.1V1] and [4.2V1]; folklore and experience added a good deal of clarification (4.1BSD was the authors' home system over most of the book's preparation time).

3.4.3 4.3BSD

The 4.3BSD information is based upon prerelease information [4.3PR] provided by the developers at Berkeley. The system is running beta-test at a number of university sites at the time of writing.

3.4.4 XENIX 2.3

XENIX 2.3 is a derivative of V7 with additions from BSD and SIII. If a XENIX 2.3 feature has no counterpart in V7, its predecessor is considered to be its counterpart in BSD. If it has no counterpart in either V7 or BSD, its predecessor is in SIII. See [TRSX].

3.4.5 XENIX 3.0 and 5.0

XENIX 3.0 is a derivative of SIII. If a XENIX 3.0 feature has no counterpart in SIII, its predecessor is considered to be the XENIX 2.3 version. Useful Berkeley-like features such as *termcap*(3) and the */etc/ttys* have been retained to assure backward compatibility.

XENIX 5.0 is an upgrade of XE3.0 that meets the System V Interface Definition. By default, the predecessor of an XE5.0 feature is the XE3.0 version and all comments describing XE3.0 should be presumed to apply. If a feature is new in XE5.0 and present in SV, the SV version is the predecessor. One group of calls—the *directory*(S) interface listed in (3)—is imported from 4.2BSD.

The information on XE3.0 is derived from IBM XENIX for the PC/AT documentation [**IBM1**]. The command information on XE5.0 derives from the Santa Cruz Operation's Release 2.0 documentation [**SCO**]. The column marked XE3.0 applies to both, except that entries marked "$" are present in XE5.0 only. The new XE5.0 commands are imported from SV2, unless explicitly noted otherwise. Commands common to XE3.0 and XE5.0 have the same features in both, unless noted otherwise.

The XE3.0 and XE5.0 manual organization discards the traditional eight-section organization found in most other dialects for an approach based on functional groups of tools. Also, XENIX has been unbundled so that many systems do not include programming tools like *cc*(1) or text-processing tools like *troff*(1). In the interests of providing a consistent single format for the tables that facilitates comparison with other dialects, the package boundaries have been ignored and the tools and services listed in their traditional sections in the tables. This is unlikely to cause any confusion except for the 23 new XE5.0 tools of sections 1M or 8, which are therefore listed below and otherwise ignored:

asx	clockrate	cmchk	copy	custom
diskcmp	diskcpy	divvy	fixperm	fdisk
imprint	ipbs	ips	lpinit	mapkey
mapscrn	mapstr	masm	mkdev	netutil
runbig	setcolor	winstall		

The PC/AT-specific commands common to XE3.0 and XE5.0 (the MS-DOS cross-development group and *dtype*(1M)) are also omitted from the tables.

The SCO XENIX Release 2.0 (XE5.0) system calls and libraries are said to pass the System V Interface Definition validation tests with the following exceptions:

1. The *matherr*(3) library does not send error messages to stderr.

2. The *shmat*(2), *shmop*(2), *shmcntl*(2), and *shmget*(2) calls have restrictions forced by the segmented architecture of the Intel 808x processor family.

Accordingly, there is no separate listing for XENIX 5.0 in Sections 2 and 3, but XE5.0-only features are indicated with a "$" in the XE3.0 column.

3.4.6 AT&T versions

System III, System V, and System V, Release 2, are, collectively, the AT&T versions (and often are referred to as such in the notes). Our sources were [**SIII1**], [**SV1**], [**3B5**], [**SVID**], and [**SV2**].

3.4.7 The P1003 Portable Operating System Environment.

We have included information from [**P1003**] to the notes to indicate differences between the P1003 proposed standard and the SVID at the system call level. P1003 library routines that differ from the corresponding SVID calls have been so flagged and described in the notes, but no effort has been made to mark the over 100 library routines that are present in SVID but omitted from the P1003 proposal (almost all of these are specified by the ANSI X3J11 C committee draft standard, to which P1003 refers).

3.5 Section 1—Commands and Utilities

Commands classified 1M (system administration tools) are listed separately in the section following this one. XENIX 3.0 and XENIX 5.0 split these commands between sections called "C" (commands), "CP" (programming commands), and "CT" (text-processing commands).

Name	Under	?	V7	BSD	SIII	XE2.3	XE3.0	SV
300		.	.	.	F	.	.	≡
300s	300	.	.	.	F	.	.	≡
4014		.	.	.	F	.	.	≡
450		.	.	.	F	.	.	≡
acctcom		*	.	.	F	.	≡	>
addbib		.	.	F$	.	.	.	.
adb		*	F	>	>	>	>	.
admin		.	.	.	F	.	≡	≡
apl		*	.	F	.	.	.	.
apply		.	.	F$	.	.	.	.
apropos		.	.	F	.	.	.	.
ar		Y*	F	≡	≡	≡	>	>
as		*	FP	XPV	>V	>PV	X	>PC
asa		.	.	.	.	.	.	F
assign		*	.	.	.	.	F	.
at		*	F	≡	.	≡	≡	X
atq		.	.	.	.	.	F	.
atrm		.	.	.	.	.	F	.
awk		Y	≡	≡	≡	≡	≡	≡
banner		*	F6	>6	X	≡6	≡	≡

Name	Under	?	V7	BSD	SIII	XE2.3	XE3.0	SV
basename		Y*	F	≡	≡	=	=	=
batch	at	.	.	.	.	.	.	F$
bc		Y	F	≡	≡	≡	≡	≡
bdiff		.	.	.	F	.	≡	≡
bfs		*	.	.	F	.	>	>
biff		.	.	F	.	.	.	.
binmail		.	.	F	.	.	.	.
bs		*	.	.	F	.	.	>
cal		Y*	F	≡	≡	≡	>	≡
calendar		Y*	F	≡	≡	≡	≡	≡
call		.	.	F	.	.	.	.
cancel	lp	.	.	.	.	.	.	F
cat		Y*	F	>	>	≡	>	>
cb		Y*	F	≡	≡	≡	≡	>
cc		Y*	F	>	>	>	>	>
ccat	compact	.	.	F	.	.	.	.
cd		Y*	F	>	≡	≡	≡	>
cdc		.	.	.	F	.	≡	≡
cflow		.	.	.	.	.	$	F
chdir		Y*	.	.	.	F	?	.
checkeq	eqn	Y	F	≡1	≡	>	.	≡
checknr		.	.	F	.	.	.	.
chfn		.	.	F	.	.	.	.
chgrp	chown	Y*	F	≡8	>	≡	≡	≡
chmod		Y*	F	≡	>	≡	>	>
chown		Y*	F	≡8	>	≡	≡	≡
chsh		*	.	F	.	.	X	.
cifplot		.	.	F	.	.	.	.
clear		.	.	F	.	.	.	.
cmp		Y	F	≡	≡	≡	≡	≡
col		Y*	F	≡	>	≡	.	>
colcrt		.	.	F	.	.	.	.
colrm		.	.	F	.	.	.	.
comb		.	.	.	F	.	≡	≡
comm		Y	F	≡	≡	≡	≡	≡
compact		*	.	F	.	.	.	.
compress		*	.	F$	.	.	.	.
conv		.	.	.	.	.	.	F
convert		*	.	.	.	.	.	F
copy		.	.	.	.	F	≡	.
cp		Y*	F	>	>	≡	=	≡
cpio		*	.	.	F	.	X	>
cpp		*	.	.	.	.	.	F
cprs		.	.	.	.	.	.	FB
cref		*	.	.	F	.	≡	.
crontab		.	.	.	.	.	.	F$
crypt		Y*	≡	≡	≡	≡	.	≡
csh		.	.	F	.	>	>	.
csplit		*	.	.	F	≡	≡	≡
ct		*	.	.	F	.	.	>
ctags		*	.	F	.	≡	≡	.
ctrace		.	.	.	.	.	.	F$

Name	Under	?	V7	BSD	SIII	XE2.3	XE3.0	SV
cu		*	F	>	X	>	≡	X
cut		.	.	.	F	.	.	≡
cw		.	.	.	F	.	.	≡
cxref		.	.	.	.	.	$	F
date		*	F	≡	X	≡	≡	≡
dbx		*	.	F	.	.	.	.
dc		Y*	F	≡	≡	≡	>	≡
dd		Y	F	≡	≡	≡	≡	≡
deassign	assign	*	.	.	.	.	.	F
delta		.	.	.	F	.	≡	≡
deroff		Y*	F	≡	>	≡	.	≡
diction		.	.	F	.	.	.	.
diff		Y*	F	>	≡	≡	≡	≡
diff3		Y	F	≡	≡	≡	≡	≡
diffmk		.	.	.	F	.	.	≡
dircmp		*	.	.	F	.	>	>
dirname	basename	*	.	.	F	.	F1	≡
dis		.	.	.	.	.	.	FB
disable	enable	*	.	.	.	.	.	F
du		Y*	F	≡	>	≡	>	≡
dump		*	.	.	.	.	.	FC
echo		Y*	F	≡	X	≡	>	≡
ed		Y*	F	≡	>	≡	≡	>
edit		*	.	.	.	.	.	F
efl		.	.	F	≡	.	.	≡
egrep	grep	Y*	F	≡	>	>1	≡	≡
enable		*	.	.	.	.	.	F
enroll	xsend	.	F	≡	.	.	.	.
env		.	.	.	F	.	≡	≡
eqn		Y	F	≡	≡	=	.	≡
error		*	.	F	.	.	.	.
ex		.	.	F	.	≡	≡	≡
expand		.	.	F	.	.	.	.
explain		.	.	F	.	.	.	.
expr		*	F	≡	X	≡	≡	≡
eyacc		.	.	F	.	.	.	.
f77		*	F	X	X	.	.	>
factor		.	F	.	≡	.	≡	≡
false	true	Y	F	≡	≡	≡1	≡	≡
fed		*	.	F	.	.	.	.
fget		.	.	.	F	.	.	≡D
fgrep	grep	Y*	F	>	>	≡	≡	≡
file		Y*	F	≡	>	>	>	>
find		Y*	F	≡	>	>	≡	≡
finger		*	.	F	.	≡	>	.
fmt		.	.	F	.	.	.	≡
fold		.	.	F	.	.	.	.
fp		.	.	F$	.	.	.	.
fpr		.	.	F$	.	.	.	.
fsplit		.	.	F$	.	.	.	.
ftp		.	.	F$	.	.	.	.
from		.	.	F	.	.	.	.

Name	Under	?	V7	BSD	SIII	XE2.3	XE3.0	SV
fsend		.	.	.	FD	.	.	≡D
fsplit		.	.	.	.	.	.	F
gath	send	.	.	.	F	.	.	≡
gcat		.	.	.	F	.	.	≡D
gcore		.	.	F$	.	.	.	.
gcosmail		.	.	.	F	.	.	≡D
ged		.	.	.	F	.	.	≡D
get		.	.	.	F	.	≡	≡
getopt		.	.	.	F	.	≡	≡
gets		.	.	F	.	>	.	.
glossary	help	.	.	.	.	.	.	F$
gprof		.	.	F$	.	.	.	.
graph		Y	.	F	=	≡	.	≡
graphics		*	.	.	F	.	.	≡
greek		.	.	.	F	.	.	≡
grep		Y*	F	>	>	≡	≡	≡
groups		.	.	F$	.	.	.	.
grpcheck		.	.	.	.	.	F$	.
hd		*	.	.	.	.	F	.
hdr		.	.	.	.	.	F	.
head		.	.	F	.	=	≡	.
help		*	.	.	F	.	≡	>
hostid		.	.	F$	.	.	.	.
hostname		.	.	F$	.	.	.	.
hp		.	.	.	F	.	.	≡
hpio		.	.	.	.	.	.	FB
hyphen		.	.	.	F	.	.	=
id		.	.	.	F	.	≡	≡
indent		*	.	F	.	.	.	.
install		.	.	F$	.	.	.	.
ipcrm		.	.	.	.	.	$	F
ipcs		.	.	.	.	.	$	F
join		Y	F	≡	≡	≡	.	=
kas		.	.	.	FD	.	.	.
kasb		.	.	.	.	.	.	FD
kill		Y*	F	>	≡	≡	≡	≡
kun		.	.	.	FD	.	.	.
kunb		.	.	.	.	.	.	FD
l		*	.	.	.	F	.	.
last		*	.	F	.	.	.	.
lastcomm		*	.	F	.	.	.	.
lc		*	.	.	.	F	>	.
ld		Y*	?	>	>	>	>	>PC
learn		.	.	F	.	≡	.	.
leave		.	.	F	.	.	.	.
lex		Y*	F	≡	>	≡	=	≡
line		.	.	.	F	.	≡	≡
lint		*	F	≡	X	≡	≡	>
lisp		.	.	F	.	.	.	.
list		*	.	.	.	.	.	FB
liszt		.	.	F	.	.	.	.
ln	cp	Y*	F1	>1	>	≡1	≡1	>

Name	Under	?	V7	BSD	SIII	XE2.3	XE3.0	SV
locate	help	.	.	.	.	.	.	F$
lock		.	.	F	.	.	.	.
logdir		.	.	.	.	.	.	F
login		Y*	F	>	>	≡	.	>
logname		Y	.	.	F	.	≡	≡
look		.	F	≡	.	≡	≡	.
lookall		.	F	.	.	.	.	.
lookbib	refer	.	F	≡	.	≡	.	.
lorder		Y	F	≡	≡	≡	≡	=
lp		*	.	.	.	.	.	F
lpq	lpr	*	.	F	.	.	.	.
lpr	lpr	*	.	F	>	>	≡	>O
lprm	lpr	*	.	F	.	.	.	.
lpstat		.	.	.	.	.	$	F
ls		Y*	F	>	>	≡	.	>
lxref		.	.	F	.	.	.	.
m4		Y*	F	≡	>	≡	≡	≡
machid		*	.	.	.	.	.	F
mail		*	F	X	>	≡	X	≡
mailx		*	.	.	.	.	.	F
make		Y*	F	≡	>	≡	≡	≡
man		*	F	X	X	X	.	X
mesg		Y	F	≡	≡	≡	≡	≡
mkdir		Y	F	≡	≡	≡	≡	≡
mkstr		.	.	F	.	≡	≡	.
mm		*	.	.	F	.	.	=
mmchek		*	.	.	F	.	.	.
mmt		.	.	.	F	.	.	=
more		.	.	F	.	≡	≡	.
msgs		.	.	F	.	.	.	.
mt		*	.	F	.	.	.	.
mv		Y*	F	≡	≡	≡	≡	≡
mvt	mmt	.	.	.	F	.	.	=
ncp		*	.	.	.	.	.	F
neqn	eqn	Y	F	≡	≡	>1	.	≡
net		*	.	F	.	.	.	XD
netcp		*	.	F	.	.	.	.
netlog		*	.	F	.	.	.	.
netlogin		*	.	F	.	.	.	.
netlpr		*	.	F	.	.	.	.
netmail		*	.	F	.	.	.	.
netq		*	.	F	.	.	.	.
netrm		*	.	F	.	.	.	.
netstat		*	.	F	.	.	.	.
netroff		*	.	F	.	.	.	.
newaliases		.	.	F	.	.	.	.
newform		.	.	.	.	.	$	F
newgrp		Y*	F	≡	>	≡	.	=
news		.	.	.	F	.	≡	≡
nice		*	F	≡	>	>	≡	≡
nkill		*	.	.	.	.	.	F
nl		*	.	.	F	.	≡	>

Name	Under	?	V7	BSD	SIII	XE2.3	XE3.0	SV
nm		Y*	F	>	>	>	>	X
nohup	nice	Y	F	≡	>1	>1	≡	=
nroff	roff	Y*	F	≡	≡	≡1	.	>1
nscstat		.	.	.	.	.	.	FD
nsctorje		.	.	.	.	.	.	FD
num		.	.	F	.	.	.	.
nusend		.	.	.	.	.	.	FD
od		Y*	F	>	≡	≡	≡	>
orjestat		.	.	.	FO	.	.	
pack		*	.	.	F	.	≡	>
pagesize		.	.	F$	.	.	.	.
passwd		Y*	F	≡	>	≡	>	≡
paste		.	.	.	F	.	.	≡
pc		*	.	F	.	.	.	.
pcc	cc	*	F	≡	.	.	.	.
pcat	pack	.	.	.	F	.	≡	≡
pdx		.	.	F$	.	.	.	.
pg		.	.	.	.	.	$	F$
pi		*	.	F	.	.	.	.
pix		.	.	F	.	.	.	.
plot		*	F	≡	.	≡	.	.
pmerge		.	.	F	.	.	.	.
pr		Y*	F	>	>	>	≡	≡
prep		.	F	.	.	≡	.	.
print	lpr	.	.	F	.	.	.	.
printenv		.	.	F	.	≡	.	.
prmail		.	.	F	.	.	.	.
prof		Y*	F	≡	>	≡	X	X
prs		.	.	.	F	.	.	≡
ps		Y*	F	>	>	>	≡	≡
pti		.	.	F	.	.	.	.
ptx		Y	F	≡	≡	≡	.	.
pubindex		.	F	.	.	.	.	.
pwd		Y	F	≡	=	≡	≡	≡
px		.	.	F	.	.	.	.
pxp		.	.	F	.	.	.	.
pxref		.	.	F	.	.	.	.
random		.	.	.	.	F	≡	.
ranlib		*	F	≡	.	≡	≡	.
ratfor		Y*	F	X	≡	≡	≡	≡
rcp		*	.	F$	.	.	F	.
rdist		*	.	F$	.	.	.	.
refer		.	F	≡	.	≡	.	.
reform		.	.	.	FO	.	.	.
regcmp		*	.	.	F	.	≡	≡
reset		.	.	F	.	.	.	.
red		.	.	.	.	.	F$	.
remote		.	.	.	.	.	F	.
rev		.	.	F	.	≡	.	.
rjestat		.	.	.	F	.	.	≡
rlogin		*	.	F	.	.	.	.
rm		Y*	F	>	≡	≡	=	≡

Name	Under	?	V7	BSD	SIII	XE2.3	XE3.0	SV
rmail	mail	.	.	.	F1	.	≡	=
rmdir	rm	Y*	F	≡	≡	≡	=	≡
rmdel		.	.	.	F	.	≡	≡
roff		.	F	.	.	.	.	.
roffbib		*	.	F$	.	.	.	.
rsh		*	.	F	F	.	.	.
ruptime		*	.	F	.	.	.	.
rwho		.	.	F$	.	.	.	.
sact		.	.	.	F	.	≡	≡
sadp		.	.	.	.	.	.	F
scat		.	.	.	.	.	.	F
sar		*	.	.	.	.	.	F
scc		.	.	.	F	.	.	≡D
sccsdiff		.	.	.	F	.	≡	≡
script		*	.	F	.	.	.	.
sdb		.	.	FV	≡	.	.	>C
sdiff		.	.	.	F	.	≡	≡
se		*	.	.	.	.	.	F
sed		Y*	F	≡	>	≡	≡	>
see		.	.	F	.	.	.	.
send		.	.	.	F	.	.	=
sendbug		.	.	F$	.	.	.	.
settime		*	.	.	.	F	X	.
sh		Y*	F	≡	>	≡	≡	>
shl		.	.	.	.	.	.	F$
size		Y*	F	≡	≡	=	≡	>
sleep		Y*	F	≡	≡	≡	≡	≡
sno		.	.	.	F	.	.	≡
soelim		.	.	F	.	.	.	.
sort		*	F	≡	X	≡	≡	>
sortbib		.	.	F$	.	.	.	.
sp		.	.	.	.	F	.	.
spell		Y*	F	≡	≡	≡	.	>
spline		Y	F	≡	≡	≡	≡	≡
split		Y	F	≡	≡	≡	≡	=
starter	help	.	.	.	.	.	.	F
stat		*	.	.	F$	.	.	≡
stlogin		.	.	.	.	.	.	FD
ststat		.	.	.	.	.	.	FD
strings		.	.	F	.	≡	≡	.
strip		Y*	F	≡	>	>	>	>
struct		.	F	=	.	≡	.	.
stty		*	F	>	X	≡	.	>
style		.	.	F	.	.	.	.
su		Y*	F	≡	>	>	≡	≡
sum		Y*	F	≡	>	≡	≡	≡
symorder		.	.	F	.	.	.	.
sysline		.	.	F$	.	.	.	.
tabs		*	F	≡	X	≡	.	>
tail		Y*	F	>	>	≡	≡	=
talk		.	.	F$	.	.	.	.
tar		Y*	F	>	>	≡	.	≡

Name	Under	?	V7	BSD	SIII	XE2.3	XE3.0	SV
tbl		Y*	F	≡	>	≡	.	>
tc		*	F	≡	>	.	.	≡
tee		Y	F	≡	≡	≡	=	≡
telnet		.	.	F$	.	.	.	.
test		Y*	F	≡	>	≡	≡	>
time		Y*	F	≡	≡	≡	≡	≡
timex		*	.	.	F	.	.	>
tip		.	.	F$	.	.	.	.
tk		.	F	≡	.	.	.	.
toc		.	.	.	F	.	.	≡$
touch		Y*	F	≡	>	.	≡	≡
tp		.	F	≡	≡O	.	.	.
tplot		*	.	.	F	.	.	≡
tput		.	.	.	.	.	.	F
tr		*	F	≡	X	≡	≡	≡
trman		.	.	F	.	.	.	.
troff		*	F	≡	X	≡	≡	>
true		Y	F	≡	≡	≡1	≡	≡
tset		.	.	F	.	≡	=	.
tsort		Y	F	≡	≡	≡	≡	≡
tty		Y*	F	≡	>	≡	≡	>
typo		.	.	.	FO	.	.	>
ul		.	.	F	.	.	.	.
umask		.	.	.	F	.	=	≡
uname		*	.	.	F	.	>	>
uncompact	compact	.	.	F	.	.	.	.
unget		.	.	.	F	.	≡	≡
uniq		Y	F	≡	=	≡	≡	≡
units		Y*	F	≡	=	≡	≡	≡
unpack	pack	.	.	.	F	.	.	≡
uptime		.	.	F	.	.	.	.
usage	help	.	.	.	.	.	.	F$
users		.	.	F	.	.	.	.
uucp		*	F	≡	>	≡	≡	X
uudecode	uuencode	.	.	F	.	.	.	.
uudiff		*	.	F	.	.	.	.
uuencode		.	.	F	.	.	.	.
uulog	uucp	*	F	≡	=	≡	≡	X
uuname		.	.	?	F	.	?	≡
uupick	uuto	.	.	.	.	.	≡	F
uusend		*	.	F	.	.	.	.
uusnap		.	.	F$	.	.	.	.
uustat		*	.	.	F	.	≡	X
uuto		.	.	.	F	.	≡	=
uux		*	F	≡	>	=	≡	X
val		.	.	.	F	.	≡	≡
vc		O	.	.	FO	.	.	≡
vfontinfo		.	.	F	.	.	.	.
vgrind		*	.	F	.	.	.	.
vi		*	.	F	.	X	≡	>
vlp		.	.	F$	.	.	.	.
vmstat		*	.	F	.	.	.	.

Name	Under	?	V7	BSD	SIII	XE2.3	XE3.0	SV
vpmc		*	.	.	F	.	.	>
vpmstart		*	.	.	F	.	.	>
vpmsnap	vpmstart	*	.	.	F	.	.	.
vpmtrace	vpmstart	*	.	.	F	.	.	>
vpr		*	.	F	>	.	.	≡
vsh		.	.	.	.	.	F	.
vtroff		.	.	F	.	.	.	.
vwidth		.	.	F$	.	.	.	.
w		.	.	F	.	.	.	.
wait		Y*	F	≡	≡	≡	=	≡
wc		Y*	F	>	=	≡	≡	≡
what		*	.	X	F	.	≡	>
whatis		.	.	F	.	.	.	.
whereis		.	.	F	.	.	.	.
which		.	.	F	.	.	.	.
who		Y*	F	≡	≡	≡	≡	>
whoami		.	.	F	.	.	.	.
write		Y	F	≡	≡	≡	≡	>
xargs		.	.	.	F	.	≡	≡
xref		*	.	.	F	.	≡	.
xget	xsend	.	F	≡	.	.	.	.
xsend		.	F	≡	.	.	.	.
xstr		.	.	F	.	>	≡	.
yacc		Y	F	≡	≡	≡	≡	>
yes		.	.	F	.	≡	≡	.

Notes on Commands and Application Programs

acctcom

This tool is part of the PWB-derived accounting system found only on SIII, XENIX 3.0/5.0, and SV versions. The XENIX versions are from SIII.

Option	SIII	SV	SV2	Function
-a	.	.	F	show some extra statistics averages
-b	F	≡	≡	show latest commands first
-C	F	≡	≡	show processes with > given total time
-d	F	≡	.	set mm/dd for later arguments
-e	F	≡	≡	show processes alive before given time
-f	F	≡	≡	print fork/exec and exit status info
-g	F	≡	≡	show processes belonging to group
-h	F	≡	≡	display hog factor
-i	F	≡	≡	print I/O count columns
-k	F	≡	≡	show total kcore-minutes
-l	F	≡	≡	show processes on given line
-m	F	≡	≡	show mean core size (default)
-n	F	≡	≡	show commands that match a pattern
-o	.	F	≡	copy process records to file

Option	SIII	SV	SV2	Function
-q	.	.	F	print average statistics only
-r	F	≡	≡	show CPU factor
-s	F	≡	≡	show processes alive after given time
-t	F	≡	≡	show separate system and user times
-u	F	≡	≡	show processes belonging to given user
-v	F	≡	≡	no column headings on output
-E	.	F	≡	show processes ending at/before time
-H	F	≡	≡	show processes with > given hog factor
-I	.	.	F	show processes with > given I/O count
-O	F	≡	≡	show processes with > given time
-S	.	F	≡	show processes alive after given time

adb

The i command of *adb*(1) disassembles to the local instruction set in roughly *as*(1) format. The V7 documentation indicates PDP-11, BSD refers to the VAX, XENIX simply says "print as machine instructions." System V subsumes *adb*(1) in *sdb*(1).

The following features of the command language are also intrinsically hardware-dependent; the output of the $r command, the size of the increment for the $p format, the register accessed for the current stack frame address, and the file magic numbers that may be values of the m variable. XENIX on the PC/AT maintains and prints addresses in segment-offset form.

The V7 $a modifier used for ALGOL 68 stack backtraces has been omitted in all subsequent versions.

One insidious difference between versions has to do with the value of dot after ? and / commands. V7 and XENIX leave dot unaltered, while BSD and SIII increment it by the length of the displayed data. In V7 and XENIX, a newline command immediately after a ? or / may be used to force dot forward by the length of the displayed data.

Conventions for the input radices of integer data also differ. V7, SIII and XENIX 3.0/5.0 have a default radix of decimal and use one set of prefix conventions; BSD and XENIX 2.3 use hexadecimal by default and use a different set of radix prefixes.

BSD on the VAX and XENIX do not support the routine.name expression element. BSD and XENIX 2.3 do not support V7's $f command.

BSD has a number of unique enhancements over V7, including the # operator, count handling for the < command, the << comand, and the $? command. 4.2BSD recognizes additional -k and -I command line options and the $p command. Changes from V7 include a more conventional control-character representation in the C and S formats. BSD notes special magic necessary to debug */dev/kmem*. 4.2BSD notes that a tilde may not prefix symbols, and omits a note found in all other versions asserting that all "appropriate" variables are maintained internally as signed 32-bit integers.

XENIX 2.3 won't show local variables in $c output and doesn't have the predefined variable m. XENIX 3.0 does, but describes it differently. XENIX 3.0 also supports the following enhancements over SIII: the -p command option; use of the QUIT character as a command interrupt; the M command; and a default prompt of *. XENIX 3.0 also notes that system calls cannot be single-stepped. The XENIX 5.0 version adds 80286 support (visibly, a few new predefineds) to the 3.0 version.

apl

The 4.2BSD version of this APL language interpreter is changed and enhanced from the 4.1BSD original.

ar

The V7, 4.1BSD, XE2.3, and SIII versions are identical; in the following table, the XENIX column refers to 3.0/5.0. All versions previous to SV use /tmp/v* temp files; SV ar(1) uses /tmp/ar* temps. BSD and SV2 support new formats with all-ASCII header information. 4.2BSD also changes x to make the last-access date of an extracted file the extraction time (rather than its stored last access date) but supports a new -o option to override this. See also arcv(1M).

Option	V7	B4.2	XENIX	SV	Function
-d	F	≡	≡	≡	delete files from archive
-m	F	≡	≡	≡	move files to archive end
-n	.	.	F	.	make x date the last-access time
-p	F	≡	≡	≡	print names of archive files
-q	F	≡	≡	≡	quick update of files
-r	F	≡	≡	≡	replace named files
-s	.	.	.	F	force symbol table creation
-t	F	≡	≡	≡	print archive contents
-x	F	≡	≡	≡	extract named files
a	F	≡	≡	≡	position after
b	F	≡	≡	≡	position before
c	F	≡	≡	≡	suppress creation message
i	F	≡	≡	≡	position before
l	F	≡	≡	≡	put temp files in local directory
n	.	.	F	.	don't use true last-modified dates
o	.	F	.	.	use true last-modified dates
u	F	≡	≡	≡	update only recent files
v	F	≡	≡	≡	verbose output

as

The V7, SIII, and SV PDP-11 versions of *as*(1) appear to be identical. 4.1BSD and SIII have versions rewritten for the VAX environment. The SV *as*(1) versions on the VAX and the 3Bx machines generate COFF (Common Object File Format); the COFF column of the following table uses V to indicate a VAX-only feature. In XENIX 5.0, this tool is replaced by the new *asx*(1).

Option	PDP11	BSD	XE 2.3	XE 3.0	SIII	COFF	meaning
-	F	.	[1]	.	.	.	make undefineds global
-J	.	F	.	.	.	.	long branches when needed
-L	.	F	.	.	.	.	save L* temp labels
-M[ux]	.	.	.	F	.	.	caseblind symbols
-O	.	.	.	F	.	.	do octal output
-R	.	F	.	.	.	X	see note [2]
-V	.	F	.	.	.	X	see note [3]
-W	.	F	.	.	.	.	suppress error messages
-X	.	.	.	F	.	.	list false IF blocks
-d[124]	.	F	.	F	>	.	see note [4]
-g	.	.	F[1]	.	.	.	make undefineds global
-l	.	.	F	≡	.	V	see note [5]
-m	.	.	.	.	.	F	prefilter input with m4
-n	.	.	.	F	.	F	see note [6]
-o	F	≡	≡	≡	≡	≡	send object to given file
-r	.	.	.	F	.	V	see note [7]
-t	.	F	.	.	.	.	specify tempfile directory
-w	.	.	.	.	.	V	force word length offsets

[1] XENIX's -g option is equivalent to the - option of the PDP-11 versions. Notice that all other systems always treat undefineds as globals

[2] On BSD, -R makes initialized data read-only. For COFF, -R instructs *as*(1) to unlink the source after assembly.

[3] On BSD, -V instructs *as*(1) to use virtual store instead of temporary files. On COFF systems, -V sends the version number of *as*(1) to stderr.

[4] On BSD, -d enables one to set the width of branch offsets. On XENIX 3.0, it enables listing for both assembler phases.

[5] On XENIX, -l causes a listing to be generated. On VAX SV, it forces quad length branch offsets.

[6] On XENIX 3.0, -n suppresses symbol table output when the -l option is also selected. On SV, it disables addressing optimizations.

[7] On XENIX 3.0 for the PC/AT, -r enables generation of hardware floating-point instructions. On SV, it disables the .data directive.

assign

See also *assign*(1M), which has a different function.

at

SV2 supports an *at*(1) that can do all the things V7/BSD's does but has a very different interface (most notably, it reads the command text to be saved from standard input rather than accepting a filename on the command line). SIII and SV1 don't have *at*(1). XENIX 5.0's *ar*(1) is the SV2 version.

banner

V7/BSD/XENIX *banner*(6) prints sideways; BSD lets you specify a print width via a -w option. SIII/SV *banner*(1) prints up to 10 chars per line in large upright letters.

basename

SIII, SV *basename*(1) includes the dirname utility, which V7/BSD doesn't have. The SV version fails on the string "/", generating a syntax error in *expr*(1) (strictly speaking, the SV version is thus incompatible with its predecessor). Since this utility is a shell script, the fix is left as an easy exercise for the reader (we have not marked it incompatible).

bfs

In XENIX 3.0/5.0, the prompt is on by default, and parentheses and brackets in regular expressions need not be escaped. SV2 adds a new "xn" command to list currently defined marks. The SV1 version is identical to that of SIII.

bs

SV *bs*(1) supports a previously unknown argument for the language's dump command.

cal

XENIX 2.3 has this, derived from System III. XENIX 3.0/5.0 *cal*(1) prints current, previous, and next months when called with no arguments.

calendar

SIII/SV calendar uses */usr/lib/calendar*, not */usr/lib/calprog* as in V7/BSD/XENIX, but they are functionally the same.

cat

SV2 seems to have imported 4.1BSD's *cat*(1), document page and all (though it doesn't support the BSD -n option). The SV1 manual page includes a warning about certain uses that clobber files. The XENIX 3.0 version and its documentation derive from SIII. The XENIX 5.0 version is SV2's.

Option	V7	BSD	XENIX	SIII	SV1	SV2	meaning
-	F	≡	≡	≡	≡	≡	read from stdin
-e	.	F	.	.	.	≡	put $s at line ends
-n	.	F	.	.	.	.	number lines
-s	.	F	.	X	≡	≡	see note [1]
-t	.	F	.	.	.	F	print tabs as ^Is
-u	F	≡	≡	≡	≡	≡	suppress buffering
-v	.	F	.	.	≡	≡	visible control chars

[1] BSD -s causes runs of blank lines to be compressed. SIII/SV/XENIX 3.0 -s suppresses error messages about nonexistent files.

cb

SV/XENIX 5.0 cb includes -sjl flags and a warning about what can confuse it.

cc

All UNIX C compilers support a superset of the language defined in Appendix A of Kernighan & Ritchie [K&R]. Only differences in command-line option handling will be discussed here. For more information, see Section 1.6.2 on the history of C and the Chapter 2 material on intercompiler differences; see also the note on *pcc*(1).

Option	V7	BSD	SIII	SV	XE2.3	XE3.0	Function
-c	F	≡	≡	≡	≡	≡	suppress linking phase
-d	.	.	V	.	[1]	.	pass option through
-dos	.	.	.	.	.	F	compile for MS-DOS
-f	F	.	D	≡	.	.	soft floating point
-g	.	F	≡	≡	.	.	generate debug info

Option	V7	BSD	SIII	SV	XE2.3	XE3.0	Function
-go	.	F$	.	.	.	.	*sdb* debug
-i	.	.	.	.	.	F	split i and d spaces
-nl	.	.	.	.	.	F	set max extern length
-l	.	.	.	.	.	F	ld: search library
-o	F	≡	≡	≡	≡	≡	specify output runfile
-p	F	≡	≡	≡	.	≡	enable profiling
-pg	.	F$	.	.	.	.	keep *gprof* info
-w	.	F	.	.	≡	≡	suppress warnings
-y	.	.	.	.	F[2]	.	set optimizer limit
-t	F	≡	≡	≡	.	.	passes to apply -B to
-B	F	≡	≡	≡	.	.	use backup version [3]
-C	.	F	≡	≡	.	≡	cpp: retain comments
-D	F	≡	≡	≡	≡	≡	cpp: define symbol
-E	F	≡	≡	≡	≡	≡	run preprocessor only
-EP	.	.	.	.	.	F	as -E, no leading #line
-F	.	.	.	.	.	F	set stack size
-Fs	.	.	.	.	.	F$	emit source listing
-I	F	≡	≡	≡	≡	≡	add #include directory
-K	.	.	.	.	F	≡	suppress stack probes
-L	.	.	.	.	.	F	generate assembler
-LARGE	.	.	.	.	.	F$	enable large model
-M	.	.	.	.	.	F	set memory model
-N[DT]	.	.	.	.	.	F[6]	set segment name
-NG[DT]	.	.	.	.	.	F	set group name
-NM	.	.	.	.	.	F	set module name
-O	F	≡	≡	≡	≡	≡	invoke optimizer
-P	F	≡[4]	≡	≡	≡	≡	cpp sources to .i files
-R	.	F	.	.	.	.	initialized data shared
-S	F	≡	≡	≡	.	≡	compile to assembler
-S3	.	.	.	.	.	F$	generate V3.0 x.out
-U	F	≡	≡	≡	≡	.	cpp: undefine a macro
-V	.	.	.	.	.	F	insert version string
-W	.	.	.	F	F	≡	see note [5]
-X	.	.	.	.	.	F	opposite of -I

Notes:

[1] SV disallows the -d option; use -W for the same effect.

[2] The -y option is only available under System V, Release 2.

[3] The default -B string is /usr/c on V7 and BSD but /lib/n on SIII/SV

[4] The -P option works on BSD, but is undocumented and gives a warning.

[5] On SV, -W is used to pass options through to compiler phases and the linker. On XENIX 3.0/5.0, it is used to set the warning level.

[6] The -NG options are not documented to be present in XENIX 5.0.

cd

BSD *cd* (under *csh*(1)) and SV2 both allow a search list specification for relative directory changes via $CDPATH. XENIX 5.0 *cd*(1) called from within the shell attempts spelling correction on path names.

chdir

XENIX *chdir*(1) is a synonym for *cd*(1).

chgrp

Unlike V7/4.1BSD/XENIX 2.3, SIII, SV, and 4.2BSD permit users to change the group of files that they own. The SV2 version clears the SUID and SGID bits of files that it operates on if the caller is not the superuser.

chmod

V7, BSD, and XENIX 2.3 use the *umask* (see *sh*(1)) as a default if the who field of a symbolic mode is omitted. SV2 documents a previously existing restriction to root of sticky-bit setting. SV2 also claims that your current group must match a file's owning group in order for the file's group id to be set, but this is incorrect (root can override it) and documented in the wrong place (should be under *chgrp*(1)). This may be a documentation error, with reference intended to the permission bits. Also note that some implementations of SV disable the SUID bit on scripts.

chown

Unlike V7/BSD/XENIX, SIII and SV permit users to change the owner of files that they own; the command is entirely restricted to super-user on BSD. SV2 *chown*(1) turns off SUID and SGID bits in the file unless the owner is super-user.

chsh

XENIX 3.0/5.0 only, derived from 4.1BSD. Unlike the original version, it prompts for arguments rather than accepting them on the command line.

col

SIII/SV *col*(1) supports -p option (pass through unknown escape sequences) as well as the same -bfx options found on V7/BSD/XENIX.

compact, compress

4.3BSD replaces the *compact*(1) tool found in earlier Berkeley versions with a new *compress*(1) utility that uses a better algorithm.

convert

SV2 *convert*(1) is used to convert archives from SV1 format to SV2 format.

cp

BSD *cp*(1) supports an -i option for interactive confirmation of copies that would clobber files. 4.2BSD supports an additional -r option for recursive copying of subdirectories. The manual entry for XENIX 3.0/5.0 *cp*(1) notes support for copying from devices and named pipes, which is presumably present in SIII also. SV2 notes that it turns off the sticky-bit of copies into directories unless the caller is super-user.

cpio

XENIX 3.0/5.0 includes a version of *cpio*(1) imported from SIII; it is marked incompatible only because the V6 conversion option is not documented. SV *cpio*(1) supports -fsSb options in addition to the -aBdcrtuvlm6 options of SIII, and documents slightly different bugs and warnings.

cpp

This utility is present everywhere but documented almost nowhere. Calling conventions may vary, so check the local documentation. SV2 *cpp*(1) adds -HT options over the -PCUDI options supported by all other systems. Notice that the #elif and ## features of SV and the defined( ) pseudofunction are not portable; see Chapter 2 for more guidelines on portable preprocessor usage.

cref

SIII *cref*(1) (and BSD *xref*) are replaced by SV *cxref*(1).

crypt

This tool is omitted from some dialects due to technology-export restrictions.

csplit

XENIX 3.0/5.0 imports *csplit*(1) from SIII.

ct

SV2 adds a -x option for debugging and notes interactions with *uugetty*(1M).

ctags

The 4.2BSD version of this tool adds support for `typedef`.

cu

4.1BSD *cu*(1) supports # (break) and ^Z (suspend) commands unknown to V7. 4.2BSD replaces *cu*(1) with a 4.1-compatible front end to the line handling utilities. XENIX 2.3 adds a no-hangup (-nh) option to the V7 features. SIII *cu*(1) has ˜nostop but SV uses ˜%nostop (for disabling DC1/DC3 protocol). The XENIX 3.0/5.0 version of *cu*(1) and documentation is SIII's rather than V7; the 5.0 version differs only in not documenting the -d flag. The SV2 version is more tightly integrated with *uucp*(1); it uses the line and foreign systems capability files associated with the latter.

Option	V7	BSD	SIII	XENIX	SV	SV2	Function
-a	F	≡	≡	≡	≡	.	specify acu
-b	.	F	.	.	.	≡	turn nulls to breaks
-d	.	.	F	.	≡	≡	print diagnostics
-e	.	.	F	.	≡	≡	generate even parity
-h	.	.	F	.	≡	≡	local echo on
-l	F	≡	≡	≡	≡	≡	specify tty line
-m	.	.	F	.	≡	.	direct line
-n	.	F	.	.	.	X	see note [1]
-nh	.	.	.	F	.	≡	don't hangup on exit
-o	.	.	F	.	≡	≡	generate odd parity

Option	V7	BSD	SIII	XENIX	SV	SV2	Function
-s	F	≡	≡	≡	≡	≡	specify speed
-t	F	≡	≡	≡	≡	≡	dial to tty

[1] BSD -n is a shorthand for specifying acu/line pairs. SV -n is a callback security option.

cxref

Not supported in SV2.

date

SIII/SV *date*(1) supports an elaborate format option, and is incompatible with the V7/BSD original. The XENIX 3.0/5.0 version of this command derives from SIII rather than V7.

dbx

This command is 4.2BSD's replacement for *sdb*(1). 4.3BSD adds many new features and works with the Pascal compiler.

dc

XENIX 3.0/5.0 adds an I command to push the input base on top of the stack.

deassign

See *assign*(1) and *assign(1M)*.

deroff

SIII and later AT&T versions of *deroff*(1) add options for excluding certain kinds of generated text (see table).

Option	V7	BSD	SIII	XENIX	SV	Function
-w	F	≡	≡	≡	≡	make wordlist
-mm	.	.	F	.	≡	running text only
-ml	.	.	F	.	≡	delete lists
-ms	.	.	.	.	F	given but undocumented

diff

BSD *diff*(1) has major enhancements over the V7 version found in all other dialects, but is rumored to break on very large files.

Option	V7	BSD	SIII	XENIX	SV	Function
-b	F	≡	≡	≡	≡	ignore whitespace
-c	.	F	.	.	.	show context of changes
-e	F	≡	≡	≡	≡	produce *ed*(1) script
-f	F	≡	≡	≡	≡	like -e but more readable
-h	F	≡	≡	≡	≡	fast & dirty for big files
-l	.	F	.	.	.	long output format
-r	.	F	.	.	.	recurse on subdirectories
-s	.	F	.	.	.	report on identical files
-D	.	F	.	.	.	merge, with cpp controls
-S	.	F	.	.	.	start file of dir. compare

dircmp

V7 and BSD don't have this tool (BSD *diff*(1) will compare subdirectories). XENIX 3.0 has this command, derived from SIII, but with additional -d and -s options; the 5.0 version is SV2's.

Option	XE3.0	SV1	SV2	Function
-d	F	≡	≡	apply *diff*(1) to files with same names
-s	F	≡	≡	suppress messages about identical files
-w	.	.	F	set report width

dirname

XENIX has *dirname*(1) in 3.0 and later versions only, derived from SIII.

disable

SV *disable*(1) is different from XENIX disable(1M).

du

Notice that System V uses a 1,024-byte disk block size, while V7, BSD, XENIX, and SIII use 512-byte blocks. 4.2BSD uses variable-size disk blocks but reports file sizes everywhere in kilobytes. XENIX 2.3's version is V7's; the table column refers to 3.0/5.0. Notice that the -f and -u flags are present in 3.0, but are not documented.

Option	V7	BSD	SIII	XENIX	SV	Function
-a	F	≡	≡	≡	≡	make entries for files
-f	.	.		F	.	report on current volume only
-r	.	.	F	≡	≡	report I/O errors
-s	F	≡	≡	≡	≡	grand totals only
-u	.	.	.	F	.	ignore links

dump

V7 and BSD have a *dump*(8) used for tape backup which is not the same as SV's *dump*(1) listed here (an object-file dumper). XENIX 2.3 and 3.0 versions have *dump*(1M) versions similar to V7/BSD's *dump*(8).

echo

SIII/SV *echo*(1) doesn't support V7's -n argument (used to suppress the newline normally output after the arguments). Instead, a \c escape given as the last character of the last argument suppresses the newline. XENIX 3.0 restores the V7 -n option and adds the -eu and -- options to the SIII version it inherited. XENIX 5.0 adopts the SV version.

ed

The BSD/XENIX documentation discusses bugs and implementation details not mentioned in the original V7 entry. SIII/SV ed has been enhanced quite a bit over the V7/BSD version; it includes many new commands and uses an enhanced regular expression syntax in which: (a) "{m,n}" after a one-character regular expression specifies a match to at least m and at most n repetitions; (b) "+" postfixing a one-character regular expression is equivalent to "{1,}"; and (c) the pattern tags "\1"..."\9" are defined during template interpretation and may be used to duplicate earlier tagged pieces into the template. XENIX 3.0/5.0 *ed*(1) is the SIII/SV version.

edit

SV2 has this as a variant of *ex*(1).

egrep

SIII/SV *egrep*(1) accepts {m,n} and + in regular expressions and allows the pattern-tag syntax to be used within templates; see the note for *ed*(1) above. The XENIX 3.0/5.0 version of this command is identical to the SIII version; the XENIX column in the following table refers to XENIX 2.3.

Option	V7	BSD	SIII	XENIX	SV	Function
-v	F	≡	≡	≡	≡	print all non-matching lines
-c	F	≡	≡	≡	≡	count matched lines
-l	F	≡	≡	≡	≡	print filenames only
-n	F	≡	≡	≡	≡	number matched lines
-b	F	≡	≡	≡	≡	prepend block numbers
-s	F	≡	X	≡	≡	see note [1]
-h	F	.	.	≡	.	suppress filename headers
-e	F	≡	≡	≡	≡	accept token starting with "−"
-f	F	≡	≡	.	≡	take RE from a file
-i	.	F	.	.	≡[2]	ignore case
-y	F	.	.	F	.	ignore case

[1] For V7/BSD/XENIX *egrep*(1), -s suppresses all output (but returns status). For SIII/SV *egrep*(1), -s suppresses file I/O error messages.
[2] SV2 only.

enable

SV *enable*(1) is different from XENIX *enable*(1M).

error

4.2BSD *error*(1) understands *troff*(1) message formats.

expr

SIII/SV *expr*(1) doesn't support parentheses for grouping in expressions. The XENIX 3.0/5.0 version is from SIII.

f77

f77(1) is frequently omitted from UNIX system implementations for smaller systems that have comparatively little mass storage. XENIX doesn't include it.

Option	V7	BSD	SIII	SV	Function
-1	.	.	.	F	same as "-onetrip" (below)
-66	.	.	.	F	disable f77 extensions
-C	F	≡	.	≡	generate bounds checks
-E	F	≡	≡	≡	apply EFL option
-F	F	≡	≡	≡	EFL/Ratfor preprocessing
-I	.	F	.	.	set #include path (4.2 only)
-N	.	.	.	F	change table sizes (SV2)
-O	F	≡[1]	≡	≡	invoke the optimizer
-R	F	≡	≡	≡	apply Ratfor option
-S	F	≡	≡	≡	generate assembly language only
-U	.	.	.	F	don't fold cases
-c	F	≡	≡	≡	link & load
-f	F	[2]	≡	≡	use software floating point
-g	.	F	.	≡	debugger mode
-i	.	F	.	.	set int size (4.2 only)
-m	F	≡	≡	≡	apply m4, then EFL/Ratfor
-o	F	≡	≡	≡	send runfile to filename
-onetrip	F	≡	≡	≡	do-loops go at least once
-p	F	≡	≡	≡	prepare for profiling
-pg	.	F	.	.	keep *gprof* info (4.2 only)
-u	F	≡	≡	≡	default type is "undefined"
-v	.	.	.	F	verbose mode
-w	F	≡	≡	≡	suppress warnings

[1] On BSD, the -O argument is undocumented but supported.

[2] The VAX has floating-point hardware; an -f will be considered a loader option and cause problems.

Notice that the BSD version is marked incompatible only due to absence of the obscure V7 -f option. SIII's lack of -C is more serious.

fed

This tool is supported only on 4.2BSD, although it is present in the 4.1BSD source distribution without documentation.

fgrep

The XENIX 3.0/5.0 version of this command is identical to the SIII version; the XENIX column in the following table refers to XENIX 2.3.

Option	V7	BSD	SIII	XENIX	SV	Function
-v	F	≡	≡	≡	≡	print nonmatching lines
-c	F	≡	≡	≡	≡	count matched lines
-l	F	≡	≡	≡	≡	print filenames only
-n	F	≡	≡	≡	≡	number matched lines
-b	F	≡	≡	≡	≡	prepend block numbers
-s	F	≡	X	≡	≡	see note [1]
-h	F	.	.	F	.	suppress filename headers
-e	F	≡	≡	≡	≡	accept token starting with "-"
-f	F	≡	≡	.	≡	take strings from a file
-x	F	≡	≡	≡	≡	match entire lines
-i	.	F	.	.	F[2]	ignore case
-y	F	.	.	F	.	ignore case

[1] For V7/BSD/XENIX *fgrep*(1), -s suppresses all output (but returns status). For SIII/SV *fgrep*(1), -s suppresses file I/O error messages.

[2] SV2 only.

file

The SV version gets the magic numbers it uses for testing from /etc/magic. The XENIX documentation gives a mapping between file types and cc flags. The XENIX 3.0/5.0 version derives from BSD.

Option	V7	BSD	SIII	XENIX	SV	Function
-f	.	.	F	≡	≡	take filenames from file
-c	.	.	.	.	F	check /etc/magic format
-m	.	.	.	F	X	see note [1]

[1] XENIX 3.0/5.0 *file*(1) accepts an -m option that sets the file's access time. SV *file*(1) has an -m option that specifies an alternate magic-numbers file.

find

Option	V7	BSD	SIII	XENIX	SV	Function
-access	.	.	.	F	.	match if access valid
-atime	F	≡	≡	≡	≡	match if accessed in n days
-cpio	.	.	F	≡	≡	write file in cpio form
-depth	.	.	.	.	F	depthmost traverse (SV2 only)
-exec	F	≡	≡	≡	≡	match if command returns 0
-group	F	≡	≡	≡	≡	match given group
-inum	F	≡	≡	≡	≡	match given inode
-links	F	≡	≡	≡	≡	match given # of links
-mtime	F	≡	≡	≡	≡	match if changed in n days
-name	F	≡	≡	≡	≡	match a given name
-newer	F	≡	≡	≡	≡	match files newer than arg.
-ok	F	≡	≡	≡	≡	like -exec with confirm
-perm	F	≡	≡	≡	≡	match given permissions
-print	F	≡	≡	≡	≡	print current pathname
-size	F	≡	≡	≡	≡	match given size in blocks
-type	F	≡	≡	≡	≡	match given file type [1]
-user	F	≡	≡	≡	≡	match given user

[1] For V7/BSD/XENIX, file types are b, c, d, or f for block special, character special, directory, or ordinary file. SIII/SV adds p for a named pipe. 4.2BSD adds l for symbolic links.

finger

There are two versions of this tool; the BSD original also found in XENIX 2.3, and an enhanced version found in XENIX 3.0/5.0.

Option	BSD	XENIX	Function
-b	.	F	briefer long output
-f	F	≡	suppress header line
-i	.	F	quick listing (users + idle times)
-l	F	≡	long output format
-p	F	≡	suppress plan printing
-q	.	F	quick listing (users only)
-s	F	≡	short output format
-w	.	F	narrow format listing

graphics

The *gdev*, *gutil*, *stat*, and *toc* groups in */usr/bin/graf* have been omitted from these tables.

grep

SIII/SV *grep*(1) accepts {m,n} and + in regular expressions and allows the pattern-tag syntax to be used within templates; see the note for *ed*(1). The XENIX 3.0/5.0 version of this command is identical to the SIII version; the XENIX column in the following table refers to XENIX 2.3.

Option	V7	BSD	SIII	XENIX	SV	Function
-v	F	≡	≡	≡	≡	print nonmatching lines
-c	F	≡	≡	≡	≡	count matched lines
-l	F	≡	≡	≡	≡	print filenames only
-n	F	≡	≡	≡	≡	number matched lines
-b	F	≡	≡	≡	≡	prepend block numbers
-s	F	≡	X	≡	≡	see note [1]
-h	F	.	.	F	.	suppress filename headers
-e	F	≡	≡	≡	≡	accept token starting with "-"
-i	.	F	.	.	F[2]	ignore case
-y	F	[3]	.	F	.	ignore case
-w	.	F	.	.	.	match words

[1] For V7/BSD/XENIX *grep*(1), -s suppresses all output (but returns status). For SIII/SV *grep*(1), -s suppresses file I/O error messages.

[2] SV2 only.

[3] BSD *grep*(1) has the -y option, although it's not documented.

hd

XENIX 5.0 adds a new t format to the existing acbwlahxdo formats.

help

SV1 only. SV2 replaces this command in the new *help*(1) facility.

indent

The *indent*(1) C-formatting utility is present as user-contributed, unsupported software on many 4.1BSD distributions, and is formally supported on 4.2BSD.

kill

This call simply passes its arguments to *kill*(2). See the material on *kill*(2) in the various dialects for differences. BSD *kill*(1) accepts certain symbolic names for signals, and SVID declares that the SV *kill*(1) will eventually do likewise.

l

XENIX *l*(1) is an alias for V7/BSD/SIII *ls*(1).

last

The 4.2BSD version of this command has some network-related enhancements.

lastcomm

The 4.2BSD version of this command displays a number of additional status flags.

lc

XENIX 3.0/5.0 adds -Ano options to the XENIX 2.3 original. XENIX 5.0 notes that *lf*(1), *lr*(1) and *lx*(1) are links to this that activate various options. Though the XENIX documentation credits this to Berkeley, no Berkeley version documents it.

ld

V7 documentation omits the entry for *ld*(1). The data in the following table was collected from a friendly expert. The XENIX column is for XENIX 2.3 on the 68000; XENIX 3.0 on the 80286 supports only -o, -i, and -F flags from the table as well as a special -A flag for standalone programs and -M[sml] flags for the three linkage models for the 80286's segmented addressing (see Section 2.4). XENIX 5.0 supports the 3.0 flags plus the -u flag in its standard meaning and -ABCDPScmnsv in meanings unique to itself.

Option	V7	BSD	SIII	XENIX	SV	Function
-d	F	≡	≡	≡	P	force common storage defined
-e	F	≡	.	≡	C	set program entry point
-f	.	.	.	.	C	set intersegment filler
-i	F	.	≡	≡	P	split i and d spaces

Option	V7	BSD	SIII	XENIX	SV	Function
-l	F	≡	≡	≡	≡	load given library
-m	.	.	F	.	≡	print load map to stdout
-n	F	≡	≡	≡	≡	sharable (read-only) text
-nn	.	.	.	F	.	.n with data after text
-nr	.	.	.	F	.	.n with text after data
-o	F	≡	≡	≡	≡	specify runfile name
-p	.	.	.	F	≡	specify -l directory
-r	F	≡	≡	≡	≡	retain relocation data [1]
-s	F	≡	≡	≡	≡	strip symbol table
-sr	.	.	.	F	.	no short relocatables
-t	.	F	X	.	≡	trace (see note [2])
-u	F	≡	≡	≡	≡	load symbol as undefined
-x	F	≡	≡	≡	≡	discard local symbols
-y	.	F	.	.	.	trace given symbol
-z	.	F	.	.	≡	demand-load
-A	.	F	.	.	≡	incremental load
-D	.	F	.	≡	.	set data segment size [3]
-F	.	.	.	F	.	set stack size
-L	.	.	.	.	C	change library search path
-M	.	F	.	.	X	see note [4]
-N	.	.	.	.	C	put data after text
-O	F	.	.	.	.	set up overlays
-R	.	.	.	F	.	set text relocation addr.
-S	.	F	.	.	.	strip all but locals/globals
-T	.	F	.	.	.	set text origin
-V	.	.	.	F	X	see note [5]
-VS	.	.	.	.	F	see note [5]
-X	F	≡	≡	≡	≡	strip out L labels

[1] On 4.1BSD, -r incorrectly makes the resulting module executable.

[2] On BSD, the -t option prints the name of each file used by the load as it is processed. On SIII, the -t option takes a symbol argument; all references to and definitions of that symbol during the load are listed. On SV2, the -t option suppresses the normal warning about multiply-defined symbols that are not all the same size.

[3] The -D option takes a decimal address on XENIX 2.3, hex on BSD.

[4] On BSD, the -M flag generates a load map. On SV2, the -M flag produces messages for each multiply-defined external.

[5] On SIII, the -V option allows the user to set a version stamp into the runfile header. On SV, this function is assumed by -VS, and -V instructs the loader to print its own version information.

lex

The SIII/SV *lex*(1) manual entry includes a good summary of the *lex* specification language. The V7/BSD column in the following table also describes XENIX 2.3; the XENIX 3.0/5.0 version is like that of SIII/SV, except that the -r switch enabling Ratfor code generation is not accepted. This should perhaps earn XENIX 3.0/5.0 an "X", but Ratfor is sufficiently obsolete that we couldn't bring ourselves to do it.

Option	V7/BSD	AT&T	Function
-c	.	F	generate C code (default)
-f	F	.	fast mode, don't pack tables
-n	F	≡	suppress table size listing
-r	.	F	generate Ratfor code
-t	F	≡	send result to stdout
-v	F	≡	verbose mode

lint

The 4.1BSD and XENIX 2.3 *lint*(1) is identical to V7 *lint*(1); the 4.2BSD version has one additional -C option used to generate lint libraries. The XENIX 3.0 version is identical to SIII's; the XENIX 5.0 version is the SV1 version.

SIII/SV *lint* reverses the significance of the -abch and -x options from their V7 meanings (which are also used in BSD and XENIX 2.3). In the following table, a "Y" means the reporting specified is normally off and is turned on by the option; an "N" means the reporting is normally on and is suppressed by the option.

SV2 supports the generation of *lint* library files from user code with the -c and -o options.

Option	V7	SIII	SV1	SV2	Function
-a	Y	N	N	N	report long assignments to ints
-b	Y	N	N	N	report unreachable break statements
-c	Y	N	N	1	report suspicious casts [1]
-h	Y	N	N	N	heuristic style and bug test
-l	.	.	F	≡	include a given lint library
-n	F	≡	≡	≡	no standard library checks
-o	.	.	.	F	create a .ln library file
-p	F	≡	≡	≡	check for IBM, GCOS portability
-u	F	≡	≡	≡	no undefined/unused complaints
-v	F	≡	≡	≡	no unused-argument complaints
-x	Y	N	N	N	report unused extern variables

[1] On SV2, the -c makes *lint* produce .ln (*lint* library) files for each .c given on the command line (there is no way to suppress reporting of suspicious casts).

list

SV2 adds a -F option to the -Vh options of SV1; the SV2 entry also includes new information on diagnostics and error warnings.

ln

SIII/SV lists *ln*(1) under *cp*(1). BSD, SIII, SV, and XENIX 3.0/5.0 will accept a final argument that is a directory name. SV2 adds a -f option to suppress warnings and queries. 4.2BSD adds a -s option to create symbolic links.

login

4.1BSD has some poorly documented enhancements over V7, such as the action of the *.hushlogin* file and the */etc/ttytype* facility. 4.2BSD *login*(1) includes more features for use with the Berkeley network servers. The *login*(1) command cannot be invoked explicitly in SIII. The following table lists the shell variables initialized at login time on different systems. XENIX 5.0 is identical to its XENIX 3.0 predecessor.

Name	V7	BSD	SIII	XE2.3	XE3.0	SV	Function
HOME	F	≡	≡	≡	≡	≡	user's home directory
LOGNAME	.	.	F	.	≡	≡	user's login name
MAIL	.	.	.	.	.	F	user's mail directory
PATH	F	≡	≡	≡	≡	≡	command search path
SHELL	.	F	.	.	.	≡	user's login shell
TERM	.	F	.	.	.	.	user's terminal type
TZ	.	.	F	.	≡	≡	site's timezone
USER	.	F	.	.	.	.	user's login name

lp

XENIX 5.0 provides both SV2-style *lp*(1) and an *lpr*(1) front end compatible with earlier versions. The other SV2 spooler system tools are also present.

lpq

This auxiliary tool has been totally rewritten as part of the redoing of the *lpr*(1) spooler system in 4.2BSD. Command line options to specify printer, job number, or user to be reported on have been added (the 4.1BSD version had no command line options) as well as various degrees of verbosity.

lpr

V7 has no *lpr*(1) command. The BSD *lpr*(1) differs considerably from the SIII/SV1 utility of the same name and function, and SV2 drops it again in favor of *lp*(1). The 4.2BSD version is a new program supporting cross-network printing and the */etc/printcap* capability database. All XENIX versions support the same *lpr*(1) interface; XENIX 5.0 has apparently made it an alternate front end to an SV2-derived spooler system.

Option	BSD4.1	BSD4.2	SIII	XENIX	SV1	Function
-#	.	F	.	.	.	print multiple copies
-[1234]	.	F	.	.	.	specify mounted fonts
-c	.	F	F	≡	≡	see note [1]
-d	.	F	.	.	.	expect DVI format
-f	.	F	.	.	F	see note [2]
-g	.	F	.	.	.	expect *graph*(3) output
-h	.	F	.	.	.	suppress burst page printing
-i	.	F	.	.	.	indent output
-l	.	F	.	.	F	print control characters
-m	F	≡	≡	≡	≡	notify user via *mail*(1)
-n	.	F	F	≡	≡	see note [3]
-p	.	.	F	.	.	pre-filter with *pr*(1)
-r	.	F	F	≡	≡	remove file after printing
-s	.	F	.	.	.	use symbolic links
-t	.	F	.	.	.	expect *troff*(1) output
-v	.	F	.	.	.	expect a raster image
-w	.	F	.	.	.	set page width
-C	.	F	.	.	.	set job class string
-J	.	F	.	.	.	set job name string
-T	.	F	.	.	.	set *pr*(1) title string

[1] On 4.2BSD, this option prints *cifplot*(1) files. On all other versions, it prints from a copy of the file made immediately.

[2] On 4.2BSD, this option prefilters the printed text with code that interprets FORTRAN carriage-control characters. On all other versions, it sets a dummy print file name for the job.

[3] On 4.2BSD, this option prepares the spooler for *ditroff*(1) output. On all other versions, it suppresses mail notification.

lprm

4.2BSD *lprm*(1) has been totally rewritten. Filenames are no longer valid arguments, but the user may specify "-" to delete all of his/her current jobs or "-P" to delete all jobs associated with a given printer.

ls

The XENIX 2.3 version of *ls*(1) is identical to V7. The XENIX 3.0 version of *ls*(1) is identical to SIII *ls*(1); the 5.0 version is SV2's.

Option	V7	BSD	SIII	SV1	SV2	Function
-1	.	F	.	.	.	1 entry per line [1]
-C	.	F	.	.	≡	force columnation [1]
-F	.	F	.	.	≡	apply * and / suffixes
-L	.	F[3]	.	.	.	list symbolic links
-R	.	F	.	.	≡	recurse on directories
-a	F	≡	≡	≡	≡	list all files
-b	.	F[3]	.	.	≡	print nongraphics visibly
-c	F	≡	≡	≡	≡	sort by creation time
-d	F	≡	≡	≡	≡	list directory by name
-f	F	≡	≡	≡	≡	force directory list
-g	F	≡	≡	≡	≡	list group, not owner
-i	F	≡	≡	≡	≡	list i-nodes of files
-l	F	≡	≡	≡	≡	long listing
-m	.	F[3]	.	.	≡	stream output format
-n	.	.	.	.	F	show numeric UID/GID
-o	.	F[3]	≡	≡	≡	suppress group display
-p	.	.	.	F	≡	/ follows directories
-q	.	F	.	.	≡	show nongraphics as ?
-r	F	≡	≡	≡	≡	reverse normal sorting
-s	F	≡	≡	≡	≡	give file sizes [2]
-t	F	≡	≡	≡	≡	sort by time modified
-u	F	≡	≡	≡	≡	sort by access time
-x	.	F[3]	.	.	≡	alternate column style

[1] V7/BSD/XENIX 2.3 *ls*(1) tries to detect when it's talking to a tty, and in that case automatically columnates its output; on BSD the -1 option is available to override this. SIII/SV/XENIX 3.0/XENIX 5.0 doesn't do this, but on SV2 the -C option is available to cause columnation.

[2] Notice that 4.2BSD reports file sizes consistently in kilobytes; all others report them in blocks.

[3] The -L option is new in 4.2BSD, which also deletes the -bmox options.

m4

The *m4*(1) of BSD and XENIX 2.3 is identical to the original V7; it is a simple filter with no options. The version found on SIII/SV/XENIX 3.0/5.0 supports -eBHSTDU options for changing buffer and table sizes and to control interactions with the C preprocessor. The set of predefined words common to both versions is:

define	undefine	ifdef	changequote
divert	undivert	divnum	dnl
ifelse	incr	eval	len
index	substr	translit	include
sinclude	syscmd	maketemp	errprint
dumpdef			

One (undocumented) difference between the V7 and USG versions is that, while the V7 version permits only single-character quote marks, USG quote marks may be strings of up to five characters.

machid

This is not a command, but a documentation entry for a number of shell commands that can be used in shell scripts to identify the type of the host machine.

mail

4.1BSD *mail*(1) is hugely enhanced over V7 (see manual). The 4.2BSD version is further elaborated in the style of the Rand MH system and supports new -vinus command options. The original V7 *mail*(1) is available on BSD as *binmail*(1). SIII *mail*(1) adds a "+" command to the V7 set and replaces the "?" command with "*" (this is why it is marked incompatible). XENIX 3.0 *mail*(1) is the BSD version, but the 5.0 mailer has been considerably enhanced. SV adds -e and -t options to the -pqr options of V7/SIII; SV2 imports an enhanced version of BSD *mail*(1) as *mailx*(1).

mailx

SV2 *mailx*(1) is almost identical in function to BSD *mail*(1).

make

SIII/SV *make*(1) is an augmented new version with useful built-in rules for SCCS access and library maintenance. The 4.1BSD version is functionally identical to the V7 original, but the 4.2BSD version has a new built-in MFLAGS macro and understands the .F suffix for FORTRAN files that are to pass through the preprocessor. The XENIX 2.3 version is from V7; the XENIX 3.0/5.0 version is from SIII.

Option	V7	AT&T	Function
-b	.	F	old make compatibility mode
-d	F[1]	≡	print diagnostics as make proceeds
-e	.	F	environment overrides macro assignments
-f	F	≡	use alternate makefile
-i	F	≡	ignore error returns
-k	F	≡	continue past errors
-m	.	F	print memory map (needs *getu(2)* call)
-n	F	≡	trace and print only
-p	.	F	print macro definitions and dependencies
-q	.	F	query up-to-dateness of given target
-r	F	≡	ignore built-in rules
-s	F	≡	don't print commands
-t	F	≡	touch targets

[1] The -d option is present on V7/BSD *make*(1) but not documented.

man

The XENIX 2.3 version of *man*(1) is identical to V7's. XENIX 3.0/5.0 has no *man*(1) command (at least, the PC/AT implementation doesn't). The SV1 version is the same as SIII's but with more documentation; the SV2 version is part of the new *help*(1) system and has been optimized for speed.

Option	V7	BSD	XENIX	SIII	SV1	SV2	Function
-	.	F	.	.	.	.	browse mode
-12	.	.	.	.	F	.	12-pitch
-c	.	.	.	F	≡	≡	apply *col*(1)
-d	.	.	.	F	≡	≡	search . for file
-e	F	.	≡	.	.	.	apply *eqn*(1)
-f	.	F	.	.	.	.	find filename
-k	F	X	.	.	.	.	see note [1]
-n	F	.	≡	.	.	.	apply *nroff*(1)

Option	V7	BSD	XENIX	SIII	SV1	SV2	Function
-s	.	.	.	F	≡	.	small format
-t	F	≡	≡	≡	≡	≡	apply *troff*(1)
-w	F	.	≡	≡	≡	≡	print pathnames
-y	.	.	.	F	≡	.	use macro sources
-T	.	.	.	F	≡	≡	terminal type [2]

[1] V7 *man*(1) interprets -k as instruction to emit Tektronix 4014 codes. BSD *man*(1) accepts a -k option argument as a keyword to be searched for.

[2] Beware! The list of valid terminal types for *man*(1) varies greatly, even between SV1 and SV2.

SV man uses a "manprog" helper that is documented on the *mail*(1) manual page. The SV2 version is faster, as it does a fetch from /usr/catman rather than an *nroff*(1). Similar behavior can be induced in BSD *man*(1); see BSD *catman*(8).

mm

The SV *mm*(1) documentation includes material on *osdd* and *checkmm* helpers, not included in the SIII documentation.

mmcheck

In SV, *checkmm* (under *mm*(1)) replaces *mmchek*(1).

mt

The 4.2BSD version of this magnetic tape handler includes a new status-querying command.

mv

Notice that SIII/SV *mv*(1) is documented under *cp*(1). The 4.2BSD version uses a system call unique to that dialect, and is thus faster and omits the restrictions on ".." in pathnames; it also permits moves of multiple directories.

Option	V7	BSD	XENIX	SIII	SV1	SV2	Function
-	.	F	.	.	.	.	no more options
-f	.	F	.	.	.	≡	ignore errors
-i	.	F	.	.	.	.	interactive mode

ncp

Not supported in 3B5 SV2.

net, netcp, netlog, netlogin, netlpr, netmail, netq, netrm, netstat, nettroff

These programs are no longer supported in 4.2BSD except *netstat*(1), which is new in this distribution.

newgrp

SIII/SV *newgrp*(1) assumes the absence of arguments to be a request to reset to the login group in the user's password-file entry. SV *newgrp*(1) accepts a "-" option that resets the user's environment to the initial login environment.

nice

SIII *nice*(1) uses a 0 to 40 range of priority values, as opposed to V7/BSD/XENIX 2.3's -20 to +20. See the notes on *nice*(2).

nkill(1)

Only SV2 supports *nkill*(1).

nl

SV *nl*(1) has -d flag in addition to the -hbfviplswn flags of SIII.

nm

SV *nm*(1) on machines that support COFF is new and incompatible with the PDP-11 derived *nm*(1) of SIII. On SV2, the -p option produces output in the old format. The XENIX column describes XENIX 2.3, 3.0, and 5.0, but see note [6].

Option	V7	BSD	XENIX	SIII	COFF	Function
-a	.	F	X	.	.	see note [1]
-c	.	.	F	:	.	C symbols only
-e	.	.	.	.	F	externs/statics only
-f	.	.	.	.	F	full output
-g	F	≡	≡	≡	.	print globals only
-h	.	.	.	.	F	suppress header
-n	F	≡	≡	≡	X	see note [2]
-o	F	≡	≡	≡	X	see note [3]
-p	F	≡	≡	≡	X	see note [4]
-r	F	≡	≡	≡	X	see note [5]
-s	.	.	F	F	.	sort by size [6]
-u	F	≡	≡	≡	≡	undefineds only
-v	.	.	F	.	X	see note [7]
-x	.	.	.	.	F	hex output
-O	.	.	F	.	.	octal output [6]
-S	.	.	F	.	.	switch display form [6]
-T	.	.	.	.	F$	truncate
-V	.	.	.	.	F	print nm version

[1] On BSD, -a directs *nm*(1) to display all (even normally suppressed redundant) symbols. On XENIX 3.0 only, -a directs *nm*(1) to display absolute symbols only.

[2] In non-COFF versions of *nm*(1), -n sorts the output numerically rather than alphabetically. In COFF versions, -n sorts the output by symbol name.

[3] In pre-COFF versions of *nm*(1), -o directed the tool to prepend the name(s) of the object file(s) being examined to each line (the new -r option does this in COFF versions). In COFF versions, it changes the base for numeric output to octal (the default is decimal).

[4] In pre-COFF versions of *nm*(1), -p suppressed all output sorting (so symbols would be printed in symbol-table order). In the COFF version on SV2, -p forces a "terse" format compatible with pre-COFF versions.

[5] In pre-COFF versions of *nm*(1), -r caused a sort in reverse order. In the COFF version on SV2, it directs the tool to prepend the name(s) of the object file(s) being analyzed to each line.

[6] XENIX 3.0/5.0 only.

[7] In XENIX -v prints an explanation of the object file format. In COFF versions, it causes extern symbols to be sorted by value.

nroff

The BSD and XENIX 2.3 and 3.0 versions appear to be identical to the V7 version; the SIII, SV1, and SV2 versions appear to be the same (their options are listed in the following table under AT&T). Some macro packages that work correctly with V7 *nroff*(1) will fail when used with the AT&T version (most notably, the Berkeley -me macros). Documentation for XENIX 5.0 *nroff*(1) was not available at the time of writing.

Option	V7	AT&T	Function
-c	.	F	use a compacted package
-e	F	≡	format for tty viewing
-h	F	≡	use tab characters
-i	.	F	read stdin after files
-k	.	F	compact a package source
-m	F	≡	use given macro package
-n	F	≡	start page numbering at argument
-o	F	≡	print pages in given range only
-q	.	F	simultaneous input for .rd
-r	F	≡	set a register
-s	F	≡	stop for paper change
-z	.	F	print .tm messages only
-T	F	≡	specify terminal type [1]

[1] The types of terminals supported vary greatly between dialects.

od

The V7, SIII, and XENIX versions of this tool appear to be identical.

Option	V7	BSD4.1	BSD4.2	SV	Function
-a	.	F	.	.	display ASCII names
-b	F	≡	=	≡	interpret bytes in octal
-c	F	≡	≡	≡	interpret bytes in ASCII
-d	F	≡	=	≡	interpret words in decimal
-o	F	≡	=	≡	interpret words in octal
-s	.	.	F	F	see note [1]
-v	.	.	F	.	show all data
-w	.	F	X	.	see note [2]
-x	F	≡	=	≡	interpret words in hex
-D	.	F	.	.	interpret longs in decimal
-O	.	F	.	.	interpret longs in octal
-X	.	F	.	.	interpret longs in hex

[1] On 4.2BSD, -s tells *od*(1) to look for null-terminated ASCII strings. On SV, it tells *od*(1) to interpret words in signed decimal.

[2] On 4.1BSD, -w produces 132-column output. On 4.2BSD, it may be used with a numeric argument to set the byte width of output lines.

pack

SV2 adds a -f option to force file packing to the - option already supported.

passwd

XENIX 3.0/5.0 adds features that define a "password configuration," including minimum length and password aging parameters. SV2 *passwd*(1) tightens up the requirements for passwords. 4.2BSD notes that concurrency interlocks on the password file have been made to work, implying that they did not in 4.1BSD.

pc

The 4.2BSD version supports a new object file format enabling separate compilation with type checking. Dynamically allocated files and random file I/O are also new in 4.2BSD. "For" loops did not have standard semantics in the 4.1BSD version, they do in 4.2BSD. Numerous other bug features and minor enhancements have been added.

pcc

This is the name under which S. C. Johnson's Portable C Compiler was supported on Version 7 and System III. Later UNIX C compilers and almost all of those on microcomputer ports are adapted versions of *pcc*(1).

pi

Dynamically allocated files and random file I/O are new in 4.2BSD. "For" loops did not have standard semantics in the 4.1BSD version, they do in 4.2BSD. Numerous other bug features and minor enhancements have been added.

plot

SIII/SV replaces V7 plot with tplot.

pr

The SIII, SV, and XENIX 3.0/5.0 versions of *pr*(1) are identical and are listed in the following table as AT&T; the XENIX column refers to

XENIX 2.3.

Option	V7	BSD	XENIX	AT&T	Function
+<n>	F	≡	≡	≡	start print with page <n>
-<n>	F	≡	≡	≡	produce <n>-column output
-a	.	.	.	F	multiple columns across page
-b	.	.	F[1]	.	formfeeds between pages
-d	.	.	.	F	double-spaced output
-e	.	.	.	F	expand input tabs
-f	.	.	.	F[1]	formfeeds between pages
-h	F	≡	≡	≡	use argument as header
-i	.	.	.	F	generate output tabs
-l	F	≡	≡	≡	set page length
-m	F	≡	≡	≡	print one file per column
-n	.	.	.	F	number lines
-o	.	.	.	F	set line offset
-p	.	.	.	F	browse mode
-r	.	.	.	F	suppress diagnostics
-s	F	≡	≡	≡	change column separator
-t	F	≡	≡	≡	suppress headers/trailers
-w	F	≡	≡	≡	set page width

[1] Note that the -b option of XENIX 2.3 is equivalent to the AT&T -f option.

prof

The V7, XENIX, SIII, and PDP-11 SV versions of this command are the same; the BSD version is a slight enhancement, and the XENIX 3.0/5.0 command lacks the -v, low-address, and high-address options. There is a completely different *prof*(1) for COFF; the SV2 version adds finer control of profile output destinations and intrafunction profile marks.

Option	V7	BSD	COFF	Function
-a	F	≡	X	see note [1]
-c	.	.	F	sort by decreasing # of calls
-g	.	.	F	include nonglobals
-h	.	.	F	suppress headers
-l	F	≡	.	list by symbol value
-m	.	.	F	send profile data to file
-n	.	F	X	see note [2]
-o	.	.	F	symbol addresses in octal
-s	.	F	X	generate summary profile [3]
-t	.	.	F	sort by decreasing % of time
-v	F	≡	.	histogram output
-x	.	.	F	symbol addresses in hex
-z	.	F	≡	include zero-usage symbols

[1] On the V7/BSD versions, -a causes reporting of all symbols including
nonexternals. On the COFF version, it causes the output lines to be
sorted by increasing symbol address.

[2] On BSD, -n sorts the output by number of calls. On the COFF version,
it sorts lexically by symbol name.

[3] On BSD, the summary goes to mon.out; on the COFF version, it goes to
stderr.

ps

The SIII, XENIX 3.0/5.0, SV1, and SV2 versions of *ps*(1) appear to
have the same interface and are listed in the following table under AT&T.

Option	V7	BSD	AT&T	Function
-a	F	≡	≡	list all processes with ttys
-c	.	F	X	see note [1]
-d	.	.	F	don't list process-group leaders
-e	.	F	X	see note [2]
-f	.	.	F	generate full listing
-g	.	F	X	see note [3]
-k	F	≡	.	use given core file; see note [1]
-l	F	≡	≡	generate long listing
-n	.	.	F	use specified namelist
-p	.	.	F	list only named PIDs
-s	.	F	X	see note [4]
-t	.	F	X	named ttys only; see note [5]
-u	.	F	X	see note [6]
-v	.	F	.	print memory-usage statistics
-w	.	F	.	wide output
-x	F	≡	.	list processes with no tty
-#	.	F	.	look at one specified pid

[1] On BSD, -c causes printing of the system's internal notion of a process's
name (as opposed to `argv[0]`, which can be tampered with). On
AT&T versions, -c followed by a filename directs *ps*(1) to examine the
given core image.

[2] On BSD, -e causes environment data to be printed. On AT&T, it directs
ps(1) to display all processes (including process group leaders and
processes without terminals).

[3] On BSD, -g causes all processes to be printed, including instances of
getty(1) and process group leaders. On AT&T versions, it restricts
ps(1) to processes whose group leaders are in a following group list.

[4] On BSD, -s enables display of the SSIZ (kernel-stack size) column. On AT&T versions, it may be used to specify a swap device.

[5] BSD and AT&T -t options are not really compatible, as they use different formats for specifying terminals of interest.

[6] On BSD, -u produces user-oriented output. On AT&T versions, it may be used to restrict *ps*(1) to a list of given user ids.

ranlib

AT&T versions of *ld*(1) don't require any equivalent of V7/BSD *ranlib*(1) preprocessing, but access can be optimized by use of *lorder*(1) and *tsort*(1). (See Chapter 5 for *mklib*, a shell script that provides a portable library building technique.) All XENIX versions (including the usually AT&T-like 3.0 and even 5.0) have *ranlib*(1) and require its use.

ratfor

BSD doesn't document any of the V7 command line options, but the synopsis implies that they are there. Therefore, we did not feel compelled to mark it incompatible. The presence of this tool in XENIX 3.0/5.0 seems odd, as there is no *f77*(1) to go with it!

rcp

This tool is a remote copy for local networking schemes supported by 4.2BSD and XENIX 3.0/5.0. Although the format of network names is similar, the transport layer and command options are both different and not mutually compatible.

rdist

This source-code management utility is available under 4.3BSD only.

regcmp

The PC/AT version notes that this will only generate small-model code. This is a result of the segmented processor architecture.

rlogin

This remote-login utility is only supported on 4.2BSD.

rm

BSD is enhanced to recognize filenames beginning with a dash. XENIX 5.0 documents the following restrictions on rm -r: no more than seventeen levels of directories will be removed and the root directories of file systems cannot be removed.

rmdir

The 4.2BSD version of this tool uses a new system call that will not accept an argument with trailing slashes. The XENIX 5.0 version will refuse to remove the root directory of any file system.

roffbib

This utility for formatting bibliographies is available only under 4.2BSD.

rsh

SV *rsh* documentation is under *sh*(1). Notice that 4.2BSD (but not 4.1BSD) supports *rsh*(1) with a completely different function (it is used to do remote command execution over a network).

ruptime

This performance measuring tool is available only on 4.2BSD.

sar

SV includes in its section 1 the report generator portion of the system activity report package prototyped in SIII. See also *sar*(1M) and *sar*(8).

script

4.2BSD adds support for job control commands in scripts.

se

SV2 eliminates *se*(1) in favor of *vi*(1).

sed

SIII/SV *sed*(1) accepts {m,n} and + in regular expressions; see the note under *ed*(1). There is a minor incompatibility between BSD and AT&T versions. The regular-expression syntax of BSD *sed*(1) appears to be based on the syntax of *ex*(1), whereas V7 and AT&T *sed*(1) versions are based on the syntax of *ed*(1). For example, if the goal is to convert

```
extern int arr[MSIZE][NSIZE];
```

to

```
extern int arr[][NSIZE];
```

the BSD *sed*(1) command to do this is

```
s/\[[^\]]*[/
```

but in the V7 and AT&T versions it is

```
s/\[[^]]*[/
```

The BSD command only matches the first character after the "arr[" when run on other versions. The second command has no effect when run on BSD (it is improper syntax). For an example of the workaround for this problem, see the *cx* script in Chapter 5.

SV2 includes two new features: a number option for the s command that can specify substitution for the nth occurrence of an expression in a line, and a comment facility.

settime

The *date*(1) format has been changed, so this is incompatible between XENIX 2.3 and 3.0.

sh

AT&T versions add a pound-sign (#) comment syntax. SV *sh*(1) allows a numeric argument to shift; it also has other new features, see $CDPATH under *cd*(1). SV2 includes new unset, type, MAILPATH, MAILCHECK, hash, and SHACCT features; shell procedures are supported, and *echo*(1) and *pwd*(1) are built-ins for faster execution. In 4.2BSD the *newgrp* command is gone due to the new group facilities. XENIX 5.0 *sh*(1) in interactive mode will attempt spelling correction on pathnames that it cannot match, requesting user confirmation for the result.

size

SV *size*(1) is identical to previous versions on the PDP-11, but has new -oxV options on COFF machines. The XENIX 3.0/5.0 version adds plus signs between the segment size columns and an equals sign before the total.

sleep

The upper bound on the number of seconds that may be specified is machine word-length dependent.

sort

SV2 and XENIX 5.0 *sort*(1) include -yzM options not supported in other versions. V7/BSD includes a -T option not supported in later AT&T versions.

spell

The *spell*(1) utility has dictionary-maintenance helpers that vary between versions.

stat

Not described in the SV1 base documentation.

strip

SV has a new *strip*(1) for COFF machines as well as a PDP-11 version compatible with previous ones. V7, BSD, and SIII support no command-line options. No options are documented for the XENIX 5.0 version.

Option	XE2.3	XE3.0	SV1	SV2	Function
-b	.	.	.	F	like -x, but don't strip scope info
-d	F	≡	.	.	strip data and data relocation records
-e	F	≡	.	.	strip extended header

Option	XE2.3	XE3.0	SV1	SV2	Function
-h	F	≡	.	.	strip header and extended header
-l	.	.	F	≡	strip line number information
-r	F	≡	X	X	see note [1]
-s	F	≡	X	.	see note [2]
-t	F	≡	.	.	strip text and text relocation records
-x	F	≡	X	≡	see note [3]
-S	.	F	.	.	strip segment table
-V	.	.	F	≡	print version to stderr

[1] In XENIX, this strips all relocation information except the *x.out*(5) short form (it is selected by default). In SV1, it resets the relocation indices into the symbol table. In SV2, it suppresses stripping of nonautomatic variable information.

[2] In XENIX, this strips the symbol table (it is the default). In SV1, it resets the line-number indices into the symbol table (but does not remove them) and performs the equivalent of a -r.

[3] In XENIX, -x strips all relocation information. In SV, -x suppresses stripping of `static` and `extern` information.

stty

There are major differences between V7/BSD *stty*(1) and SIII/SV versions that reflect the rewrite of the *tty*(4) driver for System III. Every UNIX system port tends to have its own variant option set; there are too many to list exhaustively. Generally portable stty options are: baud, 0, nl, nl[01], ff*, bs*, raw, cooked, lcase, ek, tabs, hup, erase, kill, cr*, tab*, tty3*, vt05, ti?00, tek. BSD *stty* also sets modes for job control features. The XENIX 2.3 version generally resembles V7's; the XENIX 3.0 version resembles SIII's, and the XENIX 5.0 version resembles SV2's. SV2's version differs from SIII's only in having a few more control options for the tty-layer driver [see *shl*(1)]. 4.2BSD and XENIX 5.0 use DEC-style default characters (DEL for erase, ^U for kill, and ^C for interrupt) rather than the standard #, @, and DEL.

su

The XENIX 2.3 and 3.0 versions of *su*(1) are both SIII's. SV2 adds a new -r option to invoke the restricted shell *rsh*(1), and adds a note about the su log file not given in previous versions. 4.2BSD adds a -f option for faster execution.

sum

SIII/XENIX 3.0/XENIX 5.0/SV add one -r option to the V7/BSD/XENIX 2.3 version that changes the checksum algorithm.

tabs

V7/BSD/XENIX 2.3 *tabs*(1) supports only a -n option to disable indenting (besides the terminal type spec). SIII/SV *tabs*(1) is much more elaborate and supports many different kinds of canned formats and formatting options. XENIX 3.0/5.0 has no *tabs*(1).

tail

V7 and XENIX 2.3 *tail*(1) are identical; XENIX 3.0/5.0's is the AT&T (SIII/SV) version.

Option	V7	BSD	AT&T	Function
+<n>	F	≡	≡	start at line n
-<n>	F	≡	≡	start at nth from last
-l	F	≡	≡	count by lines (default)
-b	F	≡	≡	count by blocks
-c	F	≡	≡	count by characters
-f	.	F	≡	don't stop on EOF
-r	.	F	.	read in reverse

tar

The SIII and SV1 versions of *tar*(1) have options identical to V7. The XENIX 2.3 options are exactly those of V7, except for -n, which is found in the following table. The XENIX column of this table refers to XENIX 3.0/5.0. Option letters with no preceding "−" are modifiers for the basic options. Notice that SV *tar*(1) (at least on the 3B5) cannot read tapes made with V7/BSD's default block size (20); you must use a block size of 16.

Option	V7	BSD	XENIX	SV2	Function
-	.	.	F	.	take arguments from stdin
-C	.	F	.	.	force chdir operations [1]
-A	.	.	F$	.	suppress leading / [3]
-F	.	.	F	.	take arguments from file
-c	F	≡	≡	≡	create new tape
-k	.	.	F	.	specify archive volume size
-p	.	F	≡	.	extract with stored permissions

Option	V7	BSD	XENIX	SV2	Function
-r	F	≡	≡	≡	append files to tape
-t	F	≡	≡	≡	list files from tape
-u	F	≡	≡	≡	update files to tape
-x	F	≡	≡	≡	extract files from tape
<n>	F	≡	≡	X	specify drive; see [2]
B	.	F	.	.	use 20-block records [1]
b	F	≡	≡	≡	specify blocking factor
e	.	.	F	.	don't split files across volumes
f	F	≡	≡	≡	specify archive file
l	F	≡	≡	≡	complain about bad links
m	F	≡	≡	≡	don't restore modify times
n	.	.	F	.	archive device isn't tape
v	F	≡	≡	≡	verbose mode
w	F	≡	≡	≡	interactive-confirm mode

[1] These switches supported on 4.2BSD only.

[2] All versions except SV2 use */dev/mt?* as default archive files and require only a single-digit drive argument (default is 1). SV2 uses */dev/mt/??* files and requires a digit followed by a density (default is *0m*).

Note: Not all of AT&T's System V implementations can exchange *tar*(1)-format tapes; use *cpio*(1) instead.

tbl

SIII/XENIX 3.0/XENIX 5.0/SV *tbl*(1) documents a -TX option to force use of only full-line motions. This is actually a feature of the V7 and BSD versions as well (see Lesk's paper *TBL: A Program to Format Tables* in the UNIX manual).

tc

SIII/SV tc doesn't support V7/BSD's aspect-ratio option. XENIX lacks this utility entirely.

test

The BSD and XENIX 2.3 versions of this utility are identical to V7's. The XENIX 3.0 version is from SIII; the 5.0 version is SV's. All file tests in all versions fail if the file does not exist.

Option	V7	SIII	SV	Function
-a	F	≡	≡	binary logical and
-b	.	F	≡	true if file is block special
-c	.	F	≡	true if file is character special
-d	F	≡	≡	true if file is a directory
-eq	F	≡	≡	algebraic equality test
-f	F	≡	≡	true if file is not a directory
-g	.	F	≡	true if file has set-group-id
-ge	F	≡	≡	algebraic not-less-than test
-gt	F	≡	≡	algebraic greater-than test
-k	.	F	≡	true if file's sticky bit is on
-le	F	≡	≡	algebraic not-greater-than test
-lt	F	≡	≡	algebraic less-than test
-n	F	≡	≡	true if string length is nonzero
-ne	F	≡	≡	algebraic inequality test
-o	F	≡	≡	binary logical or
-r	F	≡	≡	true if file is readable
-s	F	≡	≡	true if file size > 0
-t	F	≡	≡	true if descriptor connected to tty
-u	.	F	≡	true if file has set-user-id
-w	F	≡	≡	true if file is writeable
-x	.	F	≡	true if file is executable
-z	F	≡	≡	true if string length is zero

Note: All versions identically support infix = and !=, prefix !, and parentheses (for grouping).

time

Dialects that support *csh*(1) have two versions of *time*(1), one of which is an internal (shell) command of *csh*(1). To force use of the external one, specify */bin/time*(1).

timex

SV *timex*(1) adds a number of options and warnings about what can confuse it to the SIII version (which supports no options).

touch

The BSD and XENIX 2.3 versions of *touch*(1) are identical to V7's. XENIX 3.0 *touch(1)* is SIII's; the 5.0 version is SV's.

Option	V7	SIII	SV	Function
-c	F	≡	≡	suppress file creation if nonexistent
-a	.	F	≡	update access time only
-m	.	F	≡	update modification time only

Note: SIII/SV versions allow the touch timestamp to be specified on the command line in *date*(1) format.

tplot

This tool replaces V7's *plot*(1).

tr

SIII/XENIX 3.0/XENIX 5.0/SV *tr*(1) requires [] around character ranges and has a syntax to specify runs of repeated characters. The -c, -d, and -s options are supported by all versions.

troff

The BSD and XENIX 2.3 and 3.0 versions appear to be identical to the V7 version, except that the -g option is omitted. Since spooling to GCOS is a nonissue on any current UNIX system, we might have let *troff*(1) slip by as a portable tool; but some macro packages that work correctly with V7 *troff*(1) will fail when used with the AT&T version (most notably, the Berkeley -me macros). The SIII, SV1, and SV2 versions appear to be the same (their options are listed below under AT&T). Documentation for XENIX 5.0 *troff*(1) was not available at the time of writing.

Option	V7	AT&T	Function
-c	.	F	use a compacted package
-g	F	≡	prepare output for GCOS
-i	.	F	read stdin after files
-k	.	F	compact a package source
-m	F	≡	use given macro package
-n	F	≡	start page numbering at argument
-o	F	≡	print pages in given range only
-q	.	F	simultaneous input for .rd
-r	F	≡	set a register
-s	F	≡	stop for paper change
-z	.	F	print .tm messages only

tty

SIII/SV *tty*(1) supports the -s option to suppress printing of the tty name (in case only the return code is wanted). SV adds -l to allow querying of synchronous lines.

uname

This utility is only found on SIII and SV systems and on XENIX 3.0/5.0.

Option	SIII	XENIX	SV	Function
-a	F	≡	≡	print all version information
-d	.	F	.	print name of distributor
-m	.	F	F	see note [1]
-n	.	F$	.	print the node name
-p	.	F$	.	print the processor type
-r	F	≡	≡	print operating system release
-s	F	≡	≡	print system name (default)
-u	.	F	.	print serial number
-v	F	≡	≡	print operating system version

[1] On XENIX 3.0/5.0, this prints the manufacturer name; on SV, it prints the machine hardware type (e.g., 3B5).

units

In SIII and other AT&T-derived versions, the conversions file is */usr/lib/unittab* rather than */usr/lib/units*.

uucp

There are three major versions of the *uucp*(1) system. The V7 version was the original; 4.1BSD, XENIX 2.3, and XENIX 3.0/5.0 also feature this version, and the one found on 4.2BSD and 4.3BSD is a close derivative of it (although the 4.3BSD version has substantial enhancements such as the ability to use TCP/IP protocol). SIII and SV1 have an enhanced second version, and SV2 provides a completely rewritten and enhanced third version that uses different formats for its capability files. AT&T also has a fourth version (the legendary Honey-Danber uucp) that is only sold separately. The differences between these versions are mostly not of interest to users, though from a *uucp* administrator's point of view they deserve a chapter (and perhaps an entire book) to themselves.

Option	V7	SIII	SV2	Function
-c	F	≡	≡	use source file when copying out
-d	F	≡	≡	make all necessary directories
-e	.	F	.	execute uucp command remotely
-f	.	F	≡	don't make directories
-g	.	.	F	set the job's grade
-j	.	.	F	output a job ID to stdout
-m	F	≡	≡	notify user by *mail*(1) on completion
-n	.	F	≡	notify receiving user on console
-r	.	.	F	queue the job for next batching
-s	.	.	F	report transfer status to file
-x	F	≡	≡	set debug report level; see note [1]
-C	.	F	≡	copy file to spool directory first

[1] The -x option is documented only in SV2 but is (necessarily) present everywhere.

Note: In the SIII and SV2 versions, the default options are -cd, and the -m option may take a file argument as a destination to which to direct the notification.

uudiff

The 4.1BSD documentation warns that some versions do not include this tool. The authors have been unable to confirm that any working version of the utility was ever distributed.

uulog

The SV1 version has the same function and options as SIII's, but omits earlier notes about combining log files. SV2 has different options as part of the new uucp system.

uusend, uuto

SIII/SV *uuto*(1) and BSD *uusend*(1) are roughly equivalent. However, they are not mutually compatible, which is unfortunate since the forwarding features on SV2 and 4.2BSD rely upon them.

uustat

There are three major versions of the uucp system; see the note on *uucp*(1) above. Only the SIII, XENIX 3.0/5.0, and SV versions feature *uustat*(1).

Option	SIII	SV1	SV2	Function
-a	.	.	F	report on all jobs in the queue
-c	F	≡	.	remove old status entries
-j	F	≡	≡	report on a given job or all jobs
-k	F	≡	≡	kill a given job
-m	F	≡	X	report machine accessibility; see note [1]
-o	F	≡	.	report on old requests
-p	.	.	F	report on all locked processes
-q	.	F	≡	list jobs queued for each machine
-r	.	F	≡	rejuvenate a given job
-s	F	F	≡	report on requests to/from given site
-u	F	≡	≡	report on a given user's jobs
-v	F	.	.	verbose mode; see note [2]
-y	F	≡	.	report on young requests
-M	.	F	.	report last transactions with site
-O	.	F	.	nonverbose mode; see note [2]

[1] On SIII/SV, the -m option takes the name of a machine; on SV2, it reports on all machines.

[2] On SIII, nonverbose is the default; on SV1, verbose is the default. On SV2, only verbose output is available. All the octal status codes in SIII have the same meanings in SV2, and there are two new ones.

uux

There are three major versions of *uucp*(1); *uux*(1) is found in each of them. The 4.1BSD and XENIX versions are the same as V7's.

Option	V7	SIII	SV1	SV2	Function
-	F	≡	≡	≡	take command's stdin from stdin
-a	.	.	.	F	notify to given user id
-b	.	.	.	F	return stdin to command on fail
-c	.	F	.	≡	don't make local copy for send
-g	.	F	.	≡	set the job grade
-j	.	.	F	≡	set the job id
-l	.	F	.	.	link files to spool directory
-m	.	.	F	.	report transfer status to file
-n	.	F	X	≡	see note [1]
-p	.	F	≡	≡	take command's stdin from stdin
-r	.	F	≡	≡	don't start the job spooler
-s	.	.	.	F	report transfer status to file
-x	.	.	F	≡	set debug report level
-z	.	F	.	X	see note [2]
-C	.	.	.	F	do local copy before transfer

[1] On SV1, -n suppresses notification on success or failure. On SIII and SV2, it suppresses notification on failure only.

[2] On SIII, -z suppresses notification if the command is successful. On SV2, it has exactly the opposite effect, demanding notification on success.

Note: The -j, -p, -r, and -x are undocumented but present in System V, Release 1.

vgrind

The 4.2BSD version of this tool adds a regular-expression-based control language for describing formatting, and an -f option to permit it to act as a filter.

vi

Some early releases of SV1 do not include *vi*(1). The XENIX 2.3 version is marked incompatible with BSD because it does not support BSD's -l command line option.

vmstat

The 4.2BSD version reports all sizes in kilobytes. The output format of -s option information has changed.

vpmc, vpmstart, vpmsnap, vpmtrace

Some early releases of SV1 do not include the virtual protocol machine tools.

vpr

V7 and XENIX do not have this utility. The AT&T versions are all the same. The 4.2BSD version is a script front end to the new spooler.

Option	BSD	AT&T	Function
-l	F	.	print literal
-W	F	.	print on wide device
-[1234]	F	.	specify font for position
-m	F	≡	notify by mail when complete
-w	F	.	set width
-v	F	.	convert vector plot to raster plot
-t	F	.	typeset *troff*(1) output to plotter

Note: SIII/SV vpr also have -crnfpt and -nf options. They are marked "DEC only."

wait

SIII allows a numeric argument to specify the process-id of a single process to be waited for.

wc

All versions of this except 4.1BSD's (including 4.2BSD's) are identical.

Option	V7	BSD	Function
-b	.	F	set print speed
-c	F	≡	count characters
-l	F	≡	count lines
-p	.	≡	count pages
-s	.	F	set page size
-t	.	≡	total time to print
-u	.	F	estimate uucp transfer time
-v	.	F	verbose output
-w	F	≡	count words

what

BSD *what*(1) is a limited adaptation of the SCCS command. The full SCCS facilities are not normally supported on BSD systems.

who

The BSD, SIII, and XENIX 2.3/3.0 versions are all identical to V7's. All versions accept "am i" as a request to identify the invoking user. 4.2BSD *who*(1) knows about remote logins. Later versions accept command-line options as shown in the following table. XENIX 5.0 *who*(1) is like the SV2 version but omits the -p option.

Option	SV1	SV2	Function
-H	.	F	print column headers
-T	F	≡	show terminal state
-a	F	≡	process file with all options on
-b	F	≡	give time and date of last reboot
-d	F	≡	list expired processes
-l	F	≡	list lines waiting for login
-p	F	≡	list children of init
-q	.	F	quick option
-r	F	≡	show current run-level of init
-s	F	≡	show name, line, and time (default)
-t	F	≡	show time of last clock twiddle
-u	F	≡	list only currently logged-in users

xref

This tool is replaced by SV's *cxref*(1).

yacc

All versions prior to SV are identical to V7.

Option	V7	SV	Function
-d	F	≡	generate *y.tab.h*
-l	.	F	suppress #line generation
-t	.	F	runtime debugging on by default
-v	F	≡	generate debugging file *y.output*

3.6 Section 1M/8—Administration/Maintenance Tools

These tables have been merged due to the inconsistencies among various dialects as to which tools belong under heading (1M) and which belong under (8). The Berkeley versions have no section (1M); all tools that are under (1M) in Version 7 are under (8) in the BSD documentation. There are also differences between Version 7's notion of (1M) and that of System III and later versions, all adding up to a very confusing picture.

In the following table, tools that are not marked with a section number or letter (1, 1S, C, or M) are found in either section (1M) or (8), depending on the version.

Section (8) utilities or command groups marked as specific to a given machine have generally been omitted on grounds of extreme nonportability.

XENIX 3.0 and 5.0 place these commands in section "C", "CP", or "M". Tools introduced in XENIX 3.0 or 5.0 may have their names followed by a section letter rather than a number.

Name	Under	?	V7	BSD	SIII	XE2.3	XE3.0	SV
INSTALL		*	.	.	.	.	.	F$
MAKEDEV		.	.	F$	.	.	.	.
ac		.	F	≡	.	≡	.	.
accept		.	.	.	.	.	$	F
acct		*	.	.	F	.	$	≡
acctcms		.	.	.	F	.	.	>
acctcon		.	.	.	F	.	$	≡
acctmerg		.	.	.	F	.	.	≡
accton	sa	.	F	≡	.	≡	≡	.
acctprc		.	.	.	F	.	.	=
acctsh		.	.	.	F	.	.	>
aliashash		.	.	.	.	.	FM	.
analyze		.	.	F	.	.	.	.
arcv		.	F	X	X1	X1S	.	>1
arff		.	.	F	.	.	.	.
asktime		.	.	.	.	.	F	.
autoboot		.	.	.	.	.	F$	.
backup		*	.	.	.	.	F	.
bad144		*	.	F	.	.	.	.
badsect		.	.	F	.	.	.	.
badtrack		.	.	.	.	.	FC	.
badtrk		.	.	.	.	.	FC	.
bcopy		*	.	.	FO	.	.	≡O
boot		*	FP	.	X	X	X	X
brc		*	.	.	.	.	.	F
bugfiler		.	.	F$	.	.	.	.
catman		.	.	F	.	.	.	.
checkall		.	.	.	.	.	.	F
chroot		*	.	.	F	.	=$	≡
clri		Y	F	≡O	=	≡	.	≡
comsat		*	.	F$	.	.	.	.
config		*	.	F	X	X	.	XB
cpset		.	.	.	.	.	.	F$
crash		*	.	.	F	.	.	>
cron		*	F	≡	.	>	>	≡
daemon.mn		.	.	.	.	.	.	F
daudit		*	.	.	.	.	.	.
daudoff		*	.	.	.	.	.	.
daudon		*	.	.	.	.	.	.
dcheck		*	F	>O	.	=	.	.
dcopy		*	.	.	.	.	.	F
delivermail		*	.	F	.	.	.	.
devnm		*	.	.	F	.	≡	>
df		Y*	F	>1	>1	≡	≡	≡
dfsck	fsck	.	.	.	.	.	.	F
disable		*	.	.	.	F	>	X1
diskboot		.	.	.	F	.	.	.

Name	Under	?	V7	BSD	SIII	XE2.3	XE3.0	SV
diskpart		.	.	F$	.	.	.	.
diskusg		.	.	.	.	.	.	F$
dmesg		.	.	F$	.	.	≡	.
drtest		.	.	F$	.	.	.	.
drvinstall		.	.	.	.	.	.	F$
dump		*	F	>	≡	>	≡	X1
dumpdir		.	F	≡	.	≡	=	.
dumpfs		.	.	F$	.	.	.	.
edquota		.	.	F$	.	.	.	.
enable		*	.	.	.	F	>	.
errdead		.	.	.	F	.	.	≡
errdemon		.	.	.	F	.	.	≡
errpt		*	.	.	F	.	.	X
errstop		.	.	.	F	.	.	≡
etp		.	.	.	F	.	.	.
exer		.	.	.	.	.	.	FB
fastboot		.	.	F$	.	.	.	.
fasthalt	fastboot	.	.	F$	.	.	.	.
fdisk		.	.	.	.	.	F	X
ff		.	.	.	.	.	.	FB
filesave		.	.	.	.	.	.	F
finc		.	.	.	.	.	.	F
flcopy	arff	.	.	F	.	.	.	.
format		*	.	F	.	.	FC	.
frec		.	.	.	.	.	.	F
fsba		.	.	.	.	.	.	F
fsck		*	?	≡	≡	>	≡	>
fscp		.	.	.	.	.	.	FB
fscv		.	.	.	F	.	.	.
fsdb		.	.	.	F	.	.	≡
ftpd		.	.	F$	.	.	.	.
fuser		.	.	.	.	.	.	F
fwtmp		.	.	.	F	.	.	>
gettable		.	.	F$	.	.	.	.
getty		*	F	>	X	≡	X	>
grpck	pwck	.	.	.	F	.	.	≡
halt		.	.	F	.	.	.	.
haltsys		.	.	.	.	F	≡	.
hasp		.	.	.	FO	.	.	.
icheck		*	FO	≡	.	≡	.	.
inir		.	.	.	.	F	.	.
init		*	F	X	X	≡	≡	X
install		*	.	.	F	.	.	>
iostat		*	F	X1	.	.	.	.
ipb		.	.	.	.	.	.	FB
kgmon		.	.	F$	.	.	.	.
killall		.	.	.	.	.	.	F
labelit	volcopy	.	.	.	F	.	.	>
link		.	.	.	F	.	.	≡
lpc		.	.	F$	.	.	.	.
lpd		*	.	F$	.	F	.	.
makekey		*	F	≡	≡	≡	=	.

Name	Under	?	V7	BSD	SIII	XE2.3	XE3.0	SV
mgrproc		.	.	.	.	.	.	F
mk		.	.	.	F	.	.	>
mkboot		.	.	.	.	.	.	FB
mkconf		*	F	.	.	.	.	.
mkfs		*	F	>	>	>	>	=
mklost+found		.	.	F	.	.	.	.
mknod		Y*	F	≡	>	≡	>	=
mkunix		.	.	.	.	.	.	FB
mkuser		.	.	.	.	F	≡	.
mount		Y*	F	>	≡	≡	≡	≡
mvdir		.	.	.	F	.	.	≡
ncheck		*	F	≡	.	≡	$	.
netpasswd		.	.	.	.	.	.	F
netstart		.	.	.	.	.	.	F
newboot		.	.	.	.	.	.	FB
newfs		.	.	F$	.	.	.	.
niaddnode		.	.	.	.	.	.	F
niallow		.	.	.	.	.	.	F
nichange		.	.	.	.	.	.	F
niclrerr		.	.	.	.	.	.	F
nidisable		.	.	.	.	.	.	F
niinit		.	.	.	.	.	.	F
nipichlog		.	.	.	.	.	.	F
nireset		.	.	.	.	.	.	F
nirmnode		.	.	.	.	.	.	F
nisendstart		.	.	.	.	.	.	F
nisendstop		.	.	.	.	.	.	F
nistart		.	.	.	.	.	.	F
nistatlog		.	.	.	.	.	.	F
nistop		.	.	.	.	.	.	F
pac		.	.	F$	.	.	.	.
prfdc	profiler	.	.	.	F	.	.	≡
prfld	profiler	.	.	.	F	.	.	≡
prfpr	profiler	.	.	.	F	.	.	≡
prfsnap	profiler	.	.	.	F	.	.	≡
prfstat	profiler	.	.	.	F	.	.	≡
pstat		*	F	>	.	X	≡	.
pwadmin		*	.	.	.	.	F	.
pwcheck		*	.	.	.	.	F	.
pwck		*	.	.	F	.	.	≡
quot		.	F	.	.	≡	≡	.
quotacheck		.	.	F$	.	.	.	.
quotaoff	quotaon	.	.	F$	.	.	.	.
quotaon		.	.	F$	.	.	.	.
rc	init	*	F	>	>	≡	?	>
rdump		.	.	F$	.	.	.	.
reboot		*	.	F	.	$	.	.
reject	accept	.	.	.	.	.	$	F
renice		*	.	F	.	.	.	.
repquota		.	.	F$	.	.	.	.
restart		.	.	.	.	.	.	F
restor		*	F	>	>	≡	.	.

Name	Under	?	V7	BSD	SIII	XE2.3	XE3.0	SV
restore		*	.	F$	.	.	F	.
rexecd		.	.	F$	.	.	.	.
rlogind		.	.	F$	.	.	.	.
rmt		.	.	F$	.	.	.	.
route		.	.	F$	.	.	.	.
routed		.	.	F$	.	.	.	.
rrestore		.	.	F$	.	.	.	.
rshd		.	.	F$	.	.	.	.
rwhod		.	.	F$	.	.	.	.
rshd		.	.	F$	.	.	.	.
rxformat		.	.	.	F	.	.	≡
rmuser		.	.	.	.	F	≡	.
runacct		.	.	.	F	.	.	≡
sa		*	F	>	.	≡	.	.
sag		*	.	.	F	.	.	X
sar		*	.	.	F	.	.	>
savecore		.	.	F	.	.	.	.
sddate		.	.	.	.	F	=	.
sendmail		*	.	F$	.	.	.	.
setifaddr		.	.	F$	.	.	.	.
setclock		.	.	.	.	.	FM	.
setkey		.	.	.	.	.	FM	.
setmnt		.	.	.	F	.	$	≡
shutdown		*	.	F	F	X	X	X
snoop		.	.	.	.	.	.	F
st		.	.	.	F	.	.	.
sticky		.	.	F	.	.	.	.
swapon		.	.	F	.	.	.	.
sync		Y	F	≡	≡	≡	≡	=1
sysadmin		.	.	.	.	F	≡	.
sysdef		.	.	.	F	.	.	=B
syslog		.	.	F$	.	.	.	.
tapesave	filesave	.	.	.	F	.	.	≡
telnetd		.	.	F$	.	.	.	.
tftpd		.	.	F$	.	.	.	.
trenter		.	.	.	.	.	.	F
trpt		.	.	F$	.	.	.	.
tunefs		.	.	F$	.	.	.	.
umount	mount	Y*	F	>	≡	≡	≡	≡
unlink		.	.	.	F	.	.	≡
update		.	F	≡	.	≡	.	.
uucico		*	?	?	?	?	?	F
uuclean		*	?	>	>	≡	≡	>
uucleanup		*	.	.	.	.	.	F
uugetty		.	.	.	.	.	.	F$
uusched	uucp	.	.	.	.	.	.	F$
uusub		*	.	.	F	.	$	≡
Uutry		.	.	.	.	.	.	F$
uuxqt		*	?	?	?	?	.	F
uvac		.	.	.	FO	.	.	.
vipw		*	.	F	.	.	.	.
vlx		.	.	.	FV	.	.	.

Name	Under	?	V7	BSD	SIII	XE2.3	XE3.0	SV
volcopy		.	.	.	F	.	.	>
vpac		.	.	F	.	.	.	.
vpmboot		.	.	.	.	.	.	FB
vpmsave		.	.	.	.	.	.	F
vpmset		.	.	.	.	.	.	FB
wall		Y	F	≡	≡	≡	≡	≡
whodo		.	.	.	F	.	≡	≡
wtmpfix	fwtmp	*	.	.	.	F	.	.
xinstall		*	.	.	.	.	FM	.

Notes on System Administration Tools

INSTALL

Only SV2 supports the *INSTALL*(1M) utility. This is not to be confused with the *install*(1M) command of SV2, 4.2BSD and some other versions.

acct

This group of commands (including *acctdisk*, *acctdusg*, *accton*, and *acctwtmp*) moves to */usr/lib/acct* in SV.

backup

See the note for *dump*(1M).

bad144

The 4.2BSD version has been enhanced to reference */etc/disktab* and can consequently handle many more drive types. It also adds the -f option to mark bad sectors on some disks.

bcopy

SV1 supports this utility, but SV2 drops it.

boot, reboot

This is a documentation entry rather than a utility, and is not present on all systems. Machine startup and reboot procedures are of course heavily hardware and configuration dependent. BSD *reboot*(8) has the function of V7/SIII/SV *boot*(8).

brc

This group of shell scripts includes *brc*, *bcheckrc*, *rc*, and *powerfail*. See the manual page for a description of the SV bootup sequence.

chroot

XENIX 3.0 only.

comsat

The 4.2BSD documentation for this mail-handling tool implies a 4.1BSD predecessor, but it is not documented for 4.1bBSD. It seems *comsat*(8) was introduced with the networking facilities in 4.1cBSD.

config

This is the utility used to generate the configurable parts of UNIX system kernels. Unsurprisingly, the description formats used by different dialects are all wildly incompatible, and SV2 drops the whole mess in favor of the autoconfiguration-boot system represented by *mkunix*(1M) and *mkboot*(1M). The following table is more of a gesture than anything else.

Option	BSD	SIII	XENIX	SV1	Function
-c	.	F	≡	≡	specify configuration file
-l	.	F	.	.	specify hardware interface file
-m	.	F	≡	≡	specify system master file
-t	.	F	≡	.	give device number table

The 4.2BSD version has been extensively rewritten to handle the new Fast File System, including a new syntax for root and swap device specification.

crash

All versions except XENIX 3.0/5.0 have incompatible, hardware-dependent *crash*(8) entries that describe what one should do when the system crashes. Only SIII and SV have *crash*(8) tools that are crash dump analyzers [see also BSD *analyze*(8)]. The command language of SV2 *crash*(1M) includes several new verbs and options not present in SV1, but does not document any support for examining multiple processes.

cron

SV2 *cron*(8) is a totally rewritten version that supports user crontab files and elaborate security features. The XENIX version normally runs with the ID of a special "cron" user with group permissions that make it less omnipotent than root (this is a good idea, and can be emulated on other systems). XENIX 5.0's version is the new SV2 one.

daudit, daudon, daudoff

These utilities are not present in SV2.

dcheck

V7 *dcheck* is made obsolete by *fsck*(1M).

dcopy

SV2 *dcopy*(1M) is not documented to modify its *argv* data when running.

delivermail

4.2BSD replaces this with *sendmail*(8).

devnm

The SV version treats the name "/" differently if the swap area is on the same volume as the root filesystem.

df

The XENIX 2.3 version of this command derives from V7. The XENIX 3.0/5.0 version of this command derives from SIII. The AT&T column in the following table describes SIII and SV.

Option	V7	BSD	AT&T	Function
-f	.	.	F	count only blocks in the freelist
-i	.	F	.	report used and free i-node counts
-l	.	F	.	double-check the freelist summary
-t	.	.	F	report totals
-v	.	.	F$	used blocks as % of total (XE5.0 only)

disable

In XENIX 2.3, *disable*(1M) is used to disable tty lines and *enable*(1M) is used to activate them. XENIX 3.0/5.0 adds -d (disable) and -e (enable) options that permit either one to do the work of the other. SV has a different *enable*(1)/*disable*(1) pair used for taking printers in and out of service for *lp*(1).

dump

On V7, BSD, SIII, and XENIX 2.3, *dump(1M)* is a program for doing incremental filesystem backups. On the other hand, SV *dump*(1) is a binary file dump filter; it has nothing to do with tapes. The SIII and XENIX 2.3 versions of *dump*(1M) are identical to V7's, except that XENIX supports a -k option for dumping to block devices. Notice that 4.2BSD *dump*(8) has been rewritten for the new Fast File System. On XENIX 3.0, this command is replaced by the very similar *backup* utility, but 5.0 has both; the *dump*(1) is V7's.

Option	V7	BSD	Function
\<n>	F	≡	set dump level
d	F	≡	take density from argument
f	F	≡	send dump to given file
n	.	F	broadcast messages to operators
s	F	≡	specify tape length
u	F	≡	log the dump if successful
w	.	F	terser form of -w option
J	.	F	convert dump-log file
W	.	F	tell operator what needs dumping

enable

See the note for *disable*(1M) above.

errpt

SV *errpt*(1M) has an option format significantly different from SIII.

Option	SIII	SV	Function
-<dev>	F	.	report on particular device
-a	F	≡	include all error types
-d	.	F	report on given list of devices
-e	F	≡	ignore all records posted after given date
-f	F	≡	report only unrecovered block device errors
-int	F	.	report stray interrupt errors
-mem	F	.	report memory parity errors
-p	F	≡	set report page limit
-s	F	≡	ignore all records posted before given date

format

The 4.1BSD *format*(8) entry describes an elaborate formatting procedure involving VAX monitor mode; the 4.2BSD version describes a simpler standalone formatting utility.

fsck

The *fsck*(1M) utility originated in late V7, but is not documented in the V7 manuals. The 4.1BSD and SIII versions are the same as V7's. The 4.2BSD version has been changed for the new file system, and a support document for it has been added to the manuals. The XENIX 5.0 version is SV's with new -c and -rr flags.

Option	V7	SV	BSD2	Function
-b	.	.	F	use given block as superblock
-f	.	F	.	fast check (phases 1, 5, 6)
-n	F	≡	≡	answer no to all dialogue questions
-p	.	.	F	audit and repair inconsistencies
-q	.	F	.	quiet mode
-s	F	≡	.	reconstruct the freelist
-t	F	≡	.	specify scratch file name
-y	F	≡	≡	answer yes to all dialogue questions
-D	.	F	.	check directories for bad blocks
-S	F	≡	.	conditionally reconstruct the freelist

getty

The following table describes the significance of the speed argument of *getty*(8). All speeds are in characters per second. A set of numbers separated by slashes describes a set of speeds that the software will cycle through on a <Break> keypress.

In SV and XENIX 5.0, the speed argument becomes a label for a line in the */etc/gettydefs* table. Similarly, in 4.2BSD the speed argument is a label indexing into */etc/gettytabs*. The XENIX 2.3 version is V7's; the XENIX 5.0 version is SV's.

Option	V7	BSD	SIII	XE3.0
-	110	110	110	110
0	300/1200/150/110	300/1200/150/110	300/150/110/1200	150
1	150	150	150	300/150/110/1200
2	9600	9600	2400	300
3	1200/300	1200/300	1200/300/150/110	1200/300/150/110
4	300	300	300	2400
5	300/1200	300/1200	9600	4800
6	.	2400	4800/9600	9600
7	.	4800	.	9600
8	.	9600/300	.	.

The XENIX 3.0 documentation specifies that setting 7 is intended for an IBM 3101.

There are two minor features of SV1 *getty*(1M) that are by default missing in SV2 (although they can be compiled in by turning on a few source switches): the display of the contents of */etc/issue* and the display of the system node name.

icheck

SIII replaces *icheck*(1M) with *fsck*(1M). The 4.2BSD version of *icheck*(8) has been rewritten to go with the new filesystem.

init

4.2BSD has been substantially modified to use the new signal facilities. SIII/SV *init*(8) is driven from an actions file */etc/inittab* and command line options to set the current state; it doesn't document any non-machine-dependent signal catches. These control functions are instead performed by arguments to the *init*(1M) or *telinit*(1M) command. The following list describes signal catch actions for the versions that document them.

V7:

    SIGHUP   go to single user mode

BSD:

    SIGHUP   reinitialize ttys from the *etc/ttys* file
    SIGTSTP   lock out new logins
    SIGTERM go to single user mode

XENIX 2.3, 3.0, 5.0:

    SIGINT   reinitialize ttys from the *etc/ttys* file
    SIGQUIT   lock out new logins
    SIGHUP   go to single user mode

install

This utility (supported on SIII, SV1, and SV2) is one of the rare cases where features present in SV1 have been dropped from an otherwise compatible SV2 version. The SV2 version is identical to SIII's.

Option	SIII	SV1	Function
-c	F	≡	install file in directory if not already there
-f	F	≡	overwrite existing version if present
-g	.	F	set the group id of the installed file
-i	F	≡	ignore default directory list
-m	.	F	set the mode of the installed file
-n	F	≡	add directory to search list
-o	F	≡	back up old version when installing
-s	F	≡	suppress printing of nonerror messages
-u	.	F	set the owner id of the installed file

iostat

BSD *iostat*(8) is missing the -tisb command line options supported by V7 *iostat*(1M).

lpd

The 4.2BSD version of *lpd*(8) has been rewritten as a server process using the new interprocess communication features.

makekey

The *makekey*(8) command of SV omits the specification that the Data Encryption Standard is used.

mkconf

V7 *mkconf*(1M) is replaced in later versions by *config*(1M).

mkfs

The acceptable command line syntaxes for *mkfs*(1M) vary widely between dialects, but the command has no options in the usual sense so the variants are not describable by a simple table. The first argument is invariably a special file (device) name. All dialects except 4.2BSD accept one invocation style in which the second argument is the name of a prototype-description file (and all dialects except 4.2BSD use the same description format and even document it with the same example). On 4.2BSD, this tool usually is used through the *newfs*(8) front end.

However, there are other nonportable invocation styles in versions later than V7 that omit the prototype file name and allow the user to specify the new filesystem's size and other parameters directly. These are mutually compatible between AT&T versions but vary a great deal elsewhere.

mknod

All versions accept the same command line syntax for declaring special files of character and block type. SIII/SV *mknod*(1M) has a second form for creating named fifos. XENIX adds two more forms for creating semaphore and shared-memory objects.

mount

BSD *mount*(1M) supports an extra -a option that attempts to mount all the systems listed in */etc/fstab*; otherwise all versions are identical. XENIX mount documents a return value of 1 for command failure, and 2 for the presence of an unclean file structure on the device. The 4.2BSD version, called without arguments, will display information on the write-enable and quota-enable status of filesystems.

ncheck

In later V7 and all subsequent releases, *ncheck*(1M) is made obsolete by *fsck*(1M).

pstat

BSD *pstat*(1M) supports a -T option in addition to the -aixptuf options of V7. The XENIX 2.3 and XENIX 3.0 versions lack the -t option of V7 and are thus listed as incompatible, but the XENIX 5.0 version restores it.

pwadmin

This utility is found only on XENIX 3.0 and XENIX 5.0. The 5.0 version describes the previously undocumented -n option as a switch to disable password aging.

pwcheck, pwck

These utilities (one peculiar to XENIX 3.0/5.0, the other to AT&T versions) perform similar functions.

rc

See also *rc*(1M). 4.2BSD has an auxiliary */etc/rc.local* used for system-dependent setup.

renice

In BSD, this tool may be used to change the priorities of users and process groups. As a result, it has three options (-p, -g, and -u) where the previous version had none.

restor, restore

4.2BSD replaces V7 *restor*(8) with the new *restore*(8) utility which, among other things, can retrieve files by name. XENIX 3.0 replaces the *dump*(8)/*restor*(8) pair with a *backup*(8)/*restore*(8).

sa

This is the V7/BSD accounting tool, replaced in AT&T versions by the PWB accounting package. The following table lists the command line options supported in various versions:

Option	V7	BSD	Function
-a	F	≡	put commands used once under ***other
-b	F	≡	sort output by time-per-call index
-c	F	≡	print time percentages
-d	.	F	sort by average number of disk I/O operations
-f	.	F	force no interactive threshold compression
-i	.	F	don't read in summary file
-j	F	≡	list time as seconds per call
-k	.	F	sort by cpu-time average times memory usage
-l	F	≡	list separate user and system times
-m	F	≡	print process count and CPU minutes per user
-n	F	≡	sort by number of calls
-r	F	≡	reverse the sort order
-s	F	≡	merge accounting file into summary when done
-t	F	≡	report (real time)/(user time + system time)
-u	F	≡	print user id and command name
-v	F	≡	interactive junk-cleaning mode
-D	.	F	sort by total disk I/O operations
-K	.	F	sort by cpu-storage integral

sag

SV is missing the -ahdrcwo options supported by SIII.

sar

See also *sar*(8) and *sar*(1). SV *sar*(1M) has a group of helpers in */usr/lib* listed in 1M that includes *sadc*, *sa1*, and *sa2*.

sendmail

This replaces *delivermail*(8) in 4.2BSD.

shutdown

The SIII and BSD shutdown utilities are incompatible and have no documented common ancestor in V7. The XENIX versions are marked incompatible with their V7/SIII predecessors because they require an extra argument to get to single-user mode (rather than a reboot).

umount

BSD *umount*(1M) supports an extra -a option that attempts to unmount all the systems listed in */etc/fstab*, otherwise all versions are identical.

uucico

This command is present in all versions. SV2 is the first to document it.

uuclean, uucleanup

The *uuclean*(1M) utility dates back to late V7, but is not documented in the standard V7 manuals; the BSD version is identical to it. SV moves it to */usr/lib/uucp* and SV2 replaces it entirely with *uucleanup*(1M).

Option	V7	SIII	SV1	Function
-d	.	F	≡	clean a specified directory
-m	F	≡	≡	send mail to file owners on deletion
-n	F	≡	≡	remove files of more than given age
-p	F	≡	≡	scan for files with given prefix
-s	.	.	F	examine only files sent to given site
-w	.	.	F	generate warnings rather than delete

uusub

SV *uusub*(1M) is in */usr/uucp/lib*. SV2 eliminates it.

uuxqt

This command is present in all versions. SV2 is the first to document it.

vipw

The 4.2BSD version of *vipw*(8) is a binary runfile (not, as in other versions, a shell script) and now does correct consistency interlocks with other programs that access the password file.

wtmpfix

SV checks the validity of name fields; SIII does not admit to doing so.

xinstall

XENIX 5.0 drops this utility.

3.7 Section 2—System Calls

On XENIX 3.0 these calls are grouped with those of Section 3 under Section "S".

Name	Under	?	V7	BSD	SIII	XE2.3	XE3.0	SV
_exit	exit	*	F	≡	.	F	.	.
accept		.	.	F$	.	.	.	.
access		Y*	F	≡	≡	>	≡	≡
acct		Y	F	≡	=	≡	≡	≡
adjtime		*	.	F$	.	.	.	.
alarm		Y*	F	≡	=	≡	≡	≡
bind		.	.	F$	.	.	.	.
brk		Y*	F	=	>	≡	>	≡
chdir		Y	F	≡	=	≡	≡	≡
chmod		Y*	F	X	X	≡	=	≡
chown		Y*	F	X	>	>	≡	≡
chroot		Y*	F	≡	≡	≡	≡	≡
chsize		.	.	.	.	.	F	.
close		Y*	F	>	=	≡	≡	≡
connect		.	.	F$	.	.	.	.
creat		Y*	F	≡	=	≡	≡	≡
creatsem		.	.	.	.	F	≡	.
dismaus	maus	.	.	.	.	.	.	FP
dup		Y*	F	≡	>	≡	≡	≡
dup2	dup	*	F	≡	.	≡	≡	.
enabmaus	maus	.	.	.	.	.	.	FP
execl	exec	Y*	F	>	>	≡	=	>
execv	exec	Y*	F	>	>	≡	=	>
execle	exec	Y*	F	>	>	≡	=	>
execve	exec	Y*	F	>	>	≡	=	>
execlp	exec	*	.	F	>	.	=	>
execvp	exec	*	.	F	>	.	=	>
exit		Y*	F	=	>	≡	≡	>
fchmod		.	.	F$	.	.	.	.
fchown		.	.	F$	.	.	.	.
fcntl		*	.	F	F	.	≡	>
flock		.	.	F$	.	.	.	.
fork		*	F	≡	>	≡	X	X
freemaus	maus	.	.	.	.	.	.	FP
fstat	stat	Y*	F	≡	>	≡	≡	≡

Name	Under	?	V7	BSD	SIII	XE2.3	XE3.0	SV
fsync		.	.	F$	.	.	.	.
ftime	time	*	F	≡	.	≡	≡	.
ftruncate		.	.	F$	.	.	.	.
getdtablesize		.	.	F$	.	.	.	.
getegid	getuid	*	F	≡	=	≡	=	X
geteuid	getuid	*	F	=	>	≡	=	X
getgid	getuid	*	F	=	>	≡	=	X
getgroups		.	.	F$	.	.	.	.
gethostid		.	.	F$	.	.	.	.
gethostname		.	.	F$	.	.	.	.
getitimer		.	.	F$	.	.	.	.
getmaus	maus	.	.	.	.	.	.	FP
getpagesize		.	.	F$	.	.	.	.
getpeername		.	.	F$	.	.	.	.
getpgrp	getpid	*	.	F	F	.	≡	≡
getpid		Y	F	≡	=	≡	≡	≡
getppid	getpid	.	.	.	F	.	≡	≡
getpriority		.	.	F$	.	.	.	.
getrlimit		*	.	F$	.	.	.	.
getrusage		*	.	F$	.	.	.	.
getsockname		.	.	F$	.	.	.	.
getsockopt		*	.	F$	.	.	.	.
gettimeofday		.	.	F$	.	.	.	.
getuid		*	F	≡	=	≡	=	X
gtty	ioctl	*	F	≡	.	≡	.	.
ioctl		*	F	>	X	≡	≡	=
kill		Y*	F	>	>	≡	≡	=
killpg		*	.	F	.	.	.	.
link		Y*	F	=	=	≡	≡	=
listen		*	.	F	.	.	.	.
lock		.	F	.	.	≡	=	.
lockf		*	.	.	.	.	F	≡
locking		.	.	.	.	F	=	.
lseek		Y*	F	≡	=	≡	≡	≡
lstat		.	.	F$	.	.	.	.
mkdir		.	.	F$	.	.	.	.
mknod		Y*	F	≡	>	≡	>	≡
mount		*	F	≡	X	≡	≡	=
mpx		*	FO	≡	.	.	.	.
msgctl		*	.	.	.	.	$	F
msgget		.	.	.	.	.	$	F
msgsnd	msgop	.	.	.	.	.	$	F
msgrcv	msgop	.	.	.	.	.	$	F
nap		.	.	.	.	.	F	.
nbwaitsem		.	.	.	.	F	≡	.
nice		Y*	F	≡	>	≡	=	≡
open		Y*	F	>	>	>	>	=
opensem		.	.	.	.	F	=	.
pause		Y*	F	=	=	≡	≡	≡
phys		.	F	.	.	≡	.	.
pipe		Y*	F	>	>	≡	=	≡
pkoff	pk	.	FO	.	.	.	.	.

Name	Under	?	V7	BSD	SIII	XE2.3	XE3.0	SV
pkon	pk	.	FO	.	.	.	.	.
plock		*	.	.	.	.	F	F
proctl		.	.	.	.	.	F$	.
profil		Y*	F	≡	≡	≡	≡	≡
ptrace		*	F	≡	X	≡	X	≡
quota		.	.	F$	.	.	.	.
rdchk		.	.	.	.	F	≡	.
read		Y*	F	>	>	≡	≡	=
readlink		.	.	F$	.	.	.	.
readv	read	.	.	F$	.	.	.	.
recv		.	.	F$	.	.	.	.
recvfrom	recv	.	.	F$	.	.	.	.
recvmsg	recv	.	.	F$	.	.	.	.
rename		.	.	F$	.	.	.	.
rmdir		.	.	F$	.	.	.	.
reboot		.	.	F	.	.	.	.
sbrk	brk	Y*	F	≡	>	≡	>	≡
sdget		.	.	.	.	.	F	.
sdfree		.	.	.	.	.	F	.
sdgetv		.	.	.	.	.	F	.
sdenter		.	.	.	.	.	F	.
sdleave		.	.	.	.	.	F	.
sdwaitv		.	.	.	.	.	F	.
select		.	.	F$	.	.	.	.
send		.	.	F$	.	.	.	.
sendto	send	.	.	F$	.	.	.	.
sendmsg	send	.	.	F$	.	.	.	.
semctl		.	.	.	.	.	.	F
semget		.	.	.	.	.	.	F
semop		.	.	.	.	.	.	F
setgid	setuid	Y*	F	≡	>	>	=	≡
setgroups		.	.	F$	.	.	.	.
sethostid	gethostid	.	.	F$	.	.	.	.
sethostname	gethostname	.	.	F$	.	.	.	.
setitimer		.	.	F$	.	.	.	.
setpgrp		*	.	F	X	.	≡	≡
setpriority	getpriority	.	.	F$	.	.	.	.
setquota		.	.	F$	.	.	.	.
setregid		*	.	F$	.	.	.	.
setreuid		*	.	F$	.	.	.	.
setrlimit	getrlimit	.	.	F$	.	.	.	.
setsockopt	getsockopt	*	.	F$	.	.	.	.
settimeofday	gettimeofday	.	.	F$	.	.	.	.
setuid		Y*	F	≡	>	>	=	=
shutdn		.	.	.	.	.	F	.
shutdown		*	.	F	.	.	.	.
shmctl		.	.	.	.	.	$	F
shmget		.	.	.	.	≡	$	F
shmop		.	.	.	.	.	$	F
signal		Y*	F	=	>	>	≡	=
sigblock		*	.	F	.	.	.	.
sigpause		*	.	F	.	.	.	.

Name	Under	?	V7	BSD	SIII	XE2.3	XE3.0	SV
sigreturn		*	.	F$	.	.	.	.
sigsem		.	.	.	.	F	≡	.
sigsetmask		*	.	F	.	.	.	.
sigstack		*	.	F	.	.	.	.
sigsys		*	.	F	.	.	.	.
sigvec		*	.	F	.	.	.	.
socket		.	.	F$	.	.	.	.
socketpair		.	.	F$	.	.	.	.
stat		Y*	F	≡	=	≡	≡	≡
stime		Y*	F	≡	=	≡	>	=
stty	ioctl	*	F	≡	.	≡	≡	.
switmaus	maus	.	.	.	.	.	.	FP
symlink		.	.	F$	.	.	.	.
sync		Y*	F	≡	=	≡	≡	≡
syscall		.	.	F	.	.	.	.
tell	lseek	Y*	F	≡	.	≡	.	.
time		Y*	F	=	≡	=	≡	≡
times		*	F	X	X	≡	≡	≡
truncate		.	.	F$	.	.	.	.
ulimit		*	.	.	F	.	>	≡
umask		Y	F	≡	=	≡	=	≡
umount	mount	Y*	F	≡	=	>	≡2	≡2
uname		*	.	.	F	.	>	>
unlink		Y*	F	≡	=	≡	=	≡
ustat		*	.	.	F	.	=	≡
utime		*	F	≡	X	≡	≡	≡
utimes		*	.	F	.	.	.	.
vadvise		.	.	F	.	.	.	.
vfork		.	.	F	.	.	.	.
vhangup ·		.	.	F	.	.	.	.
vlimit		*	.	F	.	.	.	.
vread		*	.	F	.	.	.	.
vswapon		*	.	F	.	.	.	.
vtimes		*	.	F	.	.	.	.
vwrite		*	.	F	.	.	.	.
wait		Y*	F	≡	>	≡	≡	>
wait3	wait	*	.	F	.	.	.	.
waitscm		.	.	.	.	F	≡	.
write		Y*	F	>	>	>	≡	>
writev	write	*	.	F	.	.	.	.

Notes on System Calls

_exit

V7 and BSD support this as a way of avoiding the cleanup actions of *exit*(2). BSD recommends _exit(2) after a *fork*(2) or *vfork*(2) to avoid flushing I/O twice. The P1003 proposal, which documents this call but not *exit*(2), says that if the caller is a process group leader SIGHUP may be sent to all the members of this process group. This omits the requirement in existing dialects that the caller be associated with a tty. See the note for *exit*(2) for more information about signals sent on exit.

access

4.2BSD and SVID introduce identical symbolic #defines for the *mode* argument of this call. The P1003 proposal omits the ETXTBSY error return.

adjtime

This clock-adjusting function is available only on 4.3BSD.

alarm

V7 *alarm*(2) has a specified maximum argument of 65535 seconds. No such restriction is documented in any other dialect.

brk

The documentation of SV1 *brk*(2) asserts that the areas it allocates will be zeroed out. SV2 omits this assertion. In PC/AT XENIX 3.0/5.0, the call is listed under *sbrk*(2) and its semantics are modified for the Intel 80286 segmented architecture.

Whether *sbrk*(2) causes a program's data space to grow downwards (as on the PDP-11) or upwards (as on the VAX under SIII) is architecture dependent, but *sbrk*(2) is defined to increase the data space on a positive increment and decrease it on a negative one, so it should be portable. On the other hand, the *brk*(2) call uses a memory address argument and can be expected to be introduce nasty portability problems if used carelessly. The only safe arguments to *brk*(2) are the external variables from *end*(3) and the return values of *sbrk*(2) calls.

In any case, the *brk*(2) and *sbrk*(2) system calls should be used with extreme caution, if at all; the *malloc*(3) library calls provide a manageable interface to these calls, which is sufficient for most purposes. *Never* mix *malloc*(3) calls with *brk*(2) calls in the same program.

chmod

The following table describes the variations between versions in which mode bits are cleared when a *chmod*(2) is executed. The bit codes are as follows: *u* is the set-user-id bit, *g* is the set-group-id bit, and *s* is the sticky bit. The calling situations are:

1. *The caller is super-user* and has root privileges.

2. *The caller is the file's owner* or (in the case where the table refers to the *g* bit) is currently in the group that owns the target file.

3. *The caller is a stranger*, neither root, the target file's owner, or in the file's owning group.

Condition	V7	BSD	SIII	XE2.3	XE3.0	SV
caller is root	.	u	.	.	.	.
caller is owner	.	u	s	.	s	s
caller is other	.	u	s,g	.	s,g	s,g

Effects on the sticky bit have not been considered in deciding the compatibility of these calls. All the incompatibilities indicated are due solely to the side effects described in the table. The SV1, SV2, and SVID versions all act alike according to their documentation.

chown

The following table indicates which mode bits are cleared by the *chown*(2) call in various versions. Bit codes and caller types are as for the *chmod*(2) table.

Condition	V7	BSD	SIII	XE2.3	XE3.0	SV
caller is root	.	u	.	.	.	.
caller is owner	.	u	u,g	.	u,g	u,g
caller is other	.	u	u,g	.	u,g	u,g

The SV1, SV2, and SVID versions all act alike, according to their documentation.

Effects on the sticky bit have not been considered in deciding the compatibility of these calls. All the incompatibilities indicated are due solely to the side effects described in the table.

On V7 and BSD, the *chown*(2) call is limited to the super-user. On SIII and descendents, users may give their own files away. Notice also that most BSDs also clear the set-user-id bit on *write*(2).

chroot

This call has been imported into 4.2BSD from SIII. It is not supported in 4.1BSD.

close

SVID stipulates that *close*(2) releases all file extent locks owned by the calling process. If the close-on-exec bit of a file has been set, *exec*(2) will do the equivalent of a *close*(2) on it. On V7/BSD/XENIX 2.3, this bit may be manipulated using *ioctl*(2); on SIII and descendents, *fcntl*(2) should be used.

creat

The *creat*(2) call has the following undocumented properties in all versions: it is atomic (i.e., completes within 1 time-slice) and it returns the lowest available file descriptor. These properties are assumptions of a great deal of existing code and are therefore unlikely to be invalidated in future versions. SIII/SV specifies a limit of twenty open files per process; the P1003 proposal makes it sixteen.

dup, dup2

SV2 has added a C library entry point *dup*(3) to simulate the V7 *dup*(2) in order to conform with the */usr/group* and P1003 draft standards. SVID indicates this as a "future direction."

execl, execv, execle, execve, execlp, execvp

BSD *exec*(2) looks for a filename defining an interpreter to be used if "#!" are the first characters of the file. The SV and SVID documentation describes C's startup environment in more detail than do previous versions, and include a third argument which is a pointer to the environment array. Note that 4.1BSD *execvp*(2) and its 4.2BSD equivalent erroneously ignore the $SHELL environment variable. Also notice that in 4.2BSD, all forms of *exec*(2) except *execve*(2) have been moved to Section 3.

exit

Only in the SIII/SV documentation is it specified that process 1 (*init*) inherits child processes orphaned by an *exit*(2), but it's true everywhere.

In BSD versions, a special signal SIGCHLD is sent to the parent on exit. SIII and later AT&T versions do likewise, but the signal is called SIGCLD.

If the calling process is a process group leader and is associated with a terminal, special things happen. In SIII/SV, SIGHUP is sent to the whole process group; in BSD, SIGHUP and SIGCONT are sent to stopped child processes only, and SIGKILL is sent to all processes being traced. In SV, *exit*(2) takes extra steps to ensure graceful shutdown of interprocess communication facilities connected to the caller. The P1003 proposal omits this call (but the ANSI C draft includes it).

fcntl

SV2 *fcntl*(2) includes features added to implement the record-locking facilities of *lockf*(3). 4.2BSD includes an *fcntl*(2) that subsumes the SIII version (but notice that the `#defines` for file modes differ), and adds the F_GETOWN and F_SETOWN requests and the FASYNC file mode as part of the new signal facilities.

fork

V7/BSD/XENIX 2.3 gives a 30,000 limit for max legal PID value. BSD recommends use of *vfork*(2) rather than *fork*(2) if *exec*(2) is to follow shortly.

The incompatibilities marked for XENIX 3.0 and SV (SV2) are there because, according to the documentation, they omit some state information from that inherited by forked children in SIII. Most dialects inherit the same attributes across forks; the following table summarizes known differences (the BSD versions are like V7, and SV1 is like SIII):

Attribute	V7	XE3.0	SIII	SV2	SVID	P1003
alarm times	yes[1]	no	yes	no	no	yes
trace bit	no[1]	yes	no	no	yes[1]	?[2]

[1] These entries are based on folklore and USENET articles, as there is nothing in the documentation about them.

[2] The P1003 proposal does not specify the *ptrace*(2) call or associated data (it also does not specify inheritance of the tty group or file size limit if one is defined).

fstat

Notice that the use of *fstat*(2) on pipes to get the amount of data waiting via the size field is (sadly) not portable; in fact, it is known to fail on SV and 4.2BSD and is only guaranteed on 4.1BSD. 4.2BSD expands the *stat*(5) structure of 4.1BSD; see the associated note.

ftime

SIII/SV can simulate a V7/BSD *ftime*(2) by formatting *time*(2)'s return with *ctime*(3).

getegid, geteuid, getgid, getuid

In SV2, these functions return `unsigned short`, unlike all previous versions that return `int` (including SV1).

getpgrp

BSD *getpgrp*(2) is available as an extension via the -*ljobs* library, documented under *setpgrp*(2). Since the semantics of process groups are different on BSD than they are under SIII and its successors, this version is not considered a predecessor of the SIII call. See the note under *setpgrp*(2).

getrlimit, getrusage

These calls are available only on 4.2BSD. The *getrlimit*(2) and *setrlimit*(2) calls replace 4.1BSD's *vlimit*(2) call; the *getrusage*(2) call replaces *vtimes*(2).

getsockopt

4.3BSD enhances this call so it can be used to examine protocol-level options.

gtty

The V7/BSD/XENIX 2.3 calls *stty*(2) and *gtty*(2) are subsumed by *ioctl*(2) and listed under them. 4.2BSD moves these calls to Section 3 and marks them "defunct."

ioctl

SIII/SV/4.2BSD *fcntl*(2) replaces the FIOCLEX and FIONCLEX requests of V7/4.1BSD/XENIX 2.3 *ioctl*(2). The request types and arguments accepted by this call are heavily version-dependent; portable usage is discussed in Chapter 5. No proposal for a standard has gained any wide degree of acceptance at the time of this writing, although some suggestions before the P1003 committee may offer a solution; see **[P1003]**.

kill

BSD *kill*(2) protects process 2 (pager) and recognizes SIGCONT; otherwise, it is like V7/XENIX 2.3.

SIII/SV *kill*(2) will interpret a negative PID argument *-n* as a command to broadcast a signal to all processes that are members of the process group with id *n*; on BSD, this would be done with *killpg*(2). There are no sends to process groups at all on V7.

SIII, XENIX 3.0, and SV also allow a signal 0 to be specified to check the existence of a process; no signal is sent, but normal error checking including a peek at the process table is performed.

SV relaxes the permissions criteria for signal sending. In all versions, the super-user may signal any process, and any process may signal itself. Otherwise, in non-SV2 versions, it is required that the effective user ID of the sending process match the real user ID of the receiver; in SV2, any match between the real or effective user ID of the sender and real or effective user ID of the receiver enables signalling.

The P1003 proposal and the SVID "future directions" information add the error return EPERM if the signal is SIGKILL and the target process is a protected system process.

killpg

BSD *killpg*(2) is subsumed by SIII/SV *kill*(*pid, -n*), except that there is no SIGCONT. Although this is documented as a system call in 4.1BSD and 4.2BSD, it actually is a library function in 4.1BSD.

link

On some BSDs, the super-user may link to special files. This also is an undocumented feature of SV and may be present elsewhere.

listen

This call is part of the socket-based interprocess communication facilities available only in 4.2BSD.

lockf

SV2 implements the *lockf*(2) call (originally specified by the UniForum Draft Standard) call as a library routine *lockf*(3) using the new features of *fcntl*(2).

lseek

V7/BSD promises not to allocate actual disk space between end-of-file and an arbitrarily long seek. SIII/SV doesn't.

mknod

SIII/SV *mknod*(2) is like the V7/BSD/XENIX 2.3 version except for FIFO-related features. XENIX 3.0 has a unique notion of "named special file" with features added to *mknod*(2) to create them. The P1003 proposal omits *mknod*(2), but adds a new primitive *mkfifo*(2) that would replace it.

mount

BSD *mount*(2) warns that it tries to write unallocated gaps in files even if the mounted volume is read-only. This behavior may appear in other dialects. The SIII version and its descendents are documented to test the low-order bit of the read-only flag argument, whereas V7 tests whether the entire flag is nonzero. For this reason, the SIII version has been marked incompatible with its V7 predecessor. The P1003 proposal omits this call.

mpx

The *mpx*(2) facilities are notoriously unreliable and are omitted in many V7 and 4.1BSD implementations (especially microcomputer implementations). 4.2BSD drops them entirely in favor of the new socket-based interprocess communication facilities.

msgctl

SV2 slightly relaxes the SV1 restrictions on the removal of message queue identifiers.

nice

SIII/SV and XENIX 3.0 use nice values 0 to 39 rather than the V7/BSD/XENIX 2.3 values -20 to 20. V7/BSD doesn't specify a return; the AT&T versions do, but notice that the error and non-error cases of a *nice*(2) to level 19 are indistinguishable.

open

SIII/SV/SVID and P1003 have open types beyond V7/4.1BSD 0, 1, and 2 to support additional features such as file append and nonblocking read mode. They also take an optional third argument that specifies permissions with which a file is created. 4.2BSD's version has been rewritten to match SIII/SV's, except that nonblocking read mode on terminal lines requiring carrier is not supported.

Both versions of XENIX support write-through modes (but notice that the constant names and values on XENIX 2.3 and 3.0 are different).

The *open*(2) call has the following undocumented properties in all versions: it is atomic (i.e., completes within 1 time-slice) and it returns the lowest available file descriptor. Many existing programs rely on these properties and so they are unlikely to be invalidated in future versions.

SIII/SV specifies a limit of twenty open files per process; the P1003 proposal makes it sixteen and omits the error return possibilities ENXIO and ETXTBSY.

pause

V7/BSD *pause*(2) does not specify a return value. SIII/SV specifies return of -1 when a signal is caught by a handler.

pipe

BSD's documentation omits the V7 provision that pipe writes are atomic. V7 and BSD specify a maximum of 4,096 bytes for atomic pipe writes; SIII and SV raise this to 5,120 bytes.

plock

Identical versions of this appear in SV and XENIX 3.0. It is not clear which came first.

profil

The VAX 4.2BSD version changes the tick time from the usual 1/60th of a second to 10 milliseconds.

ptrace

The address argument of *ptrace* is given three different types in various dialects. In V7/BSD/XENIX 2.3, it is declared as a pointer to an int. In

SIII and SV, it is declared `int` (bad because it assumes that pointers are register-sized), and XENIX 3.0 on the PC/AT expects a structure containing segment and offset values (the segmented architecture makes pervasive changes in the semantics of this call). Notice that this call is subject to strong hardware dependencies.

read

4.1BSD notes some special behavior in connection with the SIGTTIN signal. On 4.2BSD, if a signal is handled while a terminal *read*(2) is waiting for data, the operation will automatically restart afterwards; this is a change from the behavior of 4.1BSD and other dialects. 4.3BSD enhances *sigvec*(3) so that nonrestart can be specified after particular signals.

SIII/SV has extra features on *read*(2) to go with *open*(2)'s nonblocking mode. Notice that AT&T has documented its intent to change one case of *read*(2)'s return to conform with the 1984 */usr/group* standard (now the P1003 proposal). Currently, a nonblocking read from a pipe or FIFO with no data waiting, or from one that is closed, returns 0; the change will return -1 and an EAGAIN error for the former case, allowing applications to distinguish the two.

Notice also that SIII/XENIX 3.0/SV use an unsigned rather than signed (as in V7/BSD) integer argument for the read count.

sbrk

See the note on *brk*(2).

setgid

SVID saves the effective gid from a process's parent, and this call will succeed if the argument matches it. The authors could discover no evidence that this has been implemented in a real version as of the time of writing.

setpgrp

SIII/SV *setpgrp*(2) is incompatible with BSD's original. The BSD version allows one to connect any process to any process group; the AT&T version only allows one to sever the current process from its previous process group.

setregid, setreuid

These calls are available on 4.2BSD only. The *setregid*(2) call replaces 4.1BSD's *setgid*(2); the *setreuid*(2) call similarly replaces *setuid*(2).

setsockopt

4.3BSD enhances this call so it can set buffering and protocol-level options.

setuid

SVID saves the effective uid from a process's parent, and this call will succeed if the argument matches it. The authors could discover no evidence that this has been implemented in a real version as of the time of writing.

shutdown

This interprocess communication call is available only under 4.2BSD.

signal

4.1BSD has two signal packages. The *signal*(2) call is the entry point for the V7-compatible one; the other and more versatile but nonportable one is under *sigset*(2). All UNIX system dialects support signals 1 to 15, but different versions support different interpretations of signal numbers 16 and up.

#	4.1, 4.2, and 4.3BSD	AT&T Versions
16	Not Assigned	SIGUSR1—user signal 1
17	SIGSTOP—stop signal	SIGUSR2—user signal 2
18	SIGTSTP—keyboard stop	SIGCLD—death of child
19	SIGCONT—continue after stop	SIGPWR—power failure
20	SIGCHLD—child status changed	Not assigned
21	SIGTTIN—control tty background read	Not assigned
22	SIGTTOU—control tty background write	Not assigned
23	SIGTTIN—control tty background read	Not assigned
24	SIGXCPU—cpu time limit exceeded	Not assigned
25	SIGXFSZ—file size limit exceeded	Not assigned

#	Additions and changes in 4.2 and 4.3BSD	AT&T Versions
16	SIGURG—urgent socket condition	SIGUSR1—user signal 1
23	SIGIO—I/O possible on a descriptor	Not assigned
26	SIGVTALARM—virtual timer alarm	Not assigned
27	SIGPROF—profiler timer alarm	Not assigned

#	Additions in 4.3BSD only	AT&T Versions
28	SIGWINCH—window size change	Not assigned
29	Not assigned	Not assigned
30	SIGUSR1—user-defined signal	Not assigned
31	SIGUSR2—user-defined signal	Not assigned

Notice also that the AT&T signals SIGCLD and SIGPWR are marked temporary and subject to change.

SVID introduces a number of changes from previous AT&T specifications. It doesn't give numeric equivalents for the signal names and omits the SIGIOT, SIGEMT, SIGBUS, and SIGSEGV signals. SVID claims that SIGABRT will someday be available as a synonym for SIGIOT. It defines a new SIGSYS triggered by a bad argument to a system call.

The 4.2BSD signal facilities have been completely redesigned, and there are a number of new calls that reflect this (see next note).

sigblock, sigpause, sigreturn, sigsetmask, sigstack, sigvec

These are the entry points of the new 4.2BSD signals facilities (*sigreturn*(2) is undocumented but present in 4.2BSD and formally supported in 4.3BSD). Although there is a library call *signal*(3) that superficially resembles 4.1BSD's *signal*(2), 4.2BSD signals differ from those of 4.1BSD and all other versions in some important respects (see Chapter 5 for a discussion of the differences and techniques for handling them).

4.3BSD includes an enhanced *sigvec*(2) that allows programmers to specify system call restart (4.2BSD-style) or nonrestart behavior on a per-signal basis.

sigsys

This 4.1BSD entry point is not supported in 4.2BSD.

stat

New fields have been added to the 4.1BSD *stat* structure in 4.2BSD for things such as the optimal blocking factor of the underlying physical device, the number of disk blocks allocated to the file, the file's size, and a time stamp (the latter two are not yet set correctly). The i-node number field is now 32 bits long. Two new file types may be returned for symbolic links and sockets.

stime

The XENIX 3.0 version declares the stime return to be a `time_t`, masking hardware-dependent differences in the size of a time stamp. The P1003 proposal omits this call.

stty

The V7/BSD/XENIX 2.3 calls *stty*(2) and *gtty*(2) are subsumed by *ioctl*(2) and listed under it.

sync

The P1003 proposal omits this call.

tell

V7/BSD/XENIX 2.3 *tell*(2) is portable as

```
#define tell(fd) lseek(fd, 0L, 1)
```

time

SVID omits the EFAULT error return in the case where the time buffer address is invalid.

times

Curiously enough, all versions of this call return the same data, but the names in the structure template vary a great deal. The tick unit is generally (but not always) the cycle time of the local AC mains, either 1/60 or 1/50th of a second.

Condition	V7/XE2.3	BSD/SV/XE3.0	AT&T
#include	?	sys/times.h	?
structure name	tbuffer	tms	tbuffer
1st component	proc_user_time	tms_utime	utime
2nd component	proc_system_time	tms_stime	stime
3rd component	child_user_time	tms_cutime	cutime
4th component	child_system_time	tms_cstime	cstime

SVID does not require the EFAULT error to be returned in the case where the timings buffer address is bad.

ulimit

SIII/SV gives magic numbers for the three *ulimit* request types, and XENIX 3.0 gives the constants UL_GFILLIM, UL_SFILLIM, UL_GMEMLIM but no values. Inspection of the appropriate include file on the PC/AT version reveals that they are the same. Notice that XENIX 3.0 has one additional request type UL_GTXTOFF not supported by SIII/SV. The P1003 proposal omits this call.

umount

XENIX 2.3 *umount*(2) has the new feature that a *sync*(2) is automatically performed before the actual unmounting. The P1003 proposal omits this call.

uname

XENIX 3.0 adds system origin, system oem, and system serial number fields to the *utsname* structure. SV *uname*(2)'s *utsname* structure includes a machine ID field not present in the SIII version.

unlink

4.2BSD notes that this call should no longer be used for removing directories. See *rmdir*(2) instead. The P1003 proposal omits the ETXTBSY error return.

ustat

The *ustat*(2) call is omitted from the P1003 proposal (although the */usr/group 84* standard from which it derives did include the call.

utime, utimes

The V7 version of *utime*(2) returns its results in a two-place array of *time_t* items, but SIII returns the same data in a structure. The memory layout of the data would be the same on a PDP-11, ironically, but this does create a source code incompatibility. 4.2BSD replaces this call with *utimes*(2), but the old version is still available as *utime*(3).

vlimit, vread, vswapon, vtimes, vwrite

These were all 4.1BSD calls. The *vread*(2) and *vwrite*(2) calls are dropped from 4.2BSD entirely, while *vlimit*(2) and *vtimes*(2) have been moved to Section 3 and *vswapon*(2) has been renamed *swapon*(2).

wait

New in SV is the feature that, when a process is stopped, the number of the signal that caused it is in the high 8 bits of the return code (rather than 0, in previous versions). The 4.2BSD version automatically restarts after a signal interrupt. SVID does not require an EFAULT error return if the status block address passed in is not valid.

wait3

The 4.2BSD version of this call returns its information in a new format compatible with that of the *getrusage*(2) call, and will automatically restart after a signal interrupt.

write

BSD *write*(2) may trigger a special SIGTTOU signal, see *jobs*(3). SIII and descendants use `unsigned` as the type of the write-count argument, rather than V7/BSD/XENIX 2.3's `int`; SIII notes that writes that exceed the process's file size limit are truncated. See also the note for *open*(2) on new file mode features in SV, and in particular note the effect of the O_SYNC flag on *write*(2) calls. 4.2BSD *write*(2), unlike that of other versions, resumes automatically after a signal interrupt.

The *write*(2) call's behavior in nonblocking (O_NDELAY) mode varies between implementations when writing more data to pipes than the system-defined limit for atomic write operations. For a discussion of the rather messy problems surrounding this issue, see **[P1003]**.

writev

This I/O call is only supported on 4.2BSD.

3.8 Section 3—Library Calls

On XENIX 3.0, these calls are grouped with those of Section 2 under Section "S".

The following library groups have been omitted from the table below:

curses	BSD, XENIX, SV, SV2
dbm(3X)	V7, BSD, XENIX
getfsent	BSD
j0	V7, BSD, XENIX, SIII, SV
jobs	4.1BSD
lib2648	4.2BSD
mp	V7, XENIX
net	4.2BSD
pk	V7
plot	V7, BSD, SIII, XENIX
rcmd, rexec	4.2BSD
sigset	BSD
termcap	BSD, XENIX

These libraries seem to be identical across the machines that support them, except that *curses*(3) on System V, Release 2, has some functional enhancements for *terminfo*(3) over the V7/BSD/XENIX version and is not strictly upward compatible with it.

None of the 4.2BSD or System V FORTRAN support libraries have been listed.

On SV, the *j0*(3) library is called *bessel*(3).

In this table only, the presence of a "@" in the Portability column indicates a call described by the X3J11 Draft Proposed C Standard (see [X3J11]). In general, X3J11 calls meet the System V Interface Definition (and AT&T has committed itself, in the SVID, to follow the final X3J11 standard). A few proposed X3J11 calls [*strstr*(), *onexit*(), *strerror*(), *difftime*(), *remove*(), and *rename*()] have no counterpart in SVID. A few others [*exit*() and *time*()] match with portable UNIX system calls.

Name	Under	?	V7	BSD	SIII	XE2.3	XE3.0	SV
_tolower	conv	*	.	.	F	>	≡	≡
_toupper	conv	*	.	.	F	>	≡	≡
a64l		.	.	.	F	.	≡	=
abort		Y@*	F	≡	>	≡	≡	=
abs		Y@	F	≡	≡	≡	≡	=
acos	sin	Y@*	F	≡	≡	≡	≡	≡
alphasort	scandir	.	.	F$	.	.	.	.
asctime	ctime	Y@*	F	≡	>	≡	≡	≡
asin	sin	Y@*	F	≡	≡	≡	≡	≡
assert		Y@*	F	≡	≡	≡	≡	>
atan	sin	Y@*	F	≡	≡	≡	≡	≡
atan2	sin	Y@*	F	≡	≡	≡	≡	≡
atof		Y@	F	≡	≡	≡	=	≡
atoi	atof	Y@*	F	≡	≡	≡	=	≡
atol	atof	Y@*	F	≡	≡	≡	=	≡
bcmp	bstring	*	.	F$	.	.	.	.

Name	Under	?	V7	BSD	SIII	XE2.3	XE3.0	SV
bcopy	bstring	*	.	F$	.	.	.	.
bsearch		@*	.	.	F	.	≡	=
bzero	bstring	*	.	F$	.	.	.	.
cabs	hypot	Y*	F	≡	.	≡	.	.
calloc	malloc	Y@	F	≡	≡	≡	≡	≡
ceil	floor	Y@	F	≡	≡	≡	≡	≡
clearerr	ferror	Y@	F	≡	≡	≡	≡	≡
clock		@	.	.	.	.	$	F
closedir	directory	*	.	F$	.	.	≡	.
closelog	syslog	.	.	F$	.	.	.	.
cos	sin	Y@*	F	≡	≡	≡	≡	≡
cosh	sinh	Y@	F	≡	≡	≡	≡	≡
crypt		Y*	F	≡	≡	≡	.	=
ctermid		.	.	.	F	.	≡	≡
ctime		Y@	F	≡	≡	≡	≡	≡
cuserid		*	.	.	F	.	≡	≡
defopen		.	.	.	.	F	≡	.
defread		.	.	.	.	F	≡	.
dial		.	.	.	.	.	$	F
drand48		.	.	.	.	.	$	F
ecvt		Y*	F	≡	≡	≡	≡	X
edata	end	Y*	F	≡	≡	≡	≡	>
encrypt	crypt	Y*	F	≡	≡	≡	.	≡
end		Y*	F	≡	≡	≡	≡	≡
endgrent	getgrent	Y*	F	≡	≡	≡	≡	≡
endpwent		Y*	F	≡	≡	≡	≡	≡
endutent	getut	.	.	.	.	$	.	F
etext	end	Y*	,F	≡	≡	≡	≡	>
exec	execl	Y*	.	F	.	.	.	.
exece	execl	Y*	.	F	.	.	.	.
execl		Y*	.	F	.	.	.	.
execle	execl	Y*	.	F	.	.	.	.
execlp	execl	Y*	.	F	.	.	.	.
exect	execl	*	.	F	.	.	.	.
execv	execl	Y*	.	F	.	.	.	.
execvp	execl	Y*	.	F	.	.	.	.
exp		Y@*	F	≡	≡	≡	≡	>
fabs	floor	Y@	F	≡	≡	≡	≡	≡
fclose		Y@	F	≡	≡	≡	≡	≡
fcvt	ecvt	Y	F	≡	≡	≡	≡	=
fdopen	fopen	Y*	F	>	>	=	≡	=
feof	ferror	Y@	F	≡	≡	≡	≡	≡
ferror		Y@	F	≡	≡	≡	≡	≡
fflush	fclose	Y@	F	≡	≡	≡	≡	≡
ffs	bstring	.	.	F$	.	.	.	.
fgetc	getc	Y@	F	≡	=	≡	≡	=
fgets	gets	Y@	F	≡	≡	≡	≡	=
fileno	ferror	Y	F	≡	≡	≡	≡	≡
floor		Y@	F	≡	=	≡	≡	≡
fmod	floor	@	.	.	F	.	≡	=
fopen		Y@*	F	>	>	≡	≡	=
fprintf	printf	@*	F	≡	X	≡	≡	≡

Name	Under	?	V7	BSD	SIII	XE2.3	XE3.0	SV
fptrap		.	`	.	FV	.	.	.
fputc	putc	Y@	F	≡	≡	≡	≡	=
fputs	puts	Y@	F	≡	=	≡	≡	=
fread		Y@*	F	>	≡	≡	≡	=
free	malloc	Y@	F	≡	≡	≡	≡	≡
freopen	fopen	Y@*	F	>	>	≡	≡	=
frexp		Y@	F	≡	≡	≡	≡	=
fscanf	scanf	Y@*	F	≡	≡	≡	=	>
fseek		@*	F	≡	X	≡	≡	=
ftell	fseek	Y@	F	≡	≡	≡	≡	=
ftw		.	.	.	.	.	$	F
fwrite	fread	Y@	F	≡	≡	≡	≡	=
fxlist		.	.	.	.	.	F$	.
gamma		*	.	F	>	.	≡	>
gcvt	ecvt	Y	F	≡	≡	≡	≡	≡
getc		Y@	F	≡	≡	≡	≡	=
getchar	getc	Y@	F	≡	≡	≡	≡	=
getcwd		.	.	.	.	.	$	F
getdiskbyname		.	.	F$	.	.	.	.
getenv		Y@	F	≡	≡	≡	≡	=
getgrent		Y*	F	≡	≡	≡	≡	=
getgrgid	getgrent	Y*	F	≡	≡	≡	≡	=
getgrnam	getgrent	Y*	F	≡	≡	≡	≡	=
getlogin		Y*	F	≡	=	≡	≡	≡
getopt		.	.	.	F	.	≡	=
getpass		Y*	F	≡	≡	≡	≡	>
getpw		Y	F	≡	≡O	≡	≡O	=O
getpwent		Y*	F	≡	=	≡	≡	=
getpwnam	getpwent	Y*	F	≡	=	≡	≡	=
getpwuid	getpwent	Y*	F	≡	=	≡	≡	=
gets		Y@	F	≡	≡	≡	≡	=
getutent	getut	.	.	.	.	.	$	F
getutid	getut	.	.	.	.	.	$	F
getutline	getut	.	.	.	.	.	$	F
getw	getc	Y	F	≡	≡	≡	≡	=
getwd		*	.	F	.	.	.	.
gmtime	ctime	Y@*	F	≡	>	≡	≡	≡
gsignal	ssignal	.	.	.	F	.	≡	≡
hcreate	hsearch	.	.	.	.	.	$	F
hdestroy	hsearch	.	.	.	.	.	$	F
hsearch		.	.	.	.	.	$	F
hypot		Y*	F	≡	≡	≡	≡	>
index	string	Y*	F	≡	.	≡	.	.
initgroups		.	.	F$	.	.	.	.
initstate		.	.	F$	.	.	.	.
insque		.	.	F$	.	.	.	.
isalnum	ctype	Y@*	F	≡	≡	≡	≡	≡
isalpha	ctype	Y@*	F	≡	≡	≡	≡	≡
isascii	ctype	Y@*	F	≡	≡	≡	≡	≡
isatty	ttyname	Y	F	≡	≡	≡	≡	≡
iscntrl	ctype	Y@*	F	≡	≡	≡	≡	≡
isdigit	ctype	Y@*	F	≡	≡	≡	≡	≡

Name	Under	?	V7	BSD	SIII	XE2.3	XE3.0	SV
isgraph	ctype	Y@*	.	.	F	.	≡	≡
islower	ctype	Y@*	F	≡	≡	≡	≡	≡
isprint	ctype	Y@*	F	≡	≡	≡	≡	≡
ispunct	ctype	Y@*	F	≡	≡	≡	≡	≡
isspace	ctype	Y@*	F	≡	≡	≡	≡	≡
isupper	ctype	Y@*	F	≡	≡	≡	≡	≡
isxdigit	ctype	Y@*	.	.	F	≡	≡	≡
l3tol		Y	F	≡	≡	≡	≡	≡
l64a	a64l	.	.	.	F	.	≡	≡
ldaclose		.	.	.	.	.	.	FC
ldahread		.	.	.	.	.	.	FC
ldexp	frexp	Y@	F	≡	≡	≡	≡	>
ldfhread		.	.	.	.	.	.	FC
ldgetname		.	.	.	.	.	.	F$C
ldlread		.	.	.	.	.	.	FC
ldlseek		.	.	.	.	.	.	FC
ldohseek		.	.	.	.	.	.	FC
ldopen		.	.	.	.	.	.	FC
ldrseek		.	.	.	.	.	.	FC
ldshseek		.	.	.	.	.	.	FC
ldsread		.	.	.	.	.	.	FC
ldtbindex		.	.	.	.	.	.	FC
ldtbread		.	.	.	.	.	.	FC
ldtbseek		.	.	.	.	.	.	FC
lfind	lsearch	.	.	.	.	.	.	F$
localtime	ctime	Y@	F	≡	>	≡	≡	≡
lockf		*	.	.	.	.	$	F
log	exp	@*	F	≡	X	≡	≡	>
log10	exp	@*	F	≡	.	≡	≡	>
logname		.	.	.	F	.	≡	≡
longjmp	setjmp	*	F	≡	X	≡	≡	≡
lsearch		*	.	.	F	.	≡	>
lto3l	l3tol	Y	F	≡	≡	≡	≡	≡
mallinfo	malloc	*	.	.	.	$	.	F
malloc		Y@*	F	≡	≡	≡	≡	≡
mallopt	malloc	*	.	.	.	.	$	F
matherr		.	.	.	.	.	$	F
memccpy	memory	@*	.	F$	.	.	$	F
memchr	memory	@*	.	F$	.	.	$	F
memcmp	memory	@*	.	F$	.	.	$	F
memcpy	memory	@*	.	F$	.	.	$	F
memset	memory	@*	.	F$	.	.	$	F
mktemp		*	F	≡	≡	≡	X	≡
modf	frexp	Y@	F	≡	≡	≡	≡	>
monitor		Y*	F	≡	≡	≡	≡	>
nlist		Y*	F	>	>	≡	≡	≡
opendir	directory	*	.	F$	.	.	≡	.
openlog	syslog	.	.	F$	.	.	.	.
pclose	popen	Y*	F	≡	≡	≡	≡	≡
perror		Y@*	F	≡	≡	≡	≡	≡
popen		Y*	F	≡	≡	≡	≡	≡
pow	exp	Y@*	F	≡	≡	≡	≡	>

Name	Under	?	V7	BSD	SIII	XE2.3	XE3.0	SV
printf		@*	F	≡	X	≡	>	≡
psignal		.	.	F$	.	.	.	.
putc		Y@	F	≡	≡	≡	≡	=
putchar	putc	Y@	F	≡	≡	≡	≡	=
putenv		.	.	.	.	.	$	F$
putpwent		.	.	.	F	.	≡	=
puts		Y@	F	≡	=	≡	≡	=
pututline	getut	.	.	.	.	$	.	F
putw	putc	Y	F	≡	=	≡	≡	=
qsort		Y@*	F	≡	≡	≡	≡	=
rand		Y@*	F	≡	≡	≡	≡	=
random		*	.	F	.	.	.	.
re_comp	regex	.	.	F	.	.	.	.
re_exec	regex	.	.	F	.	.	.	.
readdir	directory	*	.	F$	.	.	≡	.
realloc	malloc	Y@	F	≡	>	≡	≡	≡
regcmp	regex	*	.	.	F	.	≡	≡
regex	regex	*	.	.	F	.	≡	≡
remque	insque	.	.	F$	.	.	.	.
rewind	fseek	Y*	F	≡	≡	≡	≡	≡
rewinddir	directory	*	.	F$	.	.	≡	.
rindex	string	Y*	F	≡	.	≡	.	.
scandir		*	.	F$	.	.	.	.
scanf		Y@*	F	≡	≡	≡	=	>
seekdir	directory	*	.	F$	.	.	≡	.
setbuf		Y@*	F	=	=	≡	≡	=
setbuffer		*	.	F	.	.	.	.
setgrent		Y	F	≡	≡	≡	≡	≡
setjmp		Y@*	F	≡	≡	>	=	=
setkey	crypt	Y*	F	≡	≡	≡	≡	≡
setlinebuf		.	.	F$	.	.	.	.
setlogmask		.	.	F$	.	.	.	.
setpwent	getpwent	Y*	F	≡	≡	≡	≡	≡
setrgid	setuid	.	.	F$	.	.	.	.
setruid	setuid	.	.	F$	.	.	.	.
setstate		.	.	F$	.	.	.	.
setutent	getut	.	.	.	.	.	$	F
setvbuf	setbuf	@*	.	.	.	.	$	F$
sgetl	sputl	.	.	.	.	.	$	F
sin		Y@*	F	≡	≡	≡	≡	>
sinh		Y*	F	≡	≡	≡	≡	>
sleep		Y*	F	≡	>	≡	≡	≡
sprintf		@*	F	≡	X	≡	>	>
sputl		.	.	.	.	.	$	F
sqrt	exp	Y@*	F	≡	≡	≡	≡	>
srand	rand	Y@	F	≡	≡	≡	≡	≡
srandom	random	.	.	F$	.	.	.	.
sscanf	scanf	Y@*	F	≡	≡	≡	=	>
ssignal		.	.	.	F	.	≡	=
stdipc		.	.	.	.	.	$	F
strcat	string	Y@	F	≡	=	≡	≡	≡
strchr	string	Y@*	.	.	F	.	≡	≡

Name	Under	?	V7	BSD	SIII	XE2.3	XE3.0	SV
strcmp	string	Y@	F	≡	=	≡	≡	≡
strcpy	string	Y@	F	≡	=	≡	≡	≡
strcspn	string	@	.	.	F	.	≡	≡
strdup	string	.	.	.	.	.	F	.
strlen	string	Y@	F	≡	=	≡	≡	≡
strncat	string	Y@	F	≡	=	≡	≡	≡
strncmp	string	Y@	F	≡	=	≡	≡	≡
strncpy	string	Y@	F	≡	=	≡	≡	≡
strpbrk	string	@	.	.	F	.	≡	≡
strrchr	string	Y@*	.	.	F	.	≡	≡
strspn	string	@	.	.	F	.	≡	≡
strtod		@	.	.	.	.	$	F$
strtok	string	.	.	.	F	.	≡	≡
strtol		@	.	.	.	.	$	F
swab		Y*	F	≡	≡	≡	≡	>
syslog		.	.	F$	.	.	.	.
system		Y@*	F	≡	=	≡	=	=
tan	sin	Y@*	F	≡	≡	≡	≡	>
tanh	sinh	Y@*	F	≡	>	≡	≡	>
tdelete	tsearch	.	.	.	.	.	.	F
telldir	directory	*	.	F$	.	.	≡	.
tempname	tmpname	.	.	.	.	.	.	F
tfind	tsearch	.	.	.	.	.	.	F$
timezone	ctime	*	F	≡	X	≡	≡	=
tmpfile		@*	.	.	F	.	≡	>
tmpnam		@	.	.	F	.	≡	>
toascii	conv	.	.	.	F	≡	≡	≡
tolower	conv	*	.	.	F	X	≡	≡
toupper	conv	*	.	.	F	X	≡	≡
tsearch		.	.	.	.	.	$	F
ttyname		Y	F	≡	>	≡	.	≡
ttyslot	ttyname	*	F	≡	.	≡	≡	X
twalk	tsearch	.	.	.	.	.	$	F
tzset	ctime	*	.	.	F	.	=	=
ungetc		Y@*	F	≡	≡	≡	≡	=
utmpname	getut	.	.	.	.	$	.	F
valloc		.	.	F	.	.	.	.
varargs		.	.	F	.	=5	.	=$5
vfprintf	vprintf	@	.	.	.	$	.	F$
vprintf		@	.	.	.	.	$	F$
vsprintf	vprintf	@	.	.	.	$	.	F$
x25alnk		.	.	.	.	.	.	F
x25clnk		.	.	.	.	.	.	F
x25dlnk	x25hlnk	.	.	.	.	.	.	F
x25hlnk		.	.	.	.	.	.	F
x25ilnk	x25alnk	.	.	.	.	.	.	F
x25ipvc		.	.	.	.	.	.	F
x25rpvc	x25ipvc	.	.	.	.	.	.	F
xlist		.	.	.	.	.	$	.

Notes on C Library Functions

abort

V7/BSD/XENIX and SIII/SV send SIGIOT. SVID declares that *abort*(3) will send a defined SIGABRT in the future. SV declares the return type of this function, the others do not.

acos, asin, atan, atan2

SIII/XENIX 3.0/SV changes the name of this library to "trig".

asctime

The SIII entry includes an extra call *tzset*. In V7, the *timezone* entry point is a function; in AT&T versions, it is a variable.

assert

SV *assert*(3) uses *abort*(3) rather than *exit*(2) in order to force a core dump.

atoi, atol

SV *atoi*(3) and *atol*(3) are moved to the *strtol*(3) group.

bcmp, bcopy

These routines [equivalents of SV *memcmp*(3) and *memcpy*(3)] are supported only in 4.2BSD.

bsearch

The SV *bsearch*(3) and *qsort*(3) manual sections include a NOTES section with usage tips.

bzero

This routine for zeroing arrays is supported only under 4.2BSD, but is equivalent to a SV *memset*(3) call with the third argument set to zero.

cabs

The SIII *abs*(3) library does not include *cabs*, but it can be written using *hypot*(3).

closedir

This call is part of the new 4.2BSD directory manipulation package. An equivalent set of calls using the non-4.2BSD directory structures is reproduced in Appendix D. The P1003 proposal specifies this call, but SVID does not.

cos

In versions before SV, *cos* is in the *sin(3)* library; in SV, the name of the library becomes *trig*(3).

crypt

Encrypted files will not necessarily be transportable among UNIX system dialects, due to restrictions on distribution to users outside the U.S. of any code that uses the Data Encryption Standard.

cuserid

This routine is omitted from SVID.

ecvt

The SV *ecvt*(3) documentation doesn't mention the rounding of the low digit specified in previous versions.

encrypt

See the note for *crypt*(3).

end, edata, etext

The documentation for SV *end*(3) (including the *end*, *etext*, and *edata* entry points) doesn't include SIII's note on assembler access.

endgrent, endpwent

These calls are omitted from the SVID library specification. On SV, these calls are `void`; all other versions return `int`.

execl, execv, execle, execlp, execvp, exece, exect

These are library routines in 4.2BSD, but are listed in Section 2 in all other versions (except for *exect*(3), which is unique to 4.2BSD). See the *exec* note in the notes for Section 2.

exp

The SV versions of *exp*, *log*, *pow*, and *sqrt* use the new *matherr*(3) and have stricter error behavior than their predecessors. SIII returns HUGEVAL rather than V7's 0.

fdopen, fopen

BSD/SIII/SV *fopen*(3) modes "r+", "w+", and "a+" are also an undocumented feature of some later V7 versions. The SV *fopen*(3) manual entry adds some detail about the behavior of files opened by many writers and specifies that previously written data in files opened for append may not be overwritten. X3J11 describes a "b" qualifier for opening files as binary streams in environments with line separator conventions that require translation to and from the UNIX system newline convention.

fprintf

V7/BSD/XENIX 2.3 *fprintf*(3) uses capital letters to format long-width data. SIII/SV/XENIX 3.0 *fprintf*(3) uses capital format letters to cause capitalization in hexadecimal numeric output. Otherwise, all V7 features are upward portable; see the table under *printf*(3) for details.

fread

BSD notes that it flushes *stdout* before executing a *fread*(3).

freopen

See the note for *fopen*(3).

fscanf

See the note for *scanf*(3).

fseek

SV *fseek*(3) doesn't say that it cancels the effects of *ungetc*(3), but it still does; see the documentation for *ungetc*(3). AT&T versions simply specify a nonzero return rather than V7's -1; this is the only reason for the X in the SIII column.

gamma

See the note for *exp*(3).

getgrent, getgrgid, getgrnam

These calls are omitted from the SVID library specification.

getlogin

This routine is omitted from the SVID library specification.

getpass

SV decribes the behavior of *getpass*(3) on getting hit by a signal. The SVID omits this routine, although the format of */etc/passwd* is specified.

getpwent, getpwnam, getpwuid

These calls are omitted from the SVID library specification.

getwd

This routine is present, although not documented, in the *jobs*(3) library of 4.1BSD. 4.2BSD documents it and moves it to the main C library, and returns a special string on error rather than printing a message to *stdout*.

gmtime

See the note for *asctime*(3).

hypot

See the note for *exp*(3).

index

V7/BSD/XENIX 2.3 *index* and *rindex* are *strchr* and *strrchr* in SIII/XENIX 3.0/SV. SIII/UDS/XENIX 3.0/SV also defines *strpbrk*, *strspn*, *strspcspn*, and *strtok*. All of these functions have been added to the 4.3BSD libraries.

isalpha, islower, isupper, isdigit, isxdigit, isalnum, ispunct, isprint, iscntrl, isascii, isgraph, isspace

These are the *ctype*(3) library. Assume at most the properties described in the SIII documentation for portability. XENIX 2.3 *ctype*(3) includes the *toupper* and *tolower* macros. Notice also that SIII/SV *isspace* returns true on a vertical tab as well as on whitespace characters (space, tab, carriage-return, linefeed, or formfeed) accepted in V7.

lockf

This call is only available under SV2. It uses SV2's enhanced *fcntl*(2) file extent locking mechanism, and supports advisory locks only. AT&T has promised to support compulsory locking in the next version (System V, Release 3).

log, log10

See the note on *exp*(3). In V7/BSD, these return 0 for nonpositive arguments, but in AT&T versions they return HUGEVAL. Notice that the *log10*(3) entry point is mysteriously absent from SIII.

longjmp

XENIX 2.3 notes that `register` variables contain no useful values when *longjmp*(3) completes. AT&T versions force a 0 *longjmp*(3) second argument to 1 to avoid confusion with a real *setjmp*(3) execution; this is the reason for the X in the SIII column.

lsearch

The SV version of *lsearch*(3) uses Knuth 6.1S rather than 6.1Q as in previous incarnations.

mallinfo, malloc, mallopt

For safety's sake, don't try to allocate a block with more bytes in it than the highest value of a signed short; some (segmented) architectures will become confused if you do. The new SV2 *mallopt*(3) and *mallinfo*(3) calls are available only with Release 2's *-libmalloc* library. 4.2BSD also has a replacement that supposedly fixes some bugs, at */usr/src/local/malloc.c*.

memccpy, memchr, memcmp, memcpy, memset

These SV-originated functions have been added to the 4.3BSD libraries.

mktemp

In the XENIX 3.0 version, two calls to *mktemp*(3) with the same template argument by the same process will produce the same temp file name. Other versions will produce a different name on each call (until one runs out of distinguishing letters).

monitor

The SV1 version of this call is identical to its SIII predecessor. The SV2 version expects a third argument of a WORD type defined in */usr/include/mon.h* (usually an `unsigned short`).

nlist

For VAX BSD *nlist*(3) only, include *nlist.h* rather than *a.out.h*. According to the SV1 documentation, its *nlist*(3) expects a different second argument type than V7/BSD/XENIX/SIII/SV2, but this is probably a typo. SV specifies an error return of -1, others are silent on this subject. Notice that the name of the namelist file may differ between versions.

opendir

This call is part of the new 4.2BSD directory manipulation package. An equivalent set of calls using the non-4.2BSD directory structures is reproduced in Appendix D. The P1003 proposal specifies this call, but SVID does not.

pclose

The P1003 proposal omits this call.

perror

4.2BSD notes that this call now uses *writev*(2) to do an atomic write of all its argument data; this is important for programs that report errors through sockets. The P1003 proposal drops this from its specification, although it was included in the ancestral */usr/group 84* standard.

popen

SIII documents a restriction that only one *popen*(3) stream may be open at a time. Whether this is true in V7 or not is unknown to the authors; if so, the = in the SIII column should be an X. The P1003 proposal omits this call.

pow

See the note for *exp*(3).

printf

The following table describes the format options available under various dialects. The BSD and XENIX 2.3 versions are like V7's; the USG column describes the version found in SIII, XENIX 3.0/5.0, and SV; and the SVID column describes the System V Interface Definition version (however, see note [4]).

Char	V7	USG	SVID	Description
%	F	≡	≡	start conversion
Sign controls:				
-	F	≡	≡	left-adjust the field
+	.	F	≡	print sign of numeric value
<space>	.	F	≡	print space for positive, "-" for negative
#	.	F	≡	print in alternate form

Char	V7	USG	SVID	Description
Field-width controls:				
0	F	≡	≡	as leading char, specifies zero padding
*	.	F	≡	take width from next argument
<num>	F	≡	≡	minimum output field width
Precision:				
*	.	F	≡	take precision from next argument
<num>	F	≡	≡	float precision or max string width; see note [1]
Conversions:				
D	F	.	.	long integer, decimal; see note [2]
E	.	F	≡	"[-]m.dddE±dd" float format
G	.	F	≡	shorter of "E" and "f"
L	.	.	F	long double; see note [4]
O	F	.	.	unsigned long integer, octal; see note [2]
U	F	.	.	unsigned long integer, decimal; see note [2]
X	F	X	≡	see note [3]
c	F	≡	≡	character
d	F	≡	≡	decimal int
e	F	≡	≡	"[-]d.ddde±dd" float format
f	F	≡	≡	"[-]ddd.ddd" fixed-point format
g	F	≡	≡	shorter of "e" and "f"
h	.	.	F	short (after int conversion); see note [4]
i	.	.	F	decimal int
l	F	≡	≡	long (valid as prefix to d, o, x, and u)
n	.	.	F	store count of printed characters; see note [4]
o	F	≡	≡	octal unsigned int
p	.	.	F	value of a pointer; see note [4]
s	F	≡	≡	string
u	F	≡	≡	decimal unsigned int
x	F	≡	≡	hex unsigned int

[1] C implementations on other than UNIX systems sometimes omit the precision feature.

[2] These formats are not described in [K & R] but are in V7.

[3] In the V7 version, the X format means (unsigned) long hexadecimal. In USG versions, including the SVID/ANSI *printf*(3), X prints in hex integer format with capital ABCDEF digits. The l prefix for long is portable everywhere and should be used instead of DOXU on V7 versions.

[4] The n, h, p, and L formats are not yet specified in SVID, but will almost certainly be added due to their presence in the ANSI X3J11 draft.

qsort

The SV *qsort*(3) manual entry includes a NOTES section with usage tips. The 4.2BSD version has been tuned for speed.

rand, random

Don't assume that *rand*(3) will return in the range 0-32767 on a 32-bit machine. The SV version of *rand*(3) notes that its distribution has poor spectral properties. The new 4.2BSD *random*(3) is a replacement for *rand*(3).

readdir

This call is part of the new 4.2BSD directory manipulation package. An equivalent set of calls using the non-4.2BSD directory structures is reproduced in Appendix D. The P1003 proposal specifies this call, but SVID does not.

regcmp, regex

SV *regcmp*(3) and *regex*(3) are listed under *regcmp*(3) rather than *regex*(3) as in SIII.

rewind

SV doesn't specify a return type for this call.

rewinddir

This call is part of the new 4.2BSD directory manipulation package. An equivalent set of calls using the non-4.2BSD directory structures is reproduced in Appendix D. The P1003 proposal specifies this call, but SVID does not.

rindex

See the note for *index*(3).

scandir

This directory-scanning routine is available only under 4.2BSD.

scanf

Despite ambiguities in the V7 documentation, all versions return EOF on a I/O error before the first conversion.

The following table describes all of the format options available under various dialects. The BSD and XENIX 2.3 versions are like V7's; the USG column describes the version found in SIII, XENIX 3.0/5.0, and SV; and the SVID version describes the System V Interface Definition version (however, see note [4]).

Char	V7	USG	SVID	Description
%	F	≡	≡	start conversion
Flags:				
*	F	≡	≡	suppress assignment
Width:				
<num>	F	≡	≡	maximum input field width
Conversions:				
D	F	.	.	long integer, decimal; see note [2]
E	F	X	≡	double in V7, see note [2]; float in USG
F	F	X	≡	double in V7, see note [2]; float in USG
G	.	F	≡	float ·
L	.	.	F	long double; see note [4]
O	F	.	.	unsigned long integer, octal; see note [2]
U	F	.	.	unsigned long integer, decimal; see note [2]
X	F	X	≡	see note [3]
c	F	≡	≡	character
d	F	≡	≡	decimal int
e	F	≡	≡	float
f	F	≡	≡	float
g	.	.	F	float
h	F	X	≡	short; see note [5]
i	.	.	F	int with C-style base conversion; see note [4]
l	F	≡	≡	long (valid as prefix to d, o, x, and u)
n	.	.	F	store count of printed characters; see note [4]
o	F	≡	≡	octal unsigned int
p	.	.	F	value of a pointer; see note [4]
s	F	≡	≡	string
u	.	.	F	decimal unsigned int
x	F	≡	≡	hex unsigned int
[...]	F	≡	≡	string of chars in given set; see note [2]
[^...]	F	≡	≡	string of chars not in given set; see note [2]

[1] C implementations on other than UNIX systems sometimes omit the precision feature.

[2] These formats are not described in [K&R] but are present in V7.

[3] In the V7 version, the X format expects (unsigned) long hexadecimal. In USG versions, including the SVID/ANSI *scanf*(3), X gets a hex integer. The l prefix for long is portable everywhere and should be used instead of DOXU on V7 versions.

[4] The i, n, and p formats are not yet specified in SVID, but will almost certainly be added due to their presence in the ANSI X3J11 draft.

[5] In [K&R] and V7, h may be used as a format specifier by itself to get short int values. In V7 and all USG versions, it must be used as a prefix to d, o, or x to get a short int value in the indicated base. Only in V7 are both usages legal.

A historical note: In [K&R], it is asserted that whitespace characters are ignored entirely (rather than causing a skip of whitespace in the input stream).

seekdir

This call is part of the new 4.2BSD directory manipulation package. An equivalent set of calls using the non-4.2BSD directory structures is reproduced in Appendix D. This call is not included in the P1003 and SVID proposals.

setbuf, setbuffer

The SV *setbuf*(3) documentation notes that terminal output streams are line-buffered by default. 4.2BSD has a *setbuffer*(3) call (equivalent to SV *setvbuf*(3)) that allows the programmer to set any size of buffer for the line-buffered mode.

setjmp

SV *setjmp*(3) issues a stern warning about correctness of the environment. See also the note for *longjmp*(3). The 4.2BSD version has been enhanced to preserve signal masks in order to interact with the new signal-handling facilities. In general, the return values of *setjmp*(3) are not portable, except that whether they are zero or nonzero is consistent.

setkey

See the note for *crypt*(3).

setpwent

This function is omitted from the SVID library specification.

setvbuf

The *setvbuf* call is available on SV2 only. The 4.2BSD *setbuffer*(3) call is equivalent.

sin

SV2 moves this call from *sin*(3) to *trig*(3) and uses *matherr*(3) for error handling.

sinh

The SV2 version of this call uses the new *matherr*(3) for error handling.

sleep

SIII/SVID specifies the return from a *sleep*(3) call to be the sleep time remaining.

sprintf

See the note for *printf*(3).

sqrt

The SV2 version of this call uses the new *matherr*(3) for error handling.

sscanf

See the note for *scanf*(3).

strchr, strrchr

See the note for *index*(3). These functions have been added to the 4.3BSD libraries.

This additional entry point for the *syslog*(3) facility of 4.2BSD is supported in 4.3BSD.

swab

The SV version of *swab*(3) will accept odd length arguments (it decrements them). SV treats negative length arguments as 0.

system

SIII *system*(3) simply says it "stops" if it can't execute sh, and doesn't describe the return value; V7/BSD/XENIX documents a failure status of 127. The SV version documents a return of -1 on failure.

tan

SV2 moves this call from *sin*(3) to *trig*(3) and uses *matherr*(3) for error handling.

tanh

The SV2 version of this call uses the new *matherr*(3) for error handling.

telldir

This call is part of the new 4.2BSD directory manipulation package. An equivalent set of calls using the non-4.2BSD directory structures is reproduced in Appendix D. This call is not included in the P1003 and SVID proposals.

timezone

See the note for *asctime*(3).

tmpfile

The SV version prints a message to *stderr* using *perror*(3), and returns a NULL on failure.

tolower, toupper

All versions of these except XENIX 2.3's accept the entire ASCII character set as a domain; XENIX 2.3's are equivalent to the usual underscore-prefixed variants.

ttyslot

The SV *ttyslot*(3) searches the *utmp* file, while the V7/BSD/XENIX versions search the */etc/ttys* file.

tzset

See the note for *asctime*(3).

ungetc

SV *ungetc*(3) specifies that its effects are negated by an *fseek*(3) or an *lseek*(2).

3.9 Section 4—Device Drivers and Special Files

On System V, the device driver material is under Section 7. On XENIX 3.0 and 5.0, driver information is Section "M".

The common subset of these drivers consists of: *null*(4) and *tty*(4). The null device is a data sink and has no control functions. For a discussion of portable *tty*(4) control, see Chapter 5.

Name	Under	?	V7	BSD	SIII	XE2.3	XE3.0	SV
autoconf		.	.	F	.	.	.	.
acu		.	.	.	.	.	.	FB
acc		.	.	F$	.	.	.	.
ad		*	.	F$	.	.	.	F
adli		*	.	.	.	.	.	F$B
arp		.	.	F$	.	.	.	.
b3net		*	.	.	.	.	.	F
bk		.	.	F	.	.	.	.
cat		.	F	.	≡P	.	.	.
clock		.	.	.	.	.	F	.
cmos		.	.	.	.	.	F	.
cons		*	.	F	.	.	.	.
console		*	.	.	.	F	>	X
css		.	.	F$	.	.	.	.
ct		.	.	F	.	.	.	.
dh	dz	.	.	F	>	.	.	.
dj		.	.	.	F	.	.	.
dk		*	.	.	.	.	.	FB
dkraw		*	.	.	.	.	.	FB
dm	dh	.	.	F	.	.	.	.
dmc		*	.	F$	F	.	.	.
dmf		.	.	F$	.	.	.	.
dn		*	F	>	>	.	.	.
dp	du	.	F	.	.	.	.	.

Name	Under	?	V7	BSD	SIII	XE2.3	XE3.0	SV
dqs		.	.	.	FO	.	.	.
drum		.	.	F	.	.	.	.
du		*	F	.	>PO	.	.	.
dz		*	.	F	F	.	.	.
dzk	dz	*	.	.	F	.	.	.
ec		.	.	F$	.	.	.	.
en		.	.	F$	.	.	.	.
err		*	.	.	F	.	.	F$
error		*	.	.	.	.	.	F$
fd		.	.	.	.	F	X	.
fl		.	.	F	.	.	.	.
hd		.	.	.	.	F	X	.
hk		.	.	F	.	.	.	.
hy		.	.	F$	.	.	.	.
hp		*	F4	X	X4	.	.	.
hs		.	F	..	≡O	.	.	.
ht		*	F	X	X	.	.	.
id		.	.	.	.	.	.	F
idfc		.	.	.	.	.	.	F
ik		.	.	F$	.	.	.	.
il		.	.	F$	.	.	.	.
imp		.	.	F$	.	.	.	.
ioa		.	.	.	.	.	.	FB
keyboard		.	.	.	.	.	F$	.
kg		.	.	F$	.	.	.	.
kl		.	.	.	F	.	.	.
kmc		.	.	.	FP	.	.	.
kmem	mem	*	F	≡	≡	≡	≡	≡
lbe		.	.	.	.	.	.	FB
lo		.	.	F$	.	.	.	.
lp		*	.	F	X	X	X	.
mail		*	.	F	.	.	.	.
mem		*	F	≡	≡	.	≡	≡
mt		.	.	F	.	.	.	.
multiscreen		.	.	.	.	.	F$	.
nc		*	.	.	.	.	.	FB
ni		*	.	.	.	.	.	FB
null		Y	F	≡	≡	≡	≡	≡
parallel		*	.	.	.	.	F$	.
pcl		*	.	F$	F	.	.	.
pk		.	F	.	.	.	.	.
prf		.	.	.	F	.	.	≡
ps		.	.	F$	.	.	.	.
pty		.	.	F$	.	.	.	.
ra		*	.	F	.	.	.	.
rf		.	F	.	≡PO	.	.	.
rk		*	F	.	≡PO	.	.	.
rl		.	.	.	F	.	.	.
rp		*	F	.	XPO	.	.	.
rv		*	.	F	.	.	.	.
rx		.	.	F$	.	.	.	.
sdli		.	.	.	.	.	.	FB

Name	Under	?	V7	BSD	SIII	XE2.3	XE3.0	SV
serial		*	.	.	.	.	F	.
st		.	.	.	F	.	.	.
sxt		.	.	.	.	.	.	F$
tc		.	F	.	.	.	.	.
termio		*	.	.	.	.	.	F
tm		*	F	X	≡PO	.	.	.
trace		.	.	.	F	.	.	≡
ts		*	.	F	.	.	.	.
tti		.	.	.	.	.	.	F
tty		*	F	>	X	≡	X	>
ttyd		*	.	.	.	.	.	FB
ttys		*	.	.	.	.	.	FB
tu		*	.	F	.	.	.	.
uda		.	.	F$	.	.	.	.
un		.	.	F$	.	.	.	.
up		*	.	F	.	.	.	.
uu		.	.	F$	.	.	.	.
va		*	.	F	.	.	.	.
vp		*	F	X	?	.	.	.
vpm		.	.	.	F	.	.	=
vv		.	.	F$	.	.	.	.

Notes on Drivers and Special Files

ad, adli

SV1 has an *ad*(7) that is a predecessor of SV2 *adli*(7), and completely different from BSD *ad*(4).

b3net

This device exists on SV1 only on the AT&T 3B5.

cons, console

XENIX *console*(4) and BSD *cons*(4) are both normally handled as ttys. XENIX 5.0 eliminates the */dev/color* and */dev/monochrome* files in favor of mapping the first several ttys to the screen. XENIX 3.0 provides ANSI terminal emulation; XENIX 5.0 extends this and adds elaborate keyboard-mapping control.

dk, dkraw

These Datakit interface drivers are supported only on 3B5 SV1.

dmc

The 4.2BSD *dmc*(4) is a network interface driver for the DEC DMC-11/DMR-11 communications device. The SIII version is also a DMC-11 driver, but not the same driver.

dn

V7 and SIII use files */dev/d[0-2]*. BSD *dn*(4) uses files */dev/cul[0-9]* and */dev/cua[0-9]*. SIII and BSD added the same code for a hook-flash to the V7 command set.

du

SIII *du*(4) relaxes V7's 512-byte limit, and uses */dev/du?* instead of */dev/dp0*.

dz

BSD *dz*(4) has undocumented support for 19200 baud. SIII *dz*(4) notes that 200bps and the EXTA, EXTB speeds are not supported.

dzk

SIII *dzk*(4) is supposed to behave identically to a dz board.

err, error

The SV *error*(7) device is a descendant of the SIII *err*(4) device.

hp

The mapping between *hp*(4) minor devices and */dev* names is different in the various versions that support this driver.

ht

BSD and V7 *ht*(4) handle different physical devices. SIII *ht*(4) device-naming conventions are incompatible with V7.

kmem, mem

BSD *mem*(4) notes VAX process-table addresses as well as those of the PDP-11. PDP-11 address information tends to disappear in later versions.

lp

SIII *lp*(4) has the same translation set as V7 but is otherwise incompatible. XENIX 2.3 *lp*(4) is idiosyncratic and completely incompatible with V7, SIII. XENIX 3.0 and 5.0 versions do no translation at all (however, 5.0 provides a device that converts NLs sent through it to CR-NL pairs).

mail

4.2BSD drops support for this device; it uses sockets instead.

nc, ni

These drivers are supported only on 3B5 SV1.

parallel

This entry is another view of the XENIX 5.0 *lp* devices.

pcl

The 4.2BSD and SIII *pcl*(4) features are both drivers for the DEC PCL-11B module, but are not the same driver.

ra

This device is not supported in 4.2BSD.

rk

V7 *rk*(4) documents one bug not mentioned in SIII.

rp

V7 and SIII *rp*(4) protocols are same, but their associated minor device names are different.

rv

This device is not supported in 4.2BSD.

serial

XENIX 3.0 uses *tty00* and *tty01* for serial ports; XENIX 5.0 uses *tty1[1234]*.

termio

SV renames the *tty*(4) documentation entry as *termio*(7).

tm

BSD *tm*(4)'s block length and other parameters are incompatible with V7 and SIII.

ts

The 4.2BSD version has been enhanced to support TU-80 tape drives.

tty

BSD *tty*(4) has a "new" mode with extra features (see manual). SIII *tty*(4) lacks V7 split-speed I/O, exclusive mode, and variable start/stops, but the interface has been cleaned up and rationalized. XENIX 2.3 *tty*(4) is modelled after V7's, while XENIX 3.0/5.0's is modelled after SIII's but uses DEC-style control and interrupt characters. SV calls this entry *termio*(7); XENIX 5.0 calls it *termio*(M) and uses the *tty*(M) entry to describe */dev/tty*.

ttyd, ttys

These Datakit interfaces are only available under SV1.

tu

The 4.2BSD version is substantially enhanced over its 4.1BSD predecessor.

up

The 4.2BSD version of this driver supports ECC correction and bad sector handling, and will recognize a wider range of disks automatically.

va

The 4.2BSD Varian driver can now coexist on the UNIBUS with exclusive-use devices.

vp

BSD *vp*(4) accepts a different set of *ioctl*(2) requests than V7's version. The SIII version's command language is probably a superset of V7's, but the SIII documentation to verify this doesn't seem to exist.

3.10 Section 5—File Formats and Conventions

System V has its file format descriptions in Section 4 rather than in the traditional Section 5. XENIX 3.0 and 5.0 call this Section "F", though some of the entries in the following table are in Section "M" instead.

Name	Under	?	V7	BSD	SIII	XE2.3	XE3.0	SV
86rel		.	.	.	.	.	F$	.
a.out		*	F	X	X	X	X	=
acct		*	F	X	>	X	≡	>
aliases		*	.	F	.	.	.	.
ar		*	F	X	>	≡	≡	X
backup		*	.	.	.	.	F	.
boothdr		.	.	.	.	.	.	FB
checklist		.	.	.	F	.	≡	≡
core		*	F	X	X	≡	>	≡
cpio		.	.	.	F	.	$	≡
ddate	dump	*	F	>	>	.	≡	.
dir		*	F	>	>	>	=	≡

Name	Under	?	V7	BSD	SIII	XE2.3	XE3.0	SV
disktab		.	.	F$	.	.	.	.
dump		*	F	=	=	≡	≡	.
errfile		*	.	.	F	.	.	X
filehdr		.	.	.	.	.	.	FC
environ		Y*	F	>	>7	≡	>	≡
fblk	filsys	.	F	>	.	>	>	.
filesystem		*	.	.	.	.	F	.
filsys		*	F	X	>	X	.	.
fs		*	.	F$	F	.	.	>
fspec		.	.	.	F	.	.	≡
fstab		.	.	F	.	≡	.	.
gettytab		.	.	F$	.	.	.	.
gettydefs		.	.	.	.	.	$	F
gps		.	.	.	F	.	.	≡
group		Y	F	≡	≡	≡	≡	≡
hosts		.	.	F$	.	.	.	.
inittab		*	.	.	F	.	.	>
ino	filsys	*	F	>	>	.	>	>
inode		*	.	.	F	.	=	≡
issue		.	.	.	.	.	.	F
ldfcn		.	.	.	.	.	.	FC
linenum		.	.	.	.	.	.	FC
master		*	.	.	F	.	X	>
mnttab		*	.	.	F	.	=	>
mpxio		*	F	>	.	.	.	.
mtab		*	F	≡	.	≡	.	.
networks		.	.	F$	.	.	.	.
phones		.	.	F$	.	.	.	.
printcap		.	.	F$	.	.	.	.
protocols		.	.	F$	.	.	.	.
passwd		Y*	F	>	>	=	=	≡
physio		.	.	.	.	F	.	.
plot		*	F	≡	X	≡	.	≡
pnch		.	.	.	F	.	.	≡
profile		.	.	.	F	.	.	≡
reloc		.	.	.	.	.	.	FC
remote		.	.	F$	.	.	.	.
sccsfile		*	.	.	F	.	=	>
scnhdr		.	.	.	.	.	.	FC
services		.	.	F$	.	.	.	.
stab		*	.	F	.	.	.	.
stat		*	.	.	.	.	F	.
syms		.	.	.	.	.	.	FC
system		.	.	.	.	.	.	FB
tar		*	.	F$	.	.	X$	.
termcap		*	.	F	≡	.	>	≡
tp		.	F	X	X	.	.	.
ttys		*	F	≡	.	≡	≡	.
ttytype		.	.	.	F	.	.	.
types		*	F	X	X	X	X	.
utmp		*	F	>	>	≡	≡	X
uuencode		.	.	F	.	.	.	.

Name	Under	?	V7	BSD	SIII	XE2.3	XE3.0	SV
vfont		.	.	F	.	.	.	.
vgrindefs		.	.	F$	.	.	.	.
wtmp	utmp	*	F	>	>	≡	≡	X
x.out		.	.	.	.	F	.	.

Notes on File Formats

a.out

Executable formats before COFF are heavily machine-dependent and incompatible. COFF does not make instruction-set differences go away, although it does promise mutually readable headers.

acct

BSD *acct*(5) has a different field order from the V7 original, a different *ac_io* field and no *ac_rw* field. XENIX 2.3 *acct* is identical to it. The *acct*(5) of AT&T and XENIX 3.0/5.0 documents a process-size formula.

aliases

XENIX 3.0/5.0 has an *aliases*(M) entry that is unrelated to the BSD mail alias facility. We list it in (7).

ar

BSD *ar*(5) format is incompatible with V7's; it has all printable fields in the header. The SIII *ar*(5) documentation omits some format information given in V7 but is otherwise the same. SV *ar*(5) on PDP11 is as SIII; the COFF version is different (and has printable headers).

Note that compatible formats do not necessarily imply compatibility of the binary layouts on transport tape or other media (see *arcv*(1M) for more on this topic).

backup

See the note for *dump*(5) under *ddate, dump*.

core

The SIII, XENIX 3.0/5.0, and SV *core*(5) is identical.

ddate, dump

The BSD *dump*(5) mentions two convenience macros DUMPOUTFMT, DUMPINFMT not described in V7. SIII *dump*(5) doesn't specify the *idates* structure fields. The 4.2BSD documentation claims that its version adds new fields, but this appears to be incorrect; the only noticeable difference from 4.1BSD is that the dump history is stored at */etc/dumpdates* rather than */etc/ddates*. XENIX 3.0/5.0 calls this format *backup*(5) to go with the renaming of the dump utility; XENIX 5.0 (following SIII) documents the same format under both *dump*(F) and *backup*(F) and makes both names of the command available.

dir

4.2BSD uses a fundamentally different directory structure from that of all other versions (which otherwise are compatible with each other). It is suggested for portability that all manipulation of directories from C be directed through a package that mimics the interface of *directory*(3) from 4.2BSD. Source code for such a package is given in Appendix D.

errfile

The SV *errfile*(5) documentation has more information than the SIII entry (including 3B-specific fields) in it.

environ

See the note for *login*(1). In SV and XENIX 5.0, this entry is moved to Section "M".

filesystem, filsys, fs

The SIII/SV file system format is listed under *fs*(5), V7/BSD/XENIX under *filsys*(5), and XENIX 3.0 and 5.0 under *filesystem*(F). Only *filsys*(5) describes the free block list element format.

The BSD and XENIX 2.3 *filsys*(5) superblock structures have extra fields at the end that are not present in its predecessor V7 version, and note that some others are not maintained. SV *fs* adds *s_fill*, *s_magic*, and *s_type* fields to the SIII version to support 1K-block file systems. The 4.2BSD entry has been rewritten to reflect the new Fast File System. XENIX 3.0 and 5.0 use the SIII superblock format.

inittab

SIII/SV *inittab*(5) performs the functions of V7/BSD/XENIX *ttys*(5). SV *inittab*(5) includes a detailed description of the operation of *init*(1) that is not included in the SIII version.

ino, inode

SIII/SV *dinode* is listed under *inode*(5). V7/BSD/XENIX 2.3 specifies this under *filsys*(5). All documented I-node formats except 4.2BSD's are identical.

master

SV *master* for DEC machines is compatible with SIII; there is a different COFF version. XENIX 3.0/5.0 introduces a new and (unsurprisingly) incompatible format. Both formats intend to convey device information to a configuration program.

mnttab, mtab

SIII/SV/XE3.0/XE5.0 *mnttab*(5) is functionally the same as V7/BSD/XENIX 2.3 *mtab*(5). The 4.2BSD format has been enhanced to include a type field giving the write-enable and quota-enable state. Otherwise, all *mtab*(5) formats are mutually compatible. The SV2 format has some character-array fields lengthened from 10 to 32. Otherwise, all *mnttab*(5) formats are mutually compatible.

mpxio

4.1BSD *mpxio*(5) adds the M_SIG control message to the V7 repertoire for support of the new tty driver. 4.2BSD doesn't support this format or its associated drivers.

passwd

The BSD *passwd*(5) format uses the GCOS field for address and full name information via *finger*(1) and *chfn*(1). The SIII/SV/XE3.0/XE5.0 *passwd*(5) facility supports password aging. The XENIX 2.3 *passwd*(5) documentation mentions that some programs will fail if the "root" or "daemon" entry is missing. XENIX also refers to the GCOS field as "comment." All the password file formats are compatible.

plot

SIII/SV *plot*(5) does not mention the a and c commands of V7.

sccsfile

System V adds a new @f z flag with entirely insufficient explanation.

stab

The 4.2BSD documentation has been revised and expanded to reflect the new capabilities of *pc*(1) and *dbx*(1).

stat

In XENIX 3.0/5.0 only, there is a *stat* structure documentation entry grouped with other entries that in non-XENIX dialects are found in Section 5. See also *stat*(2).

tar

Only 4.2BSD and XENIX 5.0 document their *tar* formats. XENIX 5.0 adds three fields to the *hblock* structure to track extent sizes.

termcap

XENIX 5.0 *termcap*(M) lists some additional capabilities not supported by other versions. Notice that SV2 replaces this with the *terminfo*(3) facility, which is not strictly upward-compatible.

ttys

In 4.3BSD the *ttys*(4) format absorbs the function of the */etc/ttytype* file. The new format has four fields: (1) a tty line name; (2) a command (typically a *getty*) with arguments, to be executed on the line; (3) a termcap type; and (4) an activation and security status field. Comments are allowed after the last data field.

XENIX 3.0/5.0 lists this in Section "M".

types

Only types *d_addr*, *c_addr*, *ino_t*, *time_t*, *dev_t*, and *off_t* are compatible across the documented systems.

utmp, wtmp

The SV *utmp*(5) format has been enlarged and revamped to do more precise accounting than in previous versions. The 4.2BSD format adds a field to track remote logins. XENIX 3.0/5.0 has it in Section "M".

3.11 Section 6—Games

Many "business-oriented" packagings of these dialects (in particular, XENIX 3.0 and various SV versions) omit the games section. Those responsible will doubtless be reincarnated as worker insects of some sort. XENIX 5.0 optionally provides games but no printed documentation for them.

Name	Under	?	V7	BSD	SIII	XE2.3	SV
aardvark		*	.	F	.	.	.
adventure		.	.	F	.	.	.
aliens		*	.	F	.	.	.
arithmetic		Y	F	≡	≡	≡	≡
back		*	.	.	F	.	≡
backgammon		*	F	≡	.	>	.
banner		*	F	>	X1	.	X1
bcd		.	F	>	.	.	.
bj		.	F	.	≡	.	≡
boggle		.	.	F	.	.	.
canfield		.	.	F$	.	.	.
chase		*	.	F	.	.	.
checkers		.	F	.	.	.	.
chess		*	F	≡	>P	.	XP
ching		*	F	≡	.	≡	.
craps		.	.	.	F	.	≡
cribbage		.	.	F	.	.	.
cubic	ttt	.	F	.	≡	.	≡
doctor		.	.	F	.	.	.
factor		.	.	F$	.	.	.
fish		.	.	F	.	.	.
fortune	ching	*	F	≡	.	>	.
hangman		*	F	X	>	>	≡
jotto		.	.	.	.	.	F
maze		.	F	.	≡P	.	≡
mille		*	.	F	.	.	.

Name	Under	?	V7	BSD	SIII	XE2.3	SV
moo		.	F	.	≡	.	≡
monop		.	.	F	.	.	.
number		.	.	F	.	.	.
ppt	bcd	.	F	.	.	.	.
primes		.	.	F$	.	.	.
quiz		Y	F	≡	≡	≡	≡
rain		.	.	F	.	.	.
reversi		*	F	.	>P	.	≡P
rogue		*	.	F	.	.	.
sail		.	.	F$	.	.	.
sky		.	.	.	FP	.	≡P
snake		.	.	F	.	.	.
trek		.	.	F	.	.	.
ttt		.	F	.	≡	.	≡
words		.	F	.	.	>	.
worm		.	.	·F	.	.	.
worms		.	.	FP	.	.	≡P
wump		.	F	≡	≡P	>	.
zork		.	.	F	.	.	.

Notes on Games

aardvark

This game no longer works on 4.2BSD because the Dungeon Definition Language doesn't work, but the DDL source is still present.

aliens

This game is not included with 4.2BSD.

back, backgammon

On SIII/SV, the V7 *backgammon*(6) is replaced by a program called *back*(6), which has more features. The 4.2BSD version of *backgammon*(6) has been given a screen-oriented interface via *curses*(3).

banner

V7/BSD/XENIX *banner*(6) prints sideways; BSD lets you specify a print width via a -w option. SIII/SV *banner*(1) prints up to 10 chars per line in large upright letters.

chase

This game is not available under 4.2BSD.

chess

BSD *chess*(6) cheats; every time this author has attempted check or has trapped the queen, the program has responded "Illegal move." SIII/SV1 *chess*(6) is a different version that has on-line help and an associated tutorial. SV *chess*(6) lacks the chess rules tutorial.

ching, fortune

XENIX 2.3 lists *ching*(6) under *fortune*(6), in reverse of the practice of V7/BSD. 4.2BSD *ching*(6) pipes its output through *more*(1).

hangman

V7 *hangman* is listed under *words*(6). BSD *hangman*(6) doesn't accept V7's alternate word-list file argument. BSD adds a screen-oriented interface.

mille

The 4.2BSD version is claimed to play more intelligently than the 4.1BSD version.

reversi

SIII/SV *reversi*(6) has enhancements over the V7/BSD version including a shell escape command, and its documentation describes diagnostic messages.

rogue

The 4.2BSD version is said to have made this game more of a scoundrel.

3.12 Section 7—Miscellanea

In System V, this section is replaced by Section 5, "Miscellanea." XENIX 3.0 and 5.0 call this Section "M" (Miscellaneous), and include device driver, environment, and maintainence command descriptions that we have put in Sections 1M, 5, and 7.

Name	Under	?	V7	BSD	SIII	XE2.3	XE3.0	SV
ascii		Y*	F	>	>	≡	≡	≡
default		.	.	.	.	F	≡	.
environ		*	F	>	>	≡	>	≡
eqnchar		.	F	≡	≡	.	≡	≡
fcntl		*	.	.	F	.	.	>
greek		.	.	F	≡	>	≡	≡
hier		.	F	>	.	>	.	.
mailaddr		.	.	F$	.	.	.	.
man		Y*	F	≡	>	≡	.	≡
me		.	.	F	.	.	.	.
messages		.	.	.	.	.	F	.
micnet		.	؛	.	.	.	F	.
mm		.	.	.	F	.	≡	≡
mosdd		.	.	.	.	.	≡	F
mptx		.	.	.	.	.	.	F
ms		*	F	>	.	>	≡	.
mv		*	.	.	F	.	.	>
profile		.	.	.	.	.	F	.
regexp		.	.	.	F	.	≡	≡
stat		.	.	.	F	.	≡	≡
systemid		.	.	.	.	.	F	.
sxt		.	.	.	.	.	.	F
vsxt		.	.	.	.	.	.	F
term		*	F	>	>	≡	>	>
terminals		*	.	.	.	.	F	.
top		.	.	.	.	.	F	.
top.next		.	.	.	.	.	F	.
ttys		.	.	.	.	.	F	.
types		*	.	.	F	.	>	.

Notes on Miscellanea

ascii

BSD, SIII, and SV *ascii*(7) include a hexadecimal character map.

environ

See also *environ*(5).

fcntl

The SV1 entry for this is effectively identical to SIII's; the SV2 entry adds features related to file extent locking.

man

SIII/SV *man*(7) accepts some page-size options not supported in the V7/BSD/XENIX version and has more formatting requests.

ms

XENIX *ms*(7) omits the Bell Labs identification macros included in the ancestral V7/BSD and other versions. The 4.2BSD version has many enhancements over its 4.1BSD predecessor.

mv

The SV *mv*(7) version adds a summary of the available calls to the SIII documentation entry.

term

The SV list is similar to SIII's except that it contains a "sync" entry to describe synchronous Teletype 4540-compatible terminals. XENIX 2.3's list is the same as V7's, except for two entries ("trs16" and "adds25") added to describe TRS-specific hardware. The XENIX column in the following table refers to XENIX 3.0; notice that since the XENIX documentation describes the list as partial we have marked terminal types as portable even though they are excluded from it.

Name	?	V7	BSD	XE3.0	AT&T	Type
1520	.	.	.	F	F	Datamedia 1520
1620	Y	F	F	F	F	Diablo 1620/HiType II
1620-12	.	F	.	F	F	1620 in 12-pitch mode
2621	.	.	F	F	F	Hewlett-Packard 262x
2631	.	.	.	F	F	HP 2631 line printer
2631-c	.	.	.	F	F	HP 2631 - compressed mode
2631-c	.	.	.	F	F	HP 2631 - expanded mode
2640	.	.	.	F	F	HP 2640 series
2645	.	.	.	F	F	HP 264x, x != 1
300	Y	F	F	F	F	DASI/DTC/GSI 300/HiType I
300-12	.	F	.	F	F	300 in 12-pitch mode
300s	.	F	.	F	F	DASI/DTC 300/S
300s-12	.	F	.	F	F	300/S in 12-pitch mode
3045	.	.	.	F	F	Datamedia 3045
3101	.	.	.	F	.	IBM 3101
3270	.	.	.	F	F[1]	IBM 3270
33	Y	F	F	F	F	Teletype Model 33
37	Y	F	F	F	F	Teletype Model 37
382	.	.	.	F	F	DTC 382
40-2	.	F	.	F	F	Teletype Model 40-2

Name	?	V7	BSD	XE3.0	AT&T	Type
40-4	.	.	.	F	F	Teletype Model 40-4
4000a	.	.	.	F	F	Trendata 4000a
4014	Y	F	F	F	F	Textronix 4014
43	Y	F	F	F	F	Teletype Model 43
450	Y	F	.	F	F	DASI 450 (same as 1620)
450-12	.	F	.	.	F	DASI 450 in 12-pitch
450-12-8	.	F	.	.	F	450-12 at 8 lpi.
4540	.	.	.	.	F	Teletype Model 4540
500BCT	.	.	.	.	F[1]	Teletype Model 5541
735	Y	F	F	F	F	Texas Instruments TI725/735
745	Y	F	F	F	F	Texas Instruments TI745
adm3a	.	.	F	.	.	Lear-Siegler ADM-3A
c100	.	.	F	.	.	HDS Concept 100
dialup	.	.	F$	.	.	unknown phone dialin
dumb	Y	F	F	F	F	no special features
dw1	.	.	.	.	.	DECWriter I
dw2	.	.	.	.	.	DECWriter II
h19	.	.	F	.	.	Heathkit H19
h1000	.	.	.	.	.	Hazeltine 1000
h1500	.	.	.	.	.	Hazeltine 1500
h1510	.	.	.	.	.	Hazeltine 1510
h1520	.	.	.	.	.	Hazeltine 1520
h1552	.	.	.	.	.	Hazeltine 1552
h2000	.	.	.	.	.	Hazeltine 2000
hp	Y	F	F	F	F	Hewlett-Packard HP264x
lp	.	.	.	F	F	generic line printer
mime	.	.	F	.	.	Microterm mime
network	.	.	F$	.	.	unknown network dialin
ti700	.	.	.	.	.	Texas Instruments TI700
ti745	.	.	.	.	.	Texas Instruments TI745
tn300	.	F	.	F	F	GE TermiNet 300
tn1200	.	F	.	F	F	GE TermiNet 1200
vt05	.	F	.	.	F	DEC VT05
vt50	.	.	.	.	.	DEC VT50
vt50h	.	.	.	.	.	DEC VT50h
vt52	.	.	F	.	.	DEC VT52
vt100	.	.	.	.	.	DEC VT100
vt100s	.	.	.	.	.	DEC VT100 (132 cols, 14 rows)
vt100w	.	.	.	.	.	DEC VT100 (132 cols)
z19	.	.	.	.	.	Zenith Z19
z29	.	.	.	.	.	Zenith Z29

[1] These terminals are supported in SV only.

terminals

   Notice that BSD, XENIX 2.3 and 3.0, and SV all support *termcap*(3).
This entry, found in XENIX 3.0 and 5.0 only, is a list of terminals supported
in the termcap database. A 4.1BSD column (generated from the termcap file

of the authors' home site) is included for comparison. This table makes no claims to completeness; its main purpose is to point users at the standard names for their terminal types, so some variant names of terminals used to indicate obscure option settings have been omitted.

Name	4.1BSD	XE3.0	XE5.0	Type
1200	F	.	.	Terminet 1200
1620	F	.	.	Diablo 1620
1640	F	.	.	Diablo 1640
2621	F	.	F	Hewlett-Packard 2621
2621wl	.	.	F	2621 with labels
2640	F	.	.	Hewlett-Packard 2640a
2640b	F	.	.	Hewlett-Packard 264x series
300	F	.	.	Terminet 300
3045	F	.	F	Datamedia 3045a
4025	F	.	F	Tektronix 4024/4025/4027
4025-17	F	.	F	Tektronix 4025 w/17-line window
4025-17ws	F	.	F	Tektronix 4025 w/17-line workspace
4025ex	F	.	F	Tektronix 4025
8001	F	.	F	ISC 8001
912b	F	.	F	new Televideo 912/920
925	.	.	F	newer Televideo
TWO	.	.	F	Altos Computer Systems II
a980	F	.	F	ADDS consul 980
aaa	F	.	F	Ann Arbor ambassador/48 lines
aaadb	F	.	F	Ann Arbor ambassador 48/destructive backspace
act5s	F	.	F	skinny act5
adds	.	.	F	ADDS Viewpoint
adm2	F	.	.	Lear-Siegler ADM2
adm3	F	.	.	Lear-Siegler ADM3
adm12	.	.	F	Lear-Siegler ADM12
adm31	F	.	F	Lear-Siegler ADM31
adm3a	F	.	F	Lear-Siegler ADM3a
adm3a+	F	.	.	Lear-Siegler ADM 3a+
adm42	F	.	F	Lear-Siegler ADM42
adm5	F	.	.	Lear-Siegler ADM5
aj830	F	.	.	Anderson-Jacobson daisywheel
ampex	F	.	F	Ampex dialogue 80
annarbor	F	.	.	Ann Arbor
ansi	.	.	F	XENIX standard entry for PCs
arpanet	F	.	.	network
bh3m	F	.	F	BeehiveIIIm
big2621	F	.	.	48 line 2621
c100	F	.	F	Concept 100
c108	F	.	.	Concept 108
c3102	.	.	F	Cromemco 3102
cci	.	.	F	cci 4574
cdc456	F	.	F	dc
cdc456tst	F	.	F	dc456tst
cdi	F	.	.	cdi1203
cit	.	.	F	C. Itoh 80
compucolor	F	.	.	compucolorII

Name	4.1BSD	XE3.0	XE5.0	Type
ct220	F	.	.	Intecolor Color Trend 220
d132	F	.	F	datagraphix 132a
d800	F	.	.	Direct 800/A
datapoint	F	.	F	datapoint 3360
delta	F	.	F	Delta Data 5000
dg6053	F	.	.	Data General 6053
dialup	F	.	.	unknown phone dialin
digilog	F	.	F	Digilog 333
dm1520	F	.	F	Datamedia 1520
dm1521	F	.	F	Datamedia 1521
dm2500	F	.	F	Datamedia 2500
dm3025	F	.	F	Datamedia 3025a
dt80	F	.	F	Datamedia dt80/1
dt80132	F	.	F	Datamedia dt80/1 in 132 char mode
dtc300s	F	.	.	dtc 300s
du	.	.	F	dialup
dumb	F	.	F	unknown
dw1	F	F	.	Decwriter I
dw2	F	F	.	Decwriter II
ep40	F	.	F	Execuport 4000
ep48	F	.	F	Execuport 4080
ethernet	F	.	.	network
exidy	F	.	F	Exidy sorcerer as dm2500
fox	F	.	F	Perkin-Elmer 1100
fre100	.	.	F	Freedom 100
gt40	F	.	.	DEC gt40
gt42	F	.	.	DEC gt42
h1000	F	F	.	Hazeltine 1000
h1500	F	F	F	Hazeltine 1500
h1510	F	F	F	Hazeltine 1510
h1520	F	F	F	Hazeltine 1520
h1552	F	F	.	Hazeltine 1552
h1552rv	F	.	.	Hazeltine 1552 reverse video
h19	F	F	F	Heathkit h19
h2000	F	F	.	Hazeltine 2000
hp	.	.	F	Hewlett-Packard hp264x
hp2626	F	.	.	Hewlett-Packard 2626
hp2645	F	.	.	Hewlett-Packard 264x series
hp2648	F	.	.	Hewlett-Packard 2648a graphics terminal
i100	F	.	.	General Terminal 100A (formerly Infoton 100)
i400	F	.	.	Infoton 400
ibm	F	.	F	IBM 3101-10
inText	.	.	F	ISC-modified Owl 1200
lisa	.	.	F	Lisa console
lisawb	.	.	F	Lisa console (reverse video)
mdl110	F	.	.	Cybernex mdl-110
mdl120	F	.	.	Cybernex mdl-120
microb	F	.	F	Micro Bee series
microterm	F	.	F	Microterm act iv
microterm5	F	.	F	Microterm act v
mime	F	.	F	Microterm mime
mw2	F	.	.	Multiwriter 2

Name	4.1BSD	XE3.0	XE5.0	Type
netx	F	.	.	Netronics
oadm31	F	.	.	old ADM31
omron	F	.	.	Omron 8025AG
ovt100	F	.	.	DEC vt100
owl	F	.	F	perkin elmer 1200
pe550	F	.	.	perkin elmer 550
pixel	.	.	F	Pixel terminal
qume5	F	.	.	Qume Sprint 5
regent	F	.	F	ADDS regent series
regent100	F	.	F	ADDS regent 100
regent20	F	.	.	ADDS regent 20
regent25	F	.	F	ADDS regent 25
regent25a	.	.	F	ADDS regent 25
regent40	F	.	.	ADDS regent 40
regent60	F	.	.	ADDS Regent 60
sb1	F	.	F	Beehive SuperBee
sb2	F	.	F	fixed SuperBee
superbeeic	F	.	F	SuperBee with insert character
soroc	F	.	F	Soroc 120
switch	F	.	.	intelligent switch
swtp	F	.	.	Southwest Technical Products ct82
t1061	F	.	F	teleray 1061
t3700	F	.	F	dumb Teleray 3700
t3800	F	.	F	Teleray 3800 series
Tek	F	.	F	Tektronix 4012
Tek4013	F	.	.	Tektronix 4013
Tek4014	F	.	F	Tektronix 4014
Tek4015	F	.	.	Tektronix 4015
Tek4023	F	.	F	Tektronix 4023
teletec	F	.	.	Teletec Datascreen
terak	F	.	.	Terak emulating Datamedia 1520
ti700	F	F	.	Texas Instruments TI700
ti745	F	F	.	TI silent 745
ti800	F	.	.	TI omni 800
tty33	F	.	.	model 33 teletype
tty37	F	.	.	model 37 teletype
tty43	F	.	.	model 43 teletype
tv970	F	.	.	Televideo 970 in vt-100 mode
tvi910	.	.	F	old Televideo 910
tvi910+	.	.	F	old Televideo 910+
tvi912	F	.	F	old Televideo 912
tvi950	F	.	F	Televideo950
vc303	F	.	.	Volker-craig 303
vc303a	F	.	.	Volker-craig 303a
vc404	F	.	.	Volker-craig 404
vi50	F	.	F	Visual 50
vi55	F	.	F	Visual 55
vi200	F	.	F	Visual 200
vt100	F	F	F	DEC VT100
vt100s	F	F	F	DEC VT100 (132 cols, 14 l)
vt100w	F	F	F	DEC VT100 (132 cols)
vt132	F	.	.	vt-132

Name	4.1BSD	XE3.0	XE5.0	Type
vt50	F	F	.	DEC VT50
vt50h	F	F	.	DEC VT50h
vt52	F	F	F	DEC VT52
x1720	F	.	.	Xerox 1720
xiTex	F	.	.	xiTex sct-100
xl83	F	.	.	Cybernex XL-83
z19	.	F	.	Zenith Z19
z29	.	F	.	Zenith Z29
wy100	F	.	F	Wyse 100
zen30	F	.	F	Zentec 30

types

SV *types*(5) doesn't include the processor dependencies of its SIII counterpart, *types*(7). See also *types*(5).

4

I/O, SIGNALS,
AND DATA PORTABILITY

One place where portability problems commonly arise is in moving data between a program and its environment, whether the interface is to a terminal, a file, or another program. This problem is eased considerably with C because there are no I/O statements in C, only function calls. In many other languages that have language-defined I/O statements, extensions created to solve perceived inadequacies lead to portability problems among compiler implementations. In C, there are no predefined I/O statements. The I/O functions of the UNIX C library (usually supplied with C compilers on other systems) provide a lowest-common-denominator interface upon which a programmer can build. The programmer can replace these I/O functions to create a portable special-purpose I/O interface.

However, portability is still a problem when dealing with the UNIX *ioctl*(2) interface to *tty* device drivers and when performing I/O with other processes via interprocess communications and signals. In this chapter, we take a more detailed look at these areas.

Section 4.1 explains incompatibilities between the V7/BSD and AT&T versions of *ioctl*(2) and suggests two methods of defining portable interfaces.

Section 4.2 discusses some issues relating to the portable and safe use of signals.

Section 4.3 discusses the problem of data interchange between processes on dissimilar machines and proposes several solutions.

Section 4.4 discusses problems with portable handling of UNIX system directories due to the design changes in 4.2BSD and 4.3BSD, and indicates a solution.

4.1 The *ioctl*(2) System Call

The *ioctl*(2) call is the only major Version 7 system call that is not directly portable to all subsequent UNIX system dialects. Its general function is to pass control messages to and accept responses from the kernel I/O code and device drivers. The incompatibilities among various *ioctl* implementations are of three kinds:

1. In V7, *ioctl*(2) could be used to set or unset a flag associated with each file telling whether it is to be automatically closed during a successful *exec*(2) of the calling process. This minor and obscure use of the call did not mesh well with the rest of its uses as an I/O control mediator; SIII moved the function into its new general file control call, *fcntl*(2). The Berkeley versions, in this as in much else, retained the V7 arrangement. Code is given below that defines a portable interface to this feature for both families of systems.

2. *ioctl*(2) is used on all systems to pass requests to I/O drivers. Only the trivial null device and *tty*(4) are common to all versions. Code for masking the numerous *ioctl*(2) request differences between the original V7/BSD/XENIX 2.3 *tty* driver and the redesigned SIII/SV/XENIX 3.0 version is given in the next section.

3. The *ioctl*(2) call has often been called "the back door into the kernel." It has traditionally been used to control all manner of version-dependent, hardware-dependent, and even individual installation-dependent features via (occasionally quite large) classes of new requests. Each of these uses is highly nonportable.

The next two subsections discuss the portable uses of *ioctl*(2) in some detail.

4.1.1 Manipulation of the Close-on-Exec Flag

The close-on-exec flag is an attribute associated with each open file in a process. If it is on, and the process performs an *exec*(2) system call or any of its library variants, then the file will be closed and its resources released at the time of the *exec*(2) call.

The flag is off by default. We will define two macros, "CLEXEC" and "NCLEXEC", to expand to the appropriate calls depending on the version of the system on which the compile is taking place; see the following listings. The first version is used on AT&T and descendent systems:

```
/* clexec.h —— portable set and clear of close—on—exec flag */

/* This version is for AT&T System III and System V. */

#include <fcntl.h>

/* Set close—on—exec flag */
#define CLEXEC(fd)      fcntl(fd, F_SETFD, 1)

/* Clear close—on—exec flag */
#define NCLEXEC(fd)     fcntl(fd, F_SETFD, 0)

/* End of clexec.h */
```

The following version is used on V7, Berkeley, and descendent systems:

```
/* clexec.h —— portable set and clear of close—on—exec flag */

/* This version is for Version 7, Berkeley 4.1 and 4.2,
   and XENIX 2.3.                                        */

#include <sys/ioctl.h>

/* Set close—on—exec flag */
#define CLEXEC(fd)    ioctl(fd, FIOCLEX, 0)

/* Clear close—on—exec flag */
#define NCLEXEC(fd)   ioctl(fd, FIONCLEX, 0)

/* End of clexec.h */
```

4.1.2 Version Differences in tty Control

There are two major versions of UNIX system terminal driver. The original version is found in V7 and its direct derivatives (including XENIX 2.3 and the Berkeley versions). A redesigned version with rationalized data structures is found in AT&T versions beginning with SIII.

The Version 7 and XENIX 2.3 documentation for *tty*(4) is identical, except that XENIX refers to DEL as INTERRUPT and gives several keys that may trigger it. It also corrects a typo in the V7 manual that has TIOCSETP as the name of the last call rather than TIOCGETC, and explains the last two calls slightly more clearly.

BSD's *tty*(4) is a compatible extension of the V7 driver, but its documentation is quite different. Many features have been added to handle job control and other Berkeley extensions.

The SIII/XENIX 3.0/SV *tty*(4) driver is quite different from V7/BSD/XENIX 2.3's. The terminal parameter and terminal character structures are consolidated into one. The *ioctl*(2) request codes are not the same.

Fortunately, its functionality is similar, so it is reasonable to write a portable tty-control interface.

Before discussing the implementation of portable tty handling, it should be noted that the following V7 features are not portable:

1. Split-speed I/O (SIII doesn't support separate input and output rates).
2. Exclusive-use mode (there is no corresponding SIII ioctl call).
3. Hangup-on-last-close (the V7 and SIII calls have different side-effects).
4. Variable start and stop characters (no SIII support).
5. Delays for carriage movement, and so on, support similar functions but are not completely portable. The only one that we support here is the tab expansion control (XTABS).

4.1.3 Methods of Portable tty Control

In this section, we describe a portable interface to the version-independent features of tty drivers. The implementation consists of a header file, *ttyport.h*, that creates a common base of structures and definitions, and a set of calls that define a portable interface layer to version-dependent implementations. These calls can be written as a library of functions or as an #include file of macros, according to the reader's preference. If a macro implementation is chosen, all names should be made uppercase (see Section 2.7.2).

Header files containing necessary #defines and structures are shown in the following listings. The two versions shown define the same names, although their expansions differ considerably. The first version is used on AT&T systems and their descendents:

```
/* ttyport.h -- definitions for portable tty control
               AT&T version                              */

/* include structure definition for termio */
#include <termio.h>

/* define bit fields that aren't already in termio.h */
#define RAW          0
#define RARE         ISIG      /* no line discipline */
#define COOKED       03        /* = ICANON ¦ ISIG      */
#define OCRMOD       041       /* = ONLCR  ¦ OPOST     */
#define EVEN         01000     /* = PARENB             */
#define ODD          01400     /* = PARENB ¦ PARODD    */
#define NONE         0
#define XTABS        TAB3      /* Expand tabs          */

/* End of ttyport.h */
```

The following version is used on V7/BSD-derived systems:

```
/* ttyport.h -- definitions for portable tty control
                non-AT&T version                        */

#include <sgtty.h>    /* tty structure definitions */

/* define a termio structure - compatible
   with AT&T version in name only.           */
struct termio
{
     struct sgttyb   parms;   /* control parameters */
     struct tchars   chars;   /* special characters */
}

/* masks for sg_flags access that aren't already in sgtty.h */
#define LINEDFLD      042     /* = RAW ¦ RARE */
#define COOKED        0
#define RARE          002     /* RAW defined in sgtty.h */
#define NONE          0300    /* = EVENP ¦ ODDP */
#define EVEN          EVENP
#define ODD           ODDP
/*      XTABS         is defined in sgtty.h */

/* End of ttyport.h */
```

The following are synopses of calls that (when fully implemented) define the set of portable calls for tty control. *fd* denotes a file descriptor argument and *ptio* is a pointer to a termio structure.

The following calls do physical I/O to get or set a terminal's control parameters:

gtty(ptio, fd)	copy fd's terminal modes to local *ptio
sttynow(ptio, fd)	set terminal control from *ptio
sttywait(ptio, fd)	as sttynow, but wait for output to flush
tflush(fd)	flush terminal I/O queues

All of the following calls may be used after a *gtty* call is used to access the current terminal settings and before a *sttynow* or *sttywait* call is used to write those modified settings.

The following requests query the special-character definition fields of a *termio* structure (*ptio):

erasec(ptio)	return current erase character
killc(ptio)	return current kill character
intrc(ptio)	return current SIGINT character
quitc(ptio)	return current kill character
eofc(ptio)	return current eof character
brkc(ptio)	return current kill character

The following requests set the special character definition fields of a *termio* structure (*ptio):

seterasec(ptio, ch)	set erase character to ch
setkillc(ptio, ch)	set kill character to ch
setintrc(ptio, ch)	set interrupt character to ch
setquitc(ptio, ch)	set kill character to ch
seteofc(ptio, ch)	set eof character to ch
setbrkc(ptio, ch)	set kill character to ch

These requests may be used to query the line control fields of a *termio* structure (*ptio):

speed(ptio)	return current baud rate value
parity(ptio)	return current parity setting
protcl(ptio)	return current protocol

These requests will modify the line control fields of a local *termio* structure (*ptio):

setspeed(ptio, speed)	set baud rate to speed
setparity(ptio, par)	set parity
setprotcl(ptio, flag)	set/clear protocol according to flag

Use the #defines B0 = 0...B9600 = 15 for *setspeed()*'s speed argument and for comparisons with the return of *speed()*. Similarly use the EVEN/ODD/NONE symbolic constants for *setparity()* and comparisons with the return of *parity()*; their values differ between V7 and SIII but the symbolic names are the same.

The following requests return the current settings of I/O modes in a *termio* structure (*ptio):

iedit(ptio)	return current I/O edit mode
iecho(ptio)	return state of echo flag
ilcase(ptio)	return state of lowercase enable flag
icrmod(ptio)	return state of CR-translation flag

These requests modify the I/O mode settings in a *termio* structure (*ptio):

setiedit(ptio, mode)	set I/O edit mode (RAW, RARE, COOKED)
setiecho(ptio, flag)	set/clear input echo flag
setilcase(ptio, flag)	set/clear lowercase enable flag
seticrmod(ptio, flag)	set/clear CR-translation flag

The following steps show how to modify a terminal's behavior using these calls:

1. Allocate a *termio* structure to hold a copy of the terminal's control words. The type `struct termio` may be used as a normal C structure in all respects except that its fields must not be accessed directly (the members vary between V7 and SIII).
2. Copy the terminal's parameters into the structure with *gtty()*.
3. Use the calls described above to examine and/or modify the values of the *termio* structure.
4. Write the modified parameters to the driver with *sttynow()* or *sttywait()*.

To illustrate the usage, here is a code fragment that sets a terminal to raw mode using the foregoing definitions:

```
#include <portable.h>   /* portable definitions file */
#include "ttyport.h"    /* portable tty definitions  */

/* declare a termio structure for the terminal */
private struct termio myterm;

        /* application code ... */

        gtty(&myterm, 0);        /* get stdin's control data   */
        setiedit(&myterm, RAW);  /* set RAW mode control       */
        sttywait(&myterm, 0);    /* write stdin's control data */

        /* more application code ... */
```

We have deliberately omitted checking and handling of error returns in order to make the example more readable. Any complete implementation should include thorough handling of all error conditions.

4.2 Signal Handling

Signals and signal catching have been an area fraught with design problems, bugs, and implementation problems since before V7. One significant addition to the V7 kernel design, introduced in 4.1BSD, was an attempt to resolve this problem by a complete redesign of the signals package (the new *sygsys*(2) facility). The *signals*(2) call was left untouched for compatibility with old and imported code. This innovation proved successful and became a major argument in favor of the Berkeley versions.

In 4.2BSD, the original *signals*(2) package was replaced with a descendent of 4.1BSD *sigsys*(2) that provided both a cleaner theoretical model and a better match with the VAX hardware interrupt facilities. However, the lack of an optional compatibility package for old and imported code created some severe portability problems.

Here are the major changes that were made in 4.2BSD signal handling that functionally distinguish it from both the V7 facilities retained in 4.1BSD and the AT&T versions:

1. Signal handlers are not reset to SIG_DFL on receipt of a signal, but retain the value set by the user.
2. While a signal handler is executing, the process is blocked against the signal that triggered it. This eliminates some nasty race conditions.
3. The system calls (including I/O) have been re-implemented so that if a signal arrives during system call execution, appropriate context is saved, and when the handler exits, execution is resumed exactly where it left off. This implies that to interrupt the system call, it is necessary to unwind the stack using the *setjmp*(2)/*longjmp*(2) facilities.

Consider, as an example of these differences, the following code:

```
/* a timed read function for all versions */

#include <signal.h>

#ifdef    BSD4_2
#include <setjmp.h>
jmp_buf   ajmpbuf;       /* if in 4.2, must allocate space for context */
#endif

private int alarmtrap()
/* this is what gets executed when an alarm signal hits */
{
#ifndef   BSD4_2
    signal(SIGALRM, alarmtrap);    /* keep the signal trapped to here */
#else                              /* in 4.2 it won't be reset        */
    longjmp(ajmpbuf, 1);           /* but we have to unwind the stack */
#endif
}
```

```
rivate int timed_read(fd, timeout, buffer, buflen)
* return -1 if the read fails or times out */
nt  fd;            /* file descriptor to read from */
nt  timeout;       /* timeout in seconds          */
har *buffer;       /* where to put the output     */
nt  buflen;        /* how much output to accept   */

    int r;

    signal(SIGALRM, alarmtrap);    /* set the trap  */
    alarm(timeout);                /* set the alarm */

ifdef   BSD4_2
    if (setjmp(ajmpbuf) == 0)      /* unwind back to here in 4.2 */
endif
        r = read(0, buffer, buflen);  /* do a (blocking) read     */

    alarm(0);                      /* important if we succeeded */
    return r;
```

Notice that in 4.2BSD the longjmp(ajmpbuf, 1) causes the control flow to return to the point of the setjmp on receipt of the SIGALRM, but then fails the if (and skips reexecution of the *read*(2) call) due to the return of 1.

Notice also that a *setjmp/longjmp* control flow *will* work on non-4.2BSD versions. Thus, for portability, it is recommended that *setjmp/longjmp* be used to handle all signal interruptions of I/O calls (as in 4.2BSD). Notice further that the signal reset in the alarm trap function is not necessary in 4.2BSD, but does no harm there and is necessary everywhere else. In general, for portability, don't assume that signal traps will remain set after signal receipt; do the reset explicitly in the handler.

The 4.3BSD version retreated from the extreme 4.2BSD position by allowing the user to choose, on a per-signal basis, whether or not system calls should be restarted following a signal interrupt. This eliminated the problem mentioned under (3) above, satisfying the most serious objections to the new package.

4.3 External Data Format Portability

4.3.1 The Problem

For any program or system of programs that execute on a single processor or multiple processors of a single type, data storage formats should not be a problem and programs may share data of arbitrarily complex structure.

When data is passed between programs running on different machines, major portability problems may arise from differing representations of data. This situation can occur if:

● existing binary data files are moved to another machine as part of an application port

● the application is moved to a distributed system in which dissimilar processors must exchange data

There are several factors affecting storage of structured binary data:

Sizes of primitive data types—These are machine dependent, especially the number of bytes in an `int`.

Byte-order—Some machines store multibyte primitive data type objects from high-order to low-order byte, some do the reverse; in general, the internal byte-order of any object should be considered totally arbitrary.

Address boundary alignment—Some machines allow multibyte objects to begin on any memory address, some require alignment to even-address boundaries, and some require alignment to four-byte boundaries.

Data formats—For floating point numbers, the size of the mantissa and exponent, base of the exponent, and normalization rules may all differ. For integer numbers, a (very unlikely) problem is two's complement versus one's complement and signed-magnitude representations and arithmetic.

The varying size of data elements coupled with the address boundary alignment requirements causes differences in the amount and location of padding within a structure; for instance, the following structure:

```
struct example
    {
    char   ch;
    short  i;
    long   l;
    };
```

on a machine with no alignment requirements would look like this (the `i.x` notation refers to the bytes of the variable `i`):

```
 ┆ ch   ┆ i.0 ┆ i.1 ┆ 1.0 ┆ 1.1 ┆ 1.2 ┆ 1.3 ┆
```

but on a machine requiring even-address boundaries, padding would be required to start the `short` on an even address:

```
 ┆ ch   ┆ pad ┆ i.0 ┆ i.1 ┆ 1.0 ┆ 1.1 ┆ 1.2 ┆ 1.3 ┆
```

and, finally, on a machine requiring four-byte boundaries, padding would also be required to start the `long` at a proper address:

```
| ch  | pad | i.0 | i.1 | pad | pad | 1.0 | 1.1 | 1.2 | 1.3 |
```

Byte-order differences mean that a 16- or 32-bit quantity written by one machine will not necessarily represent the same value to another machine unless the machine reading it accounts for the byte-order. The data format differences usually mean that passing binary data from one machine to another requires significant reformatting.

4.3.2 Solution Techniques

Techniques for the solution of this problem range from simple to very complex, each with its own set of tradeoffs. Three approaches will be described.

Transfer data in text form: This probably is the most generally applicable technique. The problem of binary data portability is entirely side-stepped by defining a source-level format that is translated from and to internal form by the respective sending and receiving programs. This is especially effective for avoiding data format incompatibilities. The cost of this approach is increased code size and decreased performance, due to the code necessary to translate to and from the text representation, plus a potential increase in the volume of the data flow.

This approach has been of historical significance in UNIX systems where many simple databases (e.g., */etc/passwd* and */etc/termcap*) are stored as one line per record, the plain-text fields separated by colons.

Binary transfer with single-ended translation: This is equivalent to choosing one machine's internal data format, structure padding, byte-order, and so on, as the standard format. All programs running on dissimilar machines are required to recognize the format and to perform necessary extractions and translations. This method may be the only choice when a program must read or generate data in a format specified by an organization over which the designer has no control (e.g., tape format for reporting 1099 data to the IRS).

Binary transfer with canonical data format: Where it is preferable to transfer data in binary form and the designer has control over all programs involved, specify the file format in a canonical form and have each program access the data with well-defined rules and possibly a function library that hides the gory details. Consider the following rules for data file layout:

a. Char and byte type occupy one byte, short occupies two bytes, long occupies four bytes.

b. Pointer, float, double, and int types are not allowed.

c. Structures and bit fields are not allowed.

d. Byte-order is always from high-order to low-order.

e. There is no padding, every byte is data.

f. Higher level formats and structures must be mutually understood by the programs involved and are not defined here.

Notice that this format is defined only for character and integer data types; floating point could be included if the data format is common to all machines in the required range of portability. Pointers, however, should never be passed from one program to another as they represent memory address information valid only within the context of the originating program. The int type is excluded simply because its size is variable.

It is possible to write code to handle this data format automatically and to adapt to the needs of different target machines. The following function writes a short to *stdout*:

```
/*   Output a short integer in canonical form using
     HIBYTE and LOBYTE macros from portable.h.        */

public void putshort(var)
short var;
     {
     putchar(HIBYTE(var));
     putchar(LOBYTE(var));
     }
```

Refer to the listing of *portable.h* for an expansion of the macros; they assume only that var is a 16-bit quantity. The data extraction is done via shifting and masking techniques that are valid regardless of the byte-order of the machine. Here is the complementary program for reading that value from the file:

```
/*   Input a short integer in canonical form.  */

public void getshort(&var)
short *var;
     {
     /*   Get the first byte and move it to
          the high-order 8 bits of the short. */
     *var = getchar() << 8;

     /*   Get the second byte and put it in
          the low-order 8 bits.                 */
     *var += getchar();
     }
```

For the sake of clarity, these sample functions ignore the possibility of errors on input and output; in practice, all error returns should be dealt with. A library of such functions, including complete error checking, is easily written. Some of these may contain code that differs from machine to machine so they should become part of a "Portability Library" (see Section 1.4). In fact, only `getshort()`, `putshort()`, `getlong()`, and `putlong()` need be written: `getchar()` and `putchar()` already exist as part of *stdio*(3). The result of `getshort()` and `getlong()` should be passed by a pointer in order to allow for error returns via the value of the function. In addition, some very limited 8-bit C compilers do not support a 4-byte data type.

4.4 Directory Handling

In all UNIX system dialects, directories are read-only binary files that specify an association between segment names and i-node numbers (an *i-node* is the UNIX filesystem's internal identification block for a file.) Although it is quite unusual for an application to need to read these files directly, designers should be aware of a portability problem in doing so.

In V7, 4.1BSD, and all AT&T versions, the directory format is very simple, consisting of an array of fixed-length structures each containing a 14-character name field and a 2 byte i-node number. On these systems, directory reading is traditionally done by the *open*(2), *read*(2), and *close*(2) functions.

The 4.2BSD and 4.3BSD versions use a more complex format in order to support segment names of up to 256 characters each. They make available a new group of library functions (*opendir*(3), *readdir*(3), *seekdir*(3), *telldir*(3), *closedir*(3), and *rewinddir*(3)) for reading the new format. Programs assuming the V7 format will definitely fail on 4.2BSD.

Fortunately, the 4.2BSD interface is easily emulated on systems with a V7 directory format. The IEEE P1003 Portable Operating System proposal includes the Berkeley directory interface in its standard library. XENIX 5.0 provides it, and it seems likely to be added to future AT&T versions. Numerous emulations are available in the public domain and over USENET; one such is reproduced in Appendix D.

5

MAINTAINING PORTABLE SYSTEMS

The guidelines, advice, and detailed comparisons given in the preceding chapters make it possible to write very portable software. One area not yet well covered is the control, porting, and maintenance of a developed system. A complete treatment of this subject would require a book of its own; here, we shall briefly describe approaches, give advice, and illustrate useful techniques. Any successful port and version control system must be based on formal procedures for logging and tracking code changes as they occur; a random approach depending solely on the ability of the programming staff to remember where things are invites disaster.

In Section 5.1, we review techniques for isolating version-dependent and environment-dependent (operating system, compiler, hardware) differences in software systems. We discuss the merits of two approaches and consider the effects on porting and maintenance.

In Section 5.2, we look at the portability of *make*(1), the use of *make*(1) in the maintenance of software systems, and how it relates to the porting of code.

In Section 5.3, we describe a tool for the maintenance of interface files, and illustrate how this process is automated using *cx* and *make*(1).

In Section 5.4, we discuss the portability of shell scripts and how to use them to create portable access to nonportable commands. As an example of the latter, we provide a script for archive file maintenance.

5.1 Isolating Dependencies

Porting software to multiple systems inevitably entails some code modification. This may be due to the use of system functions or features that are not portable, or may be due to some architectural difference in implementation (e.g., networked versus non-networked).

The approach discussed here assumes that all production source code is maintained, under careful control, on a central (base) system regardless of the target system. This allows for the maintenance of a single copy of all common code to which version-dependent code is added during a port to a target system. With a single copy of common code, there is no doubt about where the up-to-date version of production code resides, and the source code control tools are required only on the base machine.

With this arrangement, ports always proceed outwards from the base machine, with updates of target-specific modules being carried back to the base machine for source code control once the port is stable.

Regardless of the reason for a change, the goal should be that all changes made during ports occur in compact, isolated areas, leaving the bulk of the code untouched. This is achieved by isolating system-dependent code into the smallest sensible areas, defining an interface between these and the independent (portable) code, then selecting a method of replacing them during a port a target system.

There are two general approaches to replacing isolated dependent code: either at the source level using the C preprocessor, or at the object level using the linker. A discussion of these methods, their implementation, and their relative merits follows.

5.1.1 Preprocessor: Header Files

The first and most generally applicable approach to replacing source code is through the `#define` facility of the C preprocessor. The *portable.h* file (introduced in Chapter 2) is an example of this, providing named constants, types, and macros that are replaced from system to system but always present a common source level interface. This method is also useful for adjusting software parameters that may affect performance tuning or the inclusion of special features. In this case a header (.h) file is created for the software system and has varying implementations depending on the target system.

5.1.2 Preprocessor: Conditional Compilation

The `#ifdef` and `#ifndef` features of the preprocessor can be used with the -D option of the compiler to selectively include or exclude version-dependent code for different systems. With this method, several versions of the dependent code are written in-line in the source file. Each version is surrounded by `#ifdef` and `#endif`; at compile time, the -D option of the compiler is used to define the appropriate selection of flags to cause compilation of the correct versions of conditional code.

This method works well when there are few areas of nonportable code, where each instance represents a straightforward replacement or a simple inclusion of code to enable a feature of the software. This also avoids duplication of common code and keeps all versions of dependent code simultaneously visible and in context.

There are disadvantages to this approach. First, in-line code has no clearly defined interface to the remainder of the source code of which it is part; there may be nonobvious side effects involved in modifying the version-dependent code section. Second, as new versions are added, it is always necessary to edit the original source code to install more dependent code sections, thereby forfeiting the goal of isolating these changes from the main source. Finally, when several versions are supported (and particularly when more than one implementation variable is involved) the combinations of conditionals may become forbiddingly complex to understand and modify.

In Chapter 4, the example code in the section on portable signal processing is rendered this way in order to highlight the differences in semantics between 4.2BSD and other UNIX system dialects.

5.1.3 Object Code Replacement

Another approach to the isolation and replacement of dependent code is to create one or more functions that encapsulate nonportable or version-dependent code, then place these functions in a separate source file which is replaced for each version. This source file is maintained and compiled separately, then combined with the portable part of the system via the linker.

This approach offers several advantages. The interface to the main code is procedural and therefore, if proper structure has been observed, is cleanly defined and documented. Each version of the dependent code is maintained in a separate source file so that no confusion exists about what code belongs to what version; this can be especially important when the different versions share little common code. Also, the portable source files (usually embodying the primary functions of the system) are not modified unless a change to the system function is necessary. This simplifies version control and tracking.

There are two forms of dependence which can be handled with slightly different methods: product-specific implementation variations and dependence on usage of nonportable features.

5.1.4 Version-Dependent Modules

In the case of implementation variations, on the base machine the version-dependent modules (commonly initialization routines and makefiles) should have multiple customized source code versions, each of which is kept separately and named to reflect the dependence. One naming convention is to give all versions of a module the same name, but to store them in subdirectories named for their dependencies. Another method is to keep all versions in the same directory, but name each version of the module according to its dependence. (See Section 5.1.7 for suggested names to use for subdirectories.)

5.1.5 Portability Libraries

To handle dependence on nonportable features, create a "Portability Library" for each target system. For each set of nonportable features (e.g., *ioctl*(2) or external data format handling, discussed in the previous chapter), define a portable interface layer that can be implemented in terms of the nonportable features of each system. For each target system, maintain a Portability Library containing all such functions.

5.1.6 Porting to the Target System

When porting a software package to one target system at a time, we recommend the following:

1. Select the correct version of *portable.h* and move it to the target system.
2. Select the correct Portability Library and port it to the target system.
3. Port the independent (portable) parts of the software package to the target system.
4. Select the required version of each dependent code file. Depending on the naming scheme used, either rename or move the file so that the selected file is in the correct directory by the correct name. Port these files to the target system.
5. A single, correct version of the software system is now on the target system and may be compiled, linked, and tested.
6. If any modifications are made to the *portable.h* file, Portability Library, or dependent code modules, port the necessary updates back to the base machine to update the controlled source code.

When distributing a software package for later customization by end users, it is necessary to include all versions of the header files, Portability Libraries, and dependent code modules along with the portable part of the code. In this case, the makefiles can help to automate the selection of the correct versions for the end user.

The general idea is that the makefile in the main directory contains production targets for each dependence that copy or link files and libraries from the corresponding subdirectories.

For example, suppose that we're in a directory that has a target *prog*. A module named *func2.c* has different implementations for Berkeley 4.1 and

System V. If the naming method chosen is to use the normal file name but store it in a subdirectory named for the dependence, there are two subdirectories: BSD4_1 and SYSV. The makefile has two similarly named productions in it that are used to copy or link the needed version from the subdirectory to the parent directory before the system target is made.

```
prog: main.o func1.o func2.o
        cc main.c func1.o func2.o -o prog

BSD4_1:
        cp BSD4_1/func2.c func2.c

SYSV:
        cp SYSV/func2.c func2.c
```

One of the BSD4_1 or SYSV make productions must be executed before making the *prog* target. For instance,

```
make BSD4_1
make prog
```

would be the command sequence to make the Berkeley 4.1 version of *prog*.

If the naming method chosen keeps version-dependent sources in the top directory under different names, use the same make file targets as above, changing only the copy commands:

```
prog: main.o func1.o func2.o
        cc main.c func1.o func2.o -o prog

BSD4_1:
        cp func2.c.4_1 func2.c

SYSV:
        cp func2.c.SV func2.c
```

The commands to make a version are the same as shown above. The *cp*(1) commands may be replaced by *ln*(1) if preferred. This reduces system overhead by avoiding unnecessary copying of files; however, be careful to remove existing links when updating the source files.

5.1.7 Recommended Naming Conventions

The following system name abbreviations can be used as subdirectory names, makefile productions, and #define symbols. Use the most general one applicable after checking for portability (e.g., don't specify the more restrictive SYSIII or SYSV if ATT can be used).

Notice that these labels have been deliberately chosen· *not* to overlap with the predefined symbols available on many compilers on the theory that it

is best that the programmer's version selection be done explicitly via switches
in the makefile.

Label	Version
V6	Bell Labs Version 6
V7	Bell Labs Version 7
SYSIII	Bell Labs System III
SYSV	Bell Labs System V
SYSV_1	Bell Labs System V, Release 1
SYSV_2	Bell Labs System V, Release 2
ATT	Code common to SIII, SYSV_1, and SYSV_2
BSD4_1	Berkeley System Distribution 4.1
BSD4_2	Berkeley System Distribution 4.2
BSD4_3	Berkeley System Distribution 4.2
BSD	Code common to Berkeley dialects
XENIX2_3	Code for XENIX 2.3
XENIX3_0	Code for XENIX 3.0
XENIX5_0	Code for XENIX 5.0
XENIX	Code common to XENIX dialects
M68000	Motorola 68000, 68010, and 68020
NS16000	National Semiconductor 16032
I8086	Intel 8086, 8088, and 80186
I80286	Intel 80286
PC_AT	IBM PC/AT
PDP11	Digital Equipment Corporation PDP-11
VAX	Digital Equipment Corporation VAX
U3B2	AT&T 3B2
U3B5	AT&T 3B5
U3B20	AT&T 3B20
U3B	code generic to the AT&T 3B series

5.2 Using Make and SCCS

The *make*(1) utility is perhaps the single most powerful tool offered by
the UNIX system for software system maintenance. It enables developers to
automate the system generation process in a way that eliminates errors and
wasted time caused by out-of-date source or object versions.

The Source Code Control System (SCCS), while not available on all
UNIX system dialects, is portable among those that do have it and is an
excellent tool for both maintaining multiple versions of and controlling
updates to source code.

Correct organization of makefiles deserves the same level of time and
forethought that goes into system code, because they form an important part
of the documentation of the system structure.

In this section, we discuss the portability of *make*(1) and offer guidelines and conventions to help developers take full advantage of *make*(1) through systematic use, and pay careful attention to the documentation function of the makefile source. These issues are particularly important when a system is ported by someone other than its originator.

5.2.1 Portability of Make

The original version of *make*(1) is found in V7 and 4.1BSD. SIII and SV have an enhanced version with several new features including:

- the ability to pick up make macro definitions from the shell environment variables
- direct support for recursive *make*(1) invocations
- built-in rules for handling libraries and SCCS files gracefully
- the capability to do includes within makefiles

None of these features are portable to V7/BSD. Some instances of V7 dependency-line syntax do not work in the AT&T version unless the -b compatibility flag is specified.

The 4.2BSD version has minor enhancements over V7's; details on these and some differences in the command line options may be found in the note on *make*(1) in Chapter 3.

5.2.2 Makefile organization

Every subsystem should have a global makefile in its top-level directory such that a "make" or "make system" command at that level attempts to make the entire system. Action lines in a makefile can themselves call *make*(1). This can provide the basis for chaining makes from the master directory of a subsystem down through every subdirectory involved.

For other subsystems and libraries upon which this subsystem depends, it is useful (but not necessary) to add productions to the makefile that check for their existence, but do not try to make them. As well as being directly useful, this is valuable documentation on the system's structure.

The basic idea of the master makefile can be seen in the following makefile fragment:

```
# There is a utility library for handling queues in
# the "qsrc" subdirectory
QDIR    = qsrc
QLIB    = $(QDIR)/queues.a

# The final system is a single executable
system: myprog

# The executable (myprog) needs an up-to-date $(QLIB)
myprog: myprog.c $(QLIB)
        cc myprog.c $(QLIB) -o myprog

# Trigger a "remote make" in the subdirectory to build $(QLIB)
$(QLIB):
        (cd $(QDIR); make `basename $(QLIB)`)
```

A "make system" command will cause make to check the status of *myprog*
and the productions upon which it depends. If the *queues.a* library is out-of-
date, the parentheses of

```
(cd $(QDIR); make `basename $(QLIB)`)
```

cause a subshell to be created that will change directory to the library subdirectory then make the library. The `basename $(QLIB)` construction extracts the last segment of the $(QLIB) pathname for use as the make
target.

Keep in mind that the makefile in *qsrc* may itself use this method. If all
of the dominos are set up correctly, a single make invocation in the master
directory can cause a large subsystem spread over any number of directories
to be updated correctly.

Organizing things this way makes porting and maintenance of large systems much easier, and clearly documents the structure and dependencies of
the system.

5.2.3 Recommended Make Productions

The following is a recommended set of standard names for common system generation and maintenance tasks that should be automated via the
makefile.

system   Regenerate the system (i.e., perform all of the actions necessary to
             go from source code to final executables). This should usually be
             the first production in the file so that a make command with no
             explicit target will invoke it by default.

print   List all of the source code files (e.g., ".c" and ".h" files).

lint   Apply *lint*(1) to all C source files.

clean   Remove generated intermediate files (e.g., ".o" files) but not exe-
            cutables and other end-products.

clobber   Like "clean", but also remove executables and system end-
            products; this should leave only the original source files.

bundle   Bundle all source files together in a source archive for file transfer.
            We often use the *bundle* utility from Kernighan and Pike's *The
            UNIX Programming Environment* (Englewood Cliffs, NJ:
            Prentice-Hall, 1984). The *shar* utility distributed with the USE-
            NET sources is also suitable.

install   Do all file moves, copies, and/or permission changes necessary to
            update the working copy of the system executables from a new
            version that was made in this directory. The user may need
            super-user permissions to run this production depending on the
            ownership and permissions of the target files being updated.

5.2.4 Supplemental Make Rules

The following lines add a default rule that is used by *make*(1) when
there are no explicit or built-in rules that can be used to create a needed target.

```
# Set up SCCS fetches
.DEFAULT:
        get s.$@
```

In this case, we have created a rule that will automatically extract files from
SCCS as necessary. This need not be added to makefiles for systems using
AT&T System III and later versions of *make*(1); they support this rule impli-
citly.

Another useful production is:

```
.SUFFIXES: .x

# To generate .x files automatically from .c files
.c.x:
        cx $*
```

This tells *make*(1) that files with a ".x" suffix are derived from files with a
".c" suffix using the tool *cx*. This automates the updating of interface files
(described in the next section).

5.3 Maintaining Interface Files

Throughout this book we have recommended the use of interface (".x") files. These files contain `extern` declarations corresponding to the `public` declarations in the related C source file. They may be thought of as external interface descriptions, and are included by any other C source file that makes reference to the public entry points described. By this method, the user file acquires valid `extern` declarations without the programmer having to explicitly determine and maintain them.

Generating interface files for C source modules by hand is tedious and error prone; furthermore, the interface file can easily become out-of-date if the C source changes. A listing of a shell script, *cx*, that can automatically generate interface files using the `public` convention follows.

Notice that if a ".h" file with the same basic name as the ".c" module exists, the script will insert an `#include` of it in the interface file. Thus, any `typedef` or #define statements needed are carried along with the generated `extern` statements. The using module need only include the ".x" file.

This script is intended to be used in makefiles to generate a new interface file as needed for any ".c" module that has been altered.

```
# cx - Bourne-shell script for making .x files from .c files
#      Note: Version 7 shells may not support pound-sign comments.
#            Lines of the form /* ..... */{} are used to put
#            comments in sed input and may be removed for speed.

case $1 in
"")        echo "usage:   cx C-filename-without-.c"
           exit 1
           ;;
esac

if [ ! -r $1.c ]
then
           # cannot find a .c file for $1.
           echo cx: $1.c not found
           exit 1
fi
```

```
if [ -r $1.h ]
then
        # include the .h file with the same name as the .c file.
        incfile="#include \"$1.h\""
else
        incfile="/* There is no $1.h file */"
fi



# Call egrep and sed to do the real work */
egrep '^[        ]*public|^#if|^#else|^#endif' $1.c | sed > /tmp/cx$$  \
                                                                       \
        '        /*        Insert leading comment and include file. */{}
        1i\
/* '$1'.x -- declarations file for module '$1' */
        1i\
'"$incfile"'

        /#if/           {
                /*      Remove empty #if ... #endif (handling   */{}
                /*      #else is much harder).                  */{}
                N
                /#if[^\n]*\n#endif/d
                P
                D
                }

        /public/        {
                /*      Change public to extern.                */{}
                s/public/extern/

                /*      Remove function parameter lists.        */{}
                s/([^*].*$/();/

                /*      Remove leftmost array dimension.         */{}
                /\[/    {
                        s/]/]CX/
                        s/\[.*CX/[]/
                        }

                /*      Remove anything trailing a semicolon.   */{}
                s/;.*/;/

                /*      Remove variable initialization.          */{}
                s/[        ]*=.*/;/
                }'


echo "/* $1.x ends here */" >> /tmp/cx$$
```

```
# If the new cx file is identical to the old, don't update the old.
# If they are different, move the new one onto the old one.

cmp -s $1.x /tmp/cx$$ > /dev/null

if [ $? = 0 ]
then
        rm -f /tmp/cx$$
        echo $1.x is up to date.
else
        mv /tmp/cx$$ $1.x
fi

exit 0

# cx ends here
```

After some preliminary checking to make sure arguments are correct and the appropriate files exist, the script filters the source with *egrep*(1) to extract interesting lines. A line is interesting if it contains a `public` or one of the `#if`/`#endif` preprocessor controls that could result in a `public` declaration not being compiled.

The script then calls *sed*(1) with an elaborate set of instructions. These first eliminate `#if`/`#endif` pairs with no intervening `public` or control lines. This is not strictly necessary, but is done to reduce clutter in the interface file.

Next, each `public` line is transformed into a corresponding `extern`. This is done in the following steps:

1. The `public` keyword is changed to `extern`.
2. The contents of function parameter lists are removed.
3. The contents of leftmost array dimensions are removed. This is not strictly necessary but might eliminate a constant that the interface file would otherwise need to know about.
4. Variable initializers are removed.
5. Anything to the right of a semicolon is removed.

The output is written to a temporary file and contains:

- a header comment identifying the C source file
- an `#include` of the corresponding ".h" file, if any, or a comment saying that there is none
- a list of `extern` statements

- a trailing comment identifying the end of the file

Finally, the new ".x" file is compared to the existing one, if any. If they are identical, no update is made to the original file; otherwise, the new ".x" file is copied over the existing one. This is important because changes may be made to the C source file that do not change its external interface but nevertheless cause *cx* to be invoked by *make*(1). If the ".x" file were to be updated, even though it is unchanged, all other productions that depend on it would be triggered unnecessarily.

This tool does have certain limitations that arise from it being written as a script using standard UNIX tools. For example,

```
public int ( *myfun)()
```

will give incorrect results due to the space before the "*". Notice also that in declarations like

```
public int i = 5,
           j = 17,
           k = 23;
```

only the first variable will have a correct `extern` generated, because *egrep*(1) only keeps the line beginning with `public` so the *sed*(1) invocation will never see the others. Each variable to be exported must be declared on the same line as a `public`, preferably one variable per declaration.

Notice also that in function declarations, at least the opening parenthesis of the argument list must be on the same line as the `public`.

These are special cases of a general problem with the shell script implementation. The full syntax of C declarations is somewhat more complex than can be handled by line-oriented tools. A C program implementing a lexical scanner and simple grammar could support all cases, but in practice we have found the limitations quite acceptable.

This script is intended to be used in makefiles to generate a new interface file for each ".c" module whenever another module uses it and its source has been altered. This can be automated by the use of the ".SUFFIXES" capability of *make*(1) (see previous section). The maintenance advantages of systematically applying this technique have been very great, and we consider *cx* to be an indispensible tool.

5.4 Shell Scripts

Much of the power of the UNIX system is embodied in the ability to solve problems by combining existing tools using shell scripts. In writing scripts, it is necessary to be aware of some portability considerations; on the other hand, shell scripts also provide a mechanism for the portable use of UNIX commands.

5.4.1 Portable Shell Usage

The most important consideration in writing portable scripts is the choice of shell: only the Bourne Shell should be considered portable. As an interactive environment, users may prefer the extra capability of Berkeley *csh*(1) or other shells, but for any production scripts (whether for internal use or as part of a product) use the Bourne Shell.

Almost all versions of the Bourne Shell are compatible except for the following considerations:

1. The "[...]" form of *test*(1) is not always implemented. This can usually be fixed by linking */bin/[* to */bin/test*.

2. The "#!filename" syntax on the first line of the script, used to invoke a particular shell to process the script, is not portable except among BSD versions. Always start Bourne Shell scripts with a blank line.

3. The comment syntax ("#") is not supported in original Version 7 — however, it has been retrofitted to most existing Version 7 implementations.

4. The System V version of this shell has some nonportable enhancements (notably, shell procedures). Also, more functions (e.g., *test*) have been built in to the shell, but this should not normally affect portability.

5. The regular expression syntax supported differs slightly. See the notes for *ed*(1) and *sed*(1) in Chapter 3.

5.4.2 Scripts that Aid Portability: mklib

One difference between the Version 7/Berkeley-descended dialects and AT&T's System III and descendents is the handling of object-code libraries. On all versions, they are built using *ar*(1), which is considered portable; but on the V7/BSD versions, the resulting archive must be additionally processed by the special tool *ranlib*(1) before it is cleanly usable in a link.

Here we give the source for *mklib*, a tool which is a portable interface to *ar*(1) or the *ar*(1)/*ranlib*(1) combination, to be used wherever an object library is made. It facilitates the writing of portable makefiles by hiding the details of determining whether to use *ranlib*(1), or *lorder*(1) and *tsort*(1), in building the library.

```
#         Bourne shell script to create libraries
#
#         This script is designed to use ranlib where it
#         exists and lorder ¦ tsort elsewhere.
#
#         mklib always creates a library from scratch; it
#         doesn't handle updates.
#
#         Copyright 1985 by Rabbit Software Corporation
case $1 in
"")   echo "Usage: mklib ar-flags libname object-files"
      exit 1
      ;;
esac
arflags=$1                       # get flags for ar
shift

libname=$1                       # get target library name
shift

tmpname=/tmp/scr.$$              # make a temp library name

if [ -f /usr/bin/ranlib -o -f /bin/ranlib ]
then

      # This portion if ranlib exists

      if ar $arflags $tmpname $*
      then
           if cp $tmpname $libname
           then
                ranlib $libname
           fi
      fi

else

      # This portion if ranlib not found

      if ar $arflags $tmpname `lorder $* ¦ tsort`
      then
           cp $tmpname $libname
      fi
fi

stat=$?

rm $tmpname                                  # clean up temp file

exit $stat
```

The *mklib* script should be called with the same flags and file argument sequence used with *ar*(1). A description of its operation follows.

The script first checks to ensure that there are arguments, as neither *ar*(1) nor *ranlib*(1) should be called without them.

On a system with *ranlib*(1), the archive operation is then done, If it succeeds, *ranlib*(1) is run on the result; if it fails, the failure status is passed back to the user.

If *ranlib*(1) is not available, the script calls *lorder*(1) and *tsort*(1) to generate a correctly sorted object module list which it then passes as arguments to *ar*(1).

If the archive command succeeds, the new archive is copied onto the original target. Finally, the temporary file is deleted and the status returned by *ar*(1) or *ranlib*(1) is returned to the user.

Notice that this script always creates a library from the given object file list, without regard for any previous contents of the library. It is possible to extend *mklib* to perform insertions and replacements in an existing library. With *ranlib*(1), the logic is identical to the creation of a new library. Without *ranlib*(1), the process is to extract all existing library members to a temporary directory, copy the new object modules over them, then build the new library from the complete set of objects as before. Since we have found that in almost all cases, the version of *mklib* shown is sufficient, we have left the implementation of the more complex case as an exercise for the interested reader.

A

PORTABILITY DEFINITIONS FILE

```
/* portable.h -- type and macro definitions for portable C */

/* Standard types */
typedef int           bool;     /* >= 16 bits used as boolean */
typedef char          flag;     /* >= 8  bits used as boolean */

typedef unsigned short word;    /* >= 16 bit unsigned type     */

typedef int           rchar;    /* I/O function return values */
typedef char          *string;  /* for readability             */

/* If void is not supported, uncomment the following line.      */
/* typedef int        void; */

/* Use this length and type for filename variables -- use
   256 on 4.2BSD since it is defined as such in dir.h           */
#ifndef MAXPATHLEN
#define MAXPATHLEN    64
#endif
typedef char          path[MAXPATHLEN];


/* Define byte and BYTE to portably support an unsigned
   8 bit data type (see Section 2.9.1 in text).                 */

/*    If char is signed by default and unsigned keyword is
      not allowed with char, byte and BYTE are:                 */
typedef char    byte;          /* 8 bit unsigned type */
#define BYTE(x)   ((x) & 0xff) /* BYTE truncates data */
```

```
/* Standard macros */
#define HIBYTE(x)   (((x) >> 8) & 0xff)        /* hi byte of short      */
#define LOBYTE(x)   ((x) & 0xff)               /* lo byte of short      */
#define HIWORD(x)   (((x)>>16) & 0xffffL)      /* upper half of long    */
#define LOWORD(x)   ((x) & 0xffffL)            /* lower half of long    */
#define CHAR(x)     ((x) & 0x7f)               /* Truncate to 7 bits    */
#define WORD(x)     ((x) & 0xffffL)            /* Truncate to 16 bits   */
#define DECODE(x)   ((int) ((x)-'0'))          /* int value of a digit  */

/* long unsigned right shift */
#define LURSHIFT(n, b) (((long)(n) >> (b)) & (0x7fffffffL >> ((b)-1)))

/* number of elements in array a */
#define DIM(a)      (sizeof(a)/sizeof(*(a)))

/* Scope control pseudo-keywords */
#define public                   /* public is C default scope  */
#define private     static       /* static really means private */

/* Standard constants */
#define TRUE        1            /* for use with booleans      */
#define FALSE       0

#define SUCCEED     0            /* for use in exit()          */
#define FAIL        (-1)         /* for exit() & error returns */

#define EOL         '\n'         /* end of line char           */
#define EOS         '\0'         /* end of string char         */
#define EOP         '\14'        /* end of page (FF) char       */

/* portable.h ends here */
```

B

PORTABLE UNIX SYSTEM FEATURES

This appendix lists the names of all UNIX system features that can be considered portable based on the comparisons detailed in Chapter 3. If your range of portable systems differs from ours, you may need to be more restrictive. We do not recommend being less restrictive unless it is certain that the range of portability will not later change.

COMMANDS

ar	crypt	ld	pr	tar
awk	dc	lex	prof	tbl
basename	dd	ln	ps	tee
bc	deroff	login	ptx	test
cal	diff	logname	pwd	time
calendar	diff3	lorder	ratfor	touch
cat	du	ls	rm	true
cb	echo	m4	rmdir	tsort
cc	ed	make	sed	tty
cd	egrep	mesg	sh	uniq
chdir	eqn	mkdir	size	units
checkeq	false	mv	sleep	wait
chgrp	fgrep	neqn	spell	wc
chmod	file	newgrp	spline	who
chown	find	nm	split	write
cmp	graph	nohup	strip	yacc
col	grep	nroff	su	
comm	join	od	sum	

cp   kill   passwd   tail

SYSTEM CALLS

access	chroot	execve	mknod	sbrk	tell
acct	close	exit	nice	setgid	time
alarm	creat	fstat	open	setuid	umask
brk	dup	getpid	pause	signal	umount
chdir	execl	kill	pipe	stat	unlink
chmod	execle	link	profil	stime	wait
chown	execv	lseek	read	sync	write

SUBROUTINES

abort	exece	getchar	isupper	setkey
abs	execlp	getenv	isxdigit	setpwent
acos	execvp	getgrent	l3tol	sin
asctime	exp	getgrgid	ldexp	sinh
asin	fabs	getgrnam	localtime	sleep
assert	fclose	getlogin	lto3l	sqrt
atan	fcvt	getpass	malloc	srand
atan2	fdopen	getpw	modf	sscanf
atof	feof	getpwent	monitor	strcat
atoi	ferror	getpwnam	nlist	strchr
atol	fflush	getpwuid	pclose	strcmp
cabs	fgetc	gets	perror	strcpy
calloc	fgets	getw	popen	strlen
ceil	fileno	gmtime	pow	· strncat
clearerr	floor	hypot	putc	strncmp
cos	fopen	index	putchar	strncpy
cosh	fputc	isalnum	puts	strrchr
crypt	fputs	isalpha	putw	swab
ctime	fread	isascii	qsort	system
ecvt	free	isatty	rand	tan
edata	freopen	iscntrl	realloc	tanh
encrypt	frexp	isdigit	rewind	ttyname
end	fscanf	isgraph	rindex	ungetc
endgrent	ftell	islower	scanf	
endpwent	fwrite	isprint	setbuf	
etext	gcvt	ispunct	setgrent	
exec	getc	isspace	setjmp	

DEVICE DRIVERS

null

SPECIAL FILE FORMATS

environ   group   passwd

GAMES

arithmetic   quiz

MISCELLANEA

ascii   man

SYSTEM ADMINISTRATION AND MAINTENANCE TOOLS

clri   mknod   sync   wall
df   mount   umount

C

OTHER DIALECTS

This appendix describes some UNIX system variants or lookalikes derived from the major dialects detailed in Chapter 3. Each dialect should be assumed identical to its given predecessor except where noted, except for facilities in the predecessor that are indicated to be hardware or configuration dependent.

The following subsections will be listed for each dialect:

UTILITIES	Tools from Section 1
KERNEL	System calls from Section 2
LIBRARIES	C run-time support functions from Section 3
DEVICES	Device drivers supported from Section 4 (7 in AT&T's new scheme)
FILE	File formats and conventions from Section 5 (4 in AT&T's new scheme)
GAMES	Game programs from Section 6
MISCELLANEA	Miscellaneous items from Section 7 (5 in AT&T's new scheme)
MAINTENANCE	System maintenance tools from Section 8.

FOR:PRO for the Fortune Systems 32:16

UTILITIES

FOR:PRO includes a large subset of the Version 7 utilities plus *vi*(1) and a proprietary debugger *fdb*(1) analogous to V7 *adb*(1).

KERNEL

The Fortune Systems kernel is a V7 port, but does include BSD-style *setpgrp*(2).

LIBRARIES

FOR:PRO has all the V7 libraries in the main table for section 3, plus BSD/SIII's *gamma*(3M), the *j0*(3M) math function group, and Berkeley *curses*(3) and *termcap*(3).

DEVICES

FOR:PRO supports a V7-compatible *tty*(4) control interface with numerous Berkeley-style enhancements (although job control is not supported) and the standard */dev/null*; in addition, *console*(4) is like V7 *cons*(4) in being handled as a tty with a fixed baud rate. Standard *mem*(4) and *kmem*(4) are supported.

Nonstandard drivers include *conf* (listed under *mem*(4)) for writing configuration information to the system EEPROMs, *floppy*(4) for accessing the system's floppy disk drive(s), *hd*(4) for access to the system hard disk, and *sio*(4) for direct control of the serial ports.

FILE FORMATS

FOR:PRO documents a mixed bag of file formats and conventions derived mostly from V7 and BSD. These are:

- The *a.out*(5) and *filsys*(5) formats have been adapted for the 68000 and are not compatible with their V7 predecessors.
- The format of *profile*(5) is as SIII's.
- The *group*(5) and *mtab*(5) formats are documented identical to their V7 predecessors.

- The *fstab*(5), *passwd*(5), *ttys*(5), *ttytype*(5), *termcap*(5) are documented identically to their Berkeley predecessors. The *motd*(5) file operates exactly as Berkeley *motd*(5), but is documented, and the *dir*(5), *utmp*(5), and *wtmp*(5) formats are (like Berkeley's) formally identical to V7's but more precisely documented.
- New formats *devtype*(5), *disk*(5), *diskconf*(5) and *disktab*(5), and *trans*(5) are documented for various device access modes.
- A new capability format for printers, *printcap*(5), is documented.

GAMES

BSD-style *worm*(6) and *worms*(6) are included, as well as *fortune*(6) and *ching*(6).

MISCELLANEA

FOR:PRO includes the V7 Section 7 facilities.

MAINTENANCE

FOR:PRO includes versions of the V7 system maintenance facilities.

PC/IX, Interactive Systems Corp. System III for the PC/AT

UTILITIES

PC/IX includes all System III utilities except the following: *arcv*(1), *ct*(1), *cu*(1), *factor*(1), *fget*(1), *fscv*(1), *fsend*(1), *gcat*(1), *gcosmail*(1), *gdev*(1), *ged*(1), the *graphics*(1) utility group, *gutil*(1), *kas*(1), *kun*(1), *lpr*(1), *mmchek*(1), *pwck*(1), *stat*(1), *tar*(1) *toc*(1), *tp*(1), *typo*(1), *vpmc*(1).

PC/IX features a suite of tools organized around a proprietary editor and special structured file format. The editor is called INed and derives from an early version of the Rand editor; the link to it is *e*(1) and associated tools are *fill*(1), *fixascii*(1), *format*(1), *ghost*(1), *history*(1), *just*(1), *newfile*(1), *readfile(1)*, *rmhist*(1), *rpl*(1), and *versions*(1).

PC/IX also replaces a few other SIII utilities with proprietary tools. The *ct*(1) and *cu*(1) programs are replaced by *connect*(1); *mmchek*(1) is replaced by *checkmm*(1) (which appears identical to the SV version); *lpr*(1) is replaced by *print*(1).

The following other utilities are new in PC/IX on the PC/AT:
chmem(1) (for changing the dynamic memory allocations of programs), *dos-del*(1), *dosdir*(1), *dosread*(1), and *doswrite*(1) (for manipulating MS-DOS
file systems), *killall*(1) (signal all processes), *l* (list with pagination),
manroff(1) (format manual pages), *memuse*(1) (report unused memory), and
splp(1) (control printer).

PC/IX *grep*(1) supports a nonportable -p option used for finding paragraphs containing a given regular expression; it is otherwise like its SIII
predecessor.

KERNEL

The PC/IX kernel is System III compatible, and adds the
Uniforum/IEEE standard's *lockf*(2) call. Both advisory and mandatory locking is supported.

LIBRARIES

All standard SIII library functions are supported. The V7 database
management routines *dbm*(3) are included, as is the Berkeley *curses*(3)
library. A *libPW*(3) library of special routines from the Programmer's Work
Bench (one of SIII's predecessors) is included for compatibility with old code,
but their use is discouraged.

DEVICES

PC/IX supports the normal SIII *tty*(4), *null*(4), *mem*(4), and *kmem*(4)
device types. A *disk*(4) entry describes logical disk partitioning; the
display(4) driver provides full support for monochrome or color PC/AT
displays; *fd*(4) describes the system floppy disk handling, and *hd*(4) describes
hard disks; *fp*(4) describes floating point support; *keyboard*(4) describes the
keyboard interface; and *lp*(4) specifies parallel-port printer control.

FILE FORMATS

Most hardware-independent SIII file entries are supported identically to
SIII. The *checklist*(5), *ddate*(5), *gps*(5), *pnch*(5), and *tp*(5) entries of SIII
are, however, omitted. The *inittab*(5) entry also is omitted, as PC/IX uses a
nonstandard boot sequence and *init*(8) acts differently from the SIII version.

Added entries include: *connect*(5) (describes *connect*(1) configuration
files), *devinfo*(5) (the format of device descriptions), *filesystems*(5) (the

filesystems configuration file), *INed*(5) (structured file formats), *param*(5) (to describe some system parameters), *primetime*(5) (accounting system prime time conventions), *qconfig*(5) (to describe spooler configuration files), *ports*(5) and *portstatus*(5) (configuration files and status structures for ports), and *termcap*(5) (as in BSD).

GAMES

PC/IX includes all the SIII games supported on non-PDP-11 machines. The *wump*(6) game also is included. The BSD *fish*(6) and *number*(6) games are included.

MISCELLANEA

PC/IX includes all SIII Section 7 entries except *ebcdic*(7). It adds a new *subset*(7) to describe the PC/IX Core System and optional tool sets.

MAINTENANCE

The *fsck*(1M) utility of SIII has been moved here, along with all related filesystem surgical instruments, the accounting tools, UUCP administration utilities, the spooler demon, and the rest of 1M. New entries have been added for *adduser*(8) and *sorry*(8) (user account management), *format*(8) (floppy formatting), *chparm*(8) (system parameter edits), *qdaemon*(8) (the spooler server), *sash*(8) and *scc*(8) (the standalone shell and compiler), and *skulker*(8) (a file-removal script). These commands are in a special *priv*(8) directory.

The *init*(8) entry and others related to the boot sequence have changed significantly.

COHERENT from the Mark Williams Co.

NOTE

COHERENT is a UNIX system lookalike rather than a port; it is entirely a development of the Mark Williams Company and contains none of Bell Labs's proprietary code. The version documented here is COHERENT 2.3.43.

The COHERENT manual does not use the conventional 8-section division. Instead, the tools and calls are grouped under functional heads. The following table gives the equivalence:

V7	COHERENT
1	<blank>
1M	Maintenance
2	System Calls
3	libc library + libm library + STDIO library
4	Device Drivers
5	File Formats
6	Games
7	Conventions
8	Maintenance (we use 1M below)

We use V7 equivalents throughout below, for consistency.

The COHERENT features related to loadable device drivers cannot be supported on the Intel 8088 or 8086 processors due to intrinsic hardware restrictions.

UTILITIES

COHERENT contains V7-compatible versions of: *ac*(1M), *accton*(1M), *ar*(1), *awk*(1), *cal*(1), *cat*(1), *cd*(1), *chgrp*(1), *chmod*(1), *chown*(1), *cmp*(1), *col*(1) *cp*(1), *crypt*(1), *date*(1), *dc*(1), *dd*(1), *deroff*(1), *df*(1), *diff*(1), *diff3*(1), *du*(1), *echo*(1), *ed*(1), *egrep*(1), *expr*(1), *file*(1), *find*(1), *join*(1), *kill*(1), *ln*(1), *login*(1), *look*(1), *ls*(1), *m4*(1), *mail*(1), *mesg*(1), *mkdir*(1), *mount*(1M), *mv*(1), *ncheck*(1M), *newgrp*(1), *pr*(1), *prep*(1), *restor*(1M), *rev*(1), *rm*(1), *rmdir*(1), *sa*(1M), *sh*(1), *size*(1), *sleep*(1), *sort*(1), *split*(1), *strip*(1), *sum*(1), *sync*(1M), *tail*(1), *tar*(1), *tee*(1), *test*(1), *time*(1), *touch*(1), *tp*(1), *tr*(1), *true*(1), *tsort*(1), *tty*(1), *umount*(1M), *uniq*(1), *units*(1), *wait*(1), *wall*(1M), *wc*(1), *who*(1), and *write*(1).

COHERENT includes SIII-compatible versions of: *banner*(1), *mknod*(1M), *su*(1), and *typo*(1).

New features have been added to *basename*(1), *cmp*(1), *col*(1), *date*(1), *dc*(1), *deroff*(1), *df*(1), *diff*(1), *ed*(1), *expr*(1), *find*(1), *grep*(1), *ln*(1), *mail*(1), *mount*(1M), *mv*(1), *nroff*(1), *od*(1), *passwd*(1), *pr*(1), *prep*(1), *pwd*(1), *quot*(1M), *ranlib*(1), *restor*(1M), *rm*(1), *rmdir*(1), *sa*(1M), *sed*(1), *tar*(1), *units*(1).

COHERENT includes functional equivalents of the following V7 commands (options, error behaviors, and associated files may differ): *as*(1), *at*(1), *bc*(1), *cc*(1), *ld*(1), *lex*(1), *make*(1), *man*(1), *mkfs*(1M), *nm*(1), *prof*(1), *ps*(1), *quot*(1M), *size*(1), *spell*(1), *stty*(1), *yacc*(1).

The V7 *enroll*(1), *xget*(1), and *xsend*(1) tools are replaced by a similar *enroll*(1), *xencode*(1), *xdecode*(1), and *xmail*(1) set.

The following V7 tools are entirely missing: *adb*(1), *bas*(1), *calendar*(1), *cb*(1), *cu*(1), *checkeq*, *eqn*(1), *neqn*(1), *f77*(1), *factor*(1), *primes*(1), *graph*(1), *lint*(1), *lookall*(1), *lookbib*(1), *lorder*(1), *mkconf*(1M), *nice*(1), *nohup*(1), *plot*(1), *pstat*(1), *ptx*(1), *pubindex*(1), *ratfor*(1), *refer*(1), *roff*(1), *spline*(1), *struct*(1), *tabs*(1), *tbl*(1), *tc*(1), *tk*(1), *troff*(1), *uucp*(1), *uulog*(1), *uux*(1).

The following COHERENT tools are entirely new: *c*(1) (a columnating filter), *conv*(1) (a base-conversion tool), *cpdir*(1) (a file-hierarchy copying utility), *db*(1) (an object-code debugger), *dumpdate*(1M) (to display dump logs), *from*(1) (to generate lists of numbers), *help*(1) (to print command synopses), *kermit*(1) (for file transfer), *lc*(1) (for directory listings by type), *learn*(1) (an interactive COHERENT tutorial), *load*(1) (for loading device drivers), *lpr*(1) (for print spooling), *msg*(1) (a message sender), *newusr*(1M) (a tool for adding accounts), *scat*(1) (a file browser), *uload*(1) (a device driver loader), and *yes*(1) (a sycophant).

The IBM PC and PC/XT versions additionally include:

- a *cu*(1) functionally equivalent to V7's
- a *disable*(1) and *enable*(1) similar to SV's
- a transfer utility (*dos*(1)) for reading and writing MS-DOS floppies
- other floppy-management tools (*fderror*(1), *fdformat*(1))
- *funkeys*(1), a utility for setting PC keyboard function keys
- print filters (*epson*(1) and *hp*(1)) for Epson and Hewlett-Packard LaserJet printers
- *hpd*(1) and *hpr*(1), a spooler for the HP LaserJet
- two screen editors, *elle*(1) and *trout*(1)
- *setclock*(1), a utility for setting the system clock from an AST board
- a port-status querying utility, *ttystat*(1)

V7-compatible *troff*(1) and *uucp*(1) are promised for future releases but are not yet present.

KERNEL

COHERENT provides a V7-compatible kernel with SIII-style named FIFOs, except that the *mpx*(2) and *phys*(2) facilities and the *nice*(2) call are not supported.

Error numbers 35 through 39 are new, COHERENT-specific error types; also, COHERENT signals 12 through 16 are processor dependent. The new calls *sload*(2) and *suload*(2) support dynamically loadable and unloadable device drivers.

LIBRARIES

COHERENT provides a complete V7-compatible C support library, with the following exceptions:

- The *ctime*(3) group follows the SIII rather than V7 model (*timezone* is a variable).
- The *dbm*(3) library is missing, an *fgetw*(3) has been added to complement V7's *getw*(3), a *getwd*(3) like BSD's has been added.
- The Bessel functions of the second kind are missing from the math library.
- A machine-name generating function *mtype*(3) has been added.
- the *monitor* execution-profiling function is missing.
- A new *pnmatch*(3) facility for regular-expression matching is included.
- The *pkopen*(3) packet-protocol library is omitted.
- The *plot*(3) library is missing.
- The *qsort*(3) library has a new *shellsort* entry point.
- A signal-name getter function *signame*(3) is supported.

Notice that the V7 *exp*(3) routines are listed under *log*(3) and the organization of the *stdio*(3) and other major function groups differs from that of the V7 manuals.

BSD-style *termcap*(3) is present but undocumented.

DEVICES

COHERENT supplies only four device descriptions: *ct*(4) (for the /dev/tty control terminal device), *mem*(4) (the usual /dev/mem device), *null*(4) (the data sink), and *tape*(4) (a description of the magnetic tape interface). On non-8088/8086 machines loadable device drivers are supported. The *tty* control interface is not described in the documentation, but is V7-compatible with added support for 19.2 kilobaud lines and a TIOCQUERY *ioctl* similar in function to BSD's FIONREAD.

The PC version documents its console device in detail and includes entries for the asynchronous line driver and for Corvus, Davong, Tecmar, and standard SASI Winchester drivers, as well as the inboard system hard disks and floppies.

FILE FORMATS

COHERENT documents the following file formats:

acct.h	functionally equivalent to V7's, but incompatible
ar.h	functionally equivalent to V7's, but incompatible
canon.h	new format for hardware-independent binary layout
core	functionally equivalent to V7's, but incompatible
dir.h	compatible with V7's
group	compatible with V7's
l.out.h	functionally equivalent to V7's *a.out*(5) entry
mtab.h	functionally equivalent to V7's, but incompatible
passwd	compatible with V7's
ttys	functionally equivalent to V7's, but incompatible
utmp.h	compatible with V7's

GAMES

COHERENT supplies a *fortune*(6) version and a Rubik's Cube simulator called *rubik*.

MISCELLANEA

COHERENT documents the following under "Conventions":

as	a new entry describing assembler calling conventions
ascii	like V7's *ascii*(7)
environ	similar to V7 *environ*(7), but with no discussion of specific environment variables
man	compatible with V7 *man*(7), but with a few more requests
ms	includes a large subset of V7 *ms*(7) plus indexing facilities.

MAINTENANCE

COHERENT includes the following V7-compatible tools: *clri*(1M), *dcheck*(1) (note the new -s option), *dump*(8) (options have been added), *icheck*(1) (note the new -v option), *cron*(8), *getty*(8) (but note the new letter options), and *update*(8). It also includes an SIII-compatible *accton*(1M).

init(8) and *rc*(8) operate similarly to V7 at boot time; *init*(8) accepts

SIGQUIT to reinitialize terminals and SIGHUP to go single-user.
New entries include:

lpd(8)	provides print-spooling services
bad(1M)	is added for maintaining bad block lists on devices
swap(8)	enables the swapper process
sysgen(8)	describes the procedure for initial load of a bootable kernel from tape on a PDP-11

The PC version includes *reboot*, a rebooting utility.

The following V7 maintenance tools are missing: *arcv*(1M), *dumpdir*(1M), *iostat*(1), and *makekey*(8).

D

PORTABLE DIRECTORY HANDLING

The following code provides an emulation of the 4.2BSD directory interface for other UNIX system dialects. It is public-domain code collected from USENET's public-domain sources bulletin board; no warranties express or implied are made by the authors or publishers as to its correctness or appropriateness in all cases.

Here is the include file for the package. It could be substituted for */usr/include/dir.h* once developers have been educated in its use (but you will need to restore the old version to regenerate your system from source).

```
/* ndir.h — 4.2BSD directory access emulation for non-4.2 systems*/

#ifndef DEV_BSIZE
#define DEV_BSIZE          512          /* device block size */
#endif

#define DIRBLKSIZ          DEV_BSIZE
#define MAXNAMLEN          255    /* name must be no longer than this */

struct  direct
{
    long    d_ino;                      /* inode number of entry   */
    short   d_reclen;                   /* length of this record   */
    short   d_namlen;                   /* length of d_name string */
    char    d_name[MAXNAMLEN + 1];  /* directory name          */
};


/*
 * The DIRSIZ macro gives the minimum record length that will hold
 * the directory entry. This requires the amount of space in struct
 * direct without the d_name field, plus enough space for the name
 * with a terminating null byte (dp->d_namlen+1), rounded up to a
 * 4 byte boundary.
 */
#undef DIRSIZ
#define DIRSIZ(dp) \
    ((sizeof (struct direct) — (MAXNAMLEN+1)) \
    + (((dp)->d_namlen+1 + 3) &~ 3))

/*
 * Definitions for library routines operating on directories.
 */
typedef struct _dirdesc
{
    int     dd_fd;
    long    dd_loc;
    long    dd_size;
    char    dd_buf[DIRBLKSIZ];
} DIR;

#ifndef NULL
#define NULL 0
#endif

extern  DIR     *opendir();
extern  struct direct *readdir();
extern  long    telldir();
extern  void    seekdir();
#define rewinddir(dirp)  seekdir((dirp), (long)0)
extern  void    closedir();

/* ndir.h ends here */
```

Here's the C code:

```c
#include <sys/param.h>
#include "ndir.h"

/*
 * support for Berkeley directory reading routine on
 * a V7 file system
 */

/*
 * open a directory.
 */
DIR *opendir(name)
char *name;
{
     register DIR *dirp;
     register int fd;

     if ((fd = open(name, 0)) == -1)
          return NULL;

     if ((dirp = (DIR *)malloc(sizeof(DIR))) == NULL)
     {
          close (fd);
          return NULL;
     }

     dirp->dd_fd = fd;
     dirp->dd_loc = 0;
     return dirp;
}


/*
 * read an old style directory entry and present it
 * as a new one
 */
#define ODIRSIZ 14

struct olddirect {
     short    od_ino;
     char     od_name[ODIRSIZ];
};

/*
 * get next entry in a directory.
 */
struct direct *readdir(dirp)
register DIR *dirp;
{
     register struct olddirect *dp;
     static struct direct dir;
```

```
        for (;;)
        {
            if (dirp->dd_loc == 0)
            {
                dirp->dd_size = read(dirp->dd_fd,
                                     dirp->dd_buf, DIRBLKSIZ);
                if (dirp->dd_size <= 0)
                    return NULL;
            }

            if (dirp->dd_loc >= dirp->dd_size)
            {
                dirp->dd_loc = 0;
                continue;
            }

            dp = (struct olddirect *)(dirp->dd_buf + dirp->dd_loc);
            dirp->dd_loc += sizeof(struct olddirect);

            if (dp->od_ino == 0)
                continue;

            dir.d_ino = dp->od_ino;
            strncpy(dir.d_name, dp->od_name, ODIRSIZ);
            dir.d_name[ODIRSIZ] = ' ';     /* ensure termination */
            dir.d_namlen = strlen(dir.d_name);
            dir.d_reclen = DIRSIZ(&dir);

            return (&dir);
        }
}


/*
 * close a directory.
 */
void closedir(dirp)
register DIR *dirp;
{
        close(dirp->dd_fd);
        dirp->dd_fd = -1;
        dirp->dd_loc = 0;
        free(dirp);
}

/* ndir.c ends here */
```

REFERENCES

K&R B. W. Kernighan and D. M. Ritchie, *The C Programming Language* (Englewood Cliffs, N.J.: Prentice-Hall, Inc., 1978).

K&P Brian Kernighan and Rob Pike, *The UNIX Programming Environment* (Englewood Cliffs, N.J.: Prentice-Hall, Inc., 1984).

RO Mark Rochkind, *Advanced UNIX Programming* (Englewood Cliffs, N.J.: Prentice-Hall, Inc., 1985).

V7 *UNIX Programmer's Manual*, Vol. 1 (Version 7) (Murray Hill, N.J.: Bell Telephone Laboratories, Inc., 1983).

4.1V1 *UNIX Programmer's Manual*, Vol. 1 (4.1BSD) (Berkeley, Calif.: Computer Science Division, University of California at Berkeley, 1981).

4.2V1 *UNIX Programmer's Manual*, Vol. 1 (4.2BSD) (Berkeley, Calif.: Computer Science Division, University of California at Berkeley).

4.3PR *Performance Improvements and Functional Enhancements in 4.3BSD*, Report #UCB/CSD 85/245 (Berkeley, Calif.: Computer Science Division (EECS), University of California at Berkeley, 1985).

SIII1 *UNIX User's Manual* (System III) (Murray Hill, N.J.: Bell Telephone Laboratories, Inc., June 1980).

TRSX *TRS-XENIX System Reference* (XENIX 2.3) (Tandy/Radio Shack Inc., 1983).

IBM1 *IBM Personal Computer XENIX Documentation* (XENIX 3.0) (Boca Raton, Fla.: International Business Machines, Inc., Dec. 1984).

SCO *SCO XENIX 5.0 Release 2 Documentation* (XENIX 5.0), Document XG-8-26-85-2.0/1.0 (Santa Cruz Operation, 1985).

SV1 *UNIX User's Manual* (System V Release 1), AT&T document 301-905, Issue 1.

3B5 *Administrator Reference Manual—3B5 Computer* (System V), AT&T Document 305-118, Issue 1, Sep. 1984.

SV21 *UNIX User's Reference Manual* (System V Release 2), AT&T document 307-103, Issue 2, April 1984.

SVID *System V Interface Definition (SVID)*, AT&T Select Code 307-127, Issue 1, Jan. 1985.

FOS *FOS 1.24 C Language Reference, FOS 1.24 Development Utilities, FOR:PRO 1.7P System Tools (pre-release documentation)*, (Belmont, Calif.: Fortune Systems Corporation).

PCIX *Personal Computer Interactive Executive User's Manual (PC/IX)*, IBM Document SH20-6365-0, Interactive Systems Corporation, Mar. 1984).

COH *COHERENT User's Manual and Version 2.3.43 Release Notes* (Chicago, Ill.: Mark Williams Company, 1985).

BSTJ *The Bell System Technical Journal*, Vol. 57, No. 6, Part 2 (July-August 1978).

LR L. Rosler, "The Evolution of C—Past and Future," *AT&T Bell Laboratories Technical Journal*, Vol. 63, No. 8, Part 2 (October 1984), pp. 1685-99.

DMR D. M. Ritchie, "The Evolution of the UNIX Time-sharing System," *AT&T Bell Laboratories Technical Journal*, Vol. 63, No. 8, Part 2 (October 1984), pp. 1577-93.

BS1 Bjarne Stroustrup, "Data Abstraction in C," *AT&T Bell Laboratories Technical Journal*, Vol. 63, No. 8, Part 2 (October 1984), pp. 1701-32.

BS2 Stroustrup, *C++ Reference Manual*, Computer Science Technical Report #108 (Murray Hill, N.J.: AT&T Bell Laboratories, January 1984).

BS3 Bjarne Stroustrup, *The C++ Programming Language* (Addison-Wesley, 1985).

P1003 *Portable Operating System Environment (P1003/D6)* November 15, 1985 draft for trial-use ballot, P1003 committee, Institute of Electrical and Electronic Engineers.

X3J11 *ANSI X3J11 Draft Standard*, ANSI Document X3J11/85-137, Nov. 1985.

INDEX